DATE DUE

MR 7 07			
MR 29 07			

DEMCO 38-296

A Nation of Adversaries

How the Litigation Explosion Is Reshaping America

A Nation of Adversaries

How the Litigation Explosion Is Reshaping America

PATRICK M. GARRY

 **INSIGHT BOOKS**

PLENUM PRESS • NEW YORK AND LONDON

g-in-Publication Data

A nation of adversaries : how the litigation explosion is
reshaping America / Patrick M. Garry.
     p.   cm.
  Includes bibliographical references and index.
  ISBN 0-306-45564-1
  1. Adversary system (Law)--Social aspects--United States.
2. Justice, Administration of--Social aspects--United States.
3. Social conflict--United States. 4. Civil society--United States.
I. Title.
KF384.G34   1997
340'.115--dc21   96-49377
                                                                 CIP

ISBN 0-306-45564-1

© 1997 Plenum Press, New York
Insight Books is a Division of Plenum Publishing Corporation
233 Spring Street, New York, N.Y. 10013-1578
http://www.plenum.com

An Insight Book

10 9 8 7 6 5 4 3 2 1

Printed in the United States of America

To my teachers,

Ray Rosol
Sr. Kenric
Bill Pohl
William Marinac
George Morgan
Martin Schirber
Donna Przybylowicz
Paul Murphy

Preface

In recent decades, the litigation explosion has become a frequently criticized social scourge. Starting in the 1970s, corporations and insurance companies—the most frequent defendants in the rising numbers of lawsuits—began complaining of a litigation system that was threatening American economic health. Congress continued this crusade in the 1990s with the House of Representatives' 1995 approval of legal-reform measures aimed at slowing the tide of litigation. Over the last several decades, the "litigation explosion" has become a common phrase to Americans; to nearly everyone except lawyers, it has come to be seen as an increasingly threatening malignancy in society.

Although the disdain for the litigation explosion is fairly widespread, the perception of its consequences is somewhat narrow. The impact of America's litigiousness is commonly seen as confined to the courts and to the corporate defendants. Court dockets are clogged, judges are overworked, lawyers are overpaid, and corporations have to shell out more and more money for higher and higher verdicts against them. The litigation explosion, according to public perceptions, decreases profitability and drives corporations to foreign countries. It increases insurance premiums and imposes countless regulations on the economy. But these are just a few of the immediate and most obvious side effects of

America's litigation explosion. The more far-reaching and longer-term consequences have, unfortunately, largely gone unrecognized.

Something so prominent as American litigiousness is not just confined in its impact on courthouses and corporate balance sheets and insurance premiums. The tremors of the litigation explosion have rippled through all of society. It has contributed to the transformation of American culture from an assimilated one to an adversarial one. The combat of the courtroom has become the newest model for social relations in the United States.

Along with the growth of litigation, the rise of conflict in society has been an often-observed social phenomenon in recent times. An edgy, uncompromising, confrontational climate has come to characterize American society. In politics, at the workplace, in the classroom, even at the playground, the mood has become more combative and less cooperative. Incivility pervades social gatherings—on the highway, in airplanes, at restaurants, in the movie theater. Countless explanations have been given for this escalation of conflict in American society—that the increasingly combative politics is a result of a growing ideological orientation bred by the media age; or, that rudeness in the theater and in the restaurant arises from a self-centered, television-addicted public not accustomed to interacting with other people; or, that tensions in the workplace flow from demands made by women and minorities. All these factors have their particular effects, but this book seeks to explore one overarching explanation for America's increasingly confrontational society. That explanation involves the litigation explosion and its breeding of an adversarial culture within the nation at large.

Because of the pervasiveness and prominence of litigation, it is orienting society toward a litigious mentality. Even those who never go to court are subtly urged to think and behave as adversarial litigants think and behave. *Liability* is becoming the universal word of social discourse. *Compromise* and *cooperation* are words of defeat. The litigation explosion may most directly impact lawyers' incomes and insurance premiums, but it is also causing a cultural fallout. It is spilling out of the courts and into the social

and cultural life of the nation. It is breeding an adversarial culture. It is fueling a society obsessively focused on a self-centered
individualism. It is encouraging people to see themselves just as
litigants do—as victims deserving of reparations. And it is transforming American politics to a litigation democracy. These cultural aspects of the litigation explosion are the focus of this book.

Contents

Introduction. The Cultural Fallout from America's Litigation
Explosion 1

Cultural Casualties 1
The New Frontier 2
A Society of Adversaries 4
The Erosion of Democratic Politics in a Litigation Age ... 6
Fueling a Culture of the Self 7
Litigation in an Age of Entitlement 8
The Rise of Victimization 9
The Empty Promises of the Litigation Explosion 11
Litigation and the Perpetuation of Conflict 13

Chapter 1. America's Litigation Obsession 15

The Litigation Explosion 15
Media Fascination with Litigation 16
The Public's Entry into the Jury Room 19
The Trial as Publicity Campaign 20
The Crowding-out Effect of a Litigation Obsession 22

Chapter 2. Pioneering on the Litigation Frontier   25

The Courtroom as the Modern Frontier   25
Litigation as an Arena for Individual Opportunity   27
New Territories Being Settled by Pioneering Litigants   29

Chapter 3. Cultural Foundations of America's Litigation
Explosion   43

Filling the Cultural Void   43
An Unattainable Alternative   46
Litigation in a Culture of the Self   48
Litigation and the Erosion of Community   51
A Litigious Cultural Mind-Set   53

Chapter 4. The Breeding of an Adversarial Culture   59

The Courtroom as America's Modern-Day Ellis Island . . .   59
The Models for a Culture of Conflict: Sports and
Litigation   61
Symptoms of an Adversarial Society   66

Chapter 5. A Litigation Democracy   89

Chapter 6. Litigation and the Rise of a New American Role
Model   103

The Appeal of the Victim   103
Victimization and the Litigation Process   105
The Creation of New Victims   108
Victimization as a Potent Political Tool   110
A Culture of Competing Victims   113
A Victim-Oriented Education   114
Blurring the Line between Victim and Criminal   119
Victimization and the Social Mind-Set   123

Chapter 7. An Explosive Partnership: Therapists and
        Lawyers   125

America's Therapeutic Culture   125
Therapy Culture and Victimization   127
Education as Therapy   128
The Litigation Explosion in a Therapy Culture   130
Repressed Memory: An Example of Therapy Litigation ..   133
The Therapeutic Culture and the Transformation of Law   135
Conclusion   138

Chapter 8. An Inadequate Social Regulator   139

The Emergence of Law as the Primary Social Regulator ..   139
The Workplace as a Legal Quagmire   141
Litigation as the Currency of Social Exchange   144
The Ineffectiveness of Law as a Sexual Regulator   146
Law's Inability to Regulate Even the Lawyers   151
The Legal Troubles of a Lawyer-Filled White House   155

Chapter 9. A Casualty of the Litigation Explosion   161

Chapter 10. False Prophets   171

Public Animosity toward Lawyers   171
A Litigation Backlash against Lawyers   173
The Evolution of Law as Big Business   176
Litigation as a Legal Business Strategy   177
Class-Action Lawsuits as Litigation-for-Lawyers   179
Conflicts between Lawyers and Their Clients   182
The Opposition to Legal Reform   185

Conclusion. The Empty Promise of Litigation   189

An Endless Maze of Conflict   189
A Culture of Fear   191

The Spreading Litigation Culture 193
Crisis within the Legal Academy 194

Notes 199

Index 212

INTRODUCTION

The Cultural Fallout from America's Litigation Explosion

CULTURAL CASUALTIES

Warnings about the litigation explosion have routinely sounded whenever a new round of statistics on the numbers of lawsuits is released, whenever crowded courthouses have to be expanded, or whenever class-action suits involving millions of plaintiffs produce more money for the lawyers than for their clients. The usual purveyors of the warnings have been physicians, insurance companies, and large corporations—the most frequent objects of America's growing litigiousness. But rich doctors and bureaucratic insurance companies do not make sympathetic victims. So the warnings continue, the stories of litigation abuses reappear, and life goes on. After all, or so it is perceived, the damage has already been done: The litigation explosion has left its crater—the law schools have been filled, the lawyers have leased their office space, the insurance companies have set their premiums. Like most explosions, however, it has impacted countless unwitting victims. Though its point of detonation was initially directed at the soldiers in the litigation war—insurance companies and deep-pocketed corporations—the litigation explosion has generated a mushroom cloud that has drifted over a much larger population of innocent bystanders, affecting those who have never been in a courtroom or party to a lawsuit. It has produced a cultural fallout that will affect generations of Americans to come, for the litigation explosion has not only resulted in new legions of lawyers and escalating numbers of lawsuits, it has also transformed American society and culture.

THE NEW FRONTIER

As will be discussed in Chapter 2, litigation is becoming the new frontier, providing the latest embodiment of the American frontier myth. This myth has uniquely characterized national identity. During the country's youth, the Western frontier epitomized the American dream—the promise of a new start "Out West." When that frontier closed in 1890, the nation looked to the urban–industrial frontier to ensure equality and individual freedom. Later, the nation's sights turned to the international frontier and then to the technological frontier. Throughout history, Americans have been in search of new frontiers on which the individual can pioneer. Presently, the litigation arena provides such a frontier, for it is in the courtroom that the trailblazing struggles of the individual are being waged.

On the litigation frontier, any individual can explore new territory and settle new ground. The endless list of lawsuits seeking to break new litigation ground is evidence of explorations into this emerging frontier: children suing parents for wrongful raising, pupils suing teachers for hostile learning environments, lovers suing each other for unfulfilled romantic promises, overweight people suing movie theaters for larger seats. The litigation surge has pushed into every area of American life, including private matters that once were immune from judicial intrusion. Religion, for instance, has become a highly litigated subject. Even in the workplace, employees sue over whether their coemployees may display or express religious beliefs. Conservative Christian groups, who once disdained legal remedies as too worldly, have become increasingly litigious in their struggle for America's soul. Litigation has also entered marital life in a new way. A developing legal specialty known as "domestic torts" now allows spouses to sue each other for "wrongful marital conduct." Whereas such civil damage claims were virtually unheard of a decade ago, there is an explosion of them today. And in the field of education, everything from class lectures, to relationships between students to athletic participation is being litigated.

The litigation frontier promises wealth to its successful pioneers, just as the gold fields of California once did. Personal injury claims offer anyone with an ability to voice believable complaints about pain and suffering the opportunity to collect a quick settlement. Punitive damages awards, like the $4 million award received by a doctor whose new BMW had incurred $4,000 of damage during shipping, are ever-present monetary windfalls just waiting for the fortunate litigant. Employment litigation offers rewards otherwise unattainable in the workplace. In one wrongful termination case in Los Angeles, for instance, a 56-year-old corporate executive received a jury verdict totalling $5.7 million for emotional distress suffered when his employer cut back his work assignments. With plaintiffs rushing to jump onto this litigation wagon train, employment discrimination lawsuits have increased by 2,200 percent since 1974.[1]

Just as it did with the Western frontier, the government is encouraging exploration of the litigation frontier. Under federal law, for instance, citizens who expose incidents of fraud perpetrated against government agencies are entitled to anywhere from 15 to 30 percent of any damages obtained in a lawsuit. In the 1990s, these "whistle-blower" suits have burgeoned—largely because of the sizable litigation rewards—and whistle-blowers themselves have become millionaires for accusing their employers of trying to cheat the government.[2] For his role in obtaining a $139 million recovery from National Health Laboratories and Corning Metpath, a former employee of the company received $21 million. Like the rewards promised to bounty hunters on the Western frontier, the economic incentives offered on the litigation frontier can be lucrative.

A SOCIETY OF ADVERSARIES

With the evolution of the litigation frontier has come a significant transformation in social identity: a realignment of American society toward an adversarial model and away from the assimilation (or "melting pot") model that prevailed largely up until the late 20th century. Under the assimilation model, society was seen as a collection of cooperating individuals who sacrificed their differences for the sake of social cohesion. In recent years, however, the nation's growing diversity has bred a respect for the country's multicultural identity. Yet while the multicultural movement may have shown that the assimilation model often denied the inherent diversity of American culture, it does not provide an accurate model of how American society actually interacts. It gives a static picture of American diversity, but it does not describe how individuals relate to each other. For this purpose, the adversarial model created by the litigation explosion and examined in Chapter 4 is needed. As accurately predicted by this model, even individuals with similar ethnic and racial identities have become real or potential adversaries during the litigation age. It has been America's adversarial conversion, not its multicultural realizations, that has most significantly eroded the traditional assimilation model. Diversity is, after all, quite different from adversity.

An adversarial culture, bred by the values and lessons of the litigation explosion, is taking hold in the United States. It is a culture that pushes individuals to conflict and confrontation, and to continually challenge community authority and institutions. It is also a culture whose adversarial values are reinforced by and reflected in America's growing sports culture. In today's media-hyped world of sports, just as in the litigation culture, an obsession with individual conflict has risen to new heights. With athletes becoming multimillionaire folk heroes, and increasing numbers of litigants finding wealth and fame in the courtroom, dominance over one's rivals has been elevated to a social ideal. From the football field to the basketball court, the old ideal of sportsmanlike conduct has degenerated into a fiesta of trash talk and aggressive taunting. This "in your face" style is loud and boastful, and it seeks not only to beat but also to humiliate the opponent. But for most people, who will never participate in any professional sports, lawsuits are the only available avenue for achieving a social victory over an adversary. In the litigation arena, any individual can enter the combat and eventually triumph.

This combative and adversarial edge, so prevalent in both the litigation and sports cultures, is intensifying within society at large. In a country that once had "Have a Nice Day" as its national slogan, citizens now wear sweatshirts that scream "Back Off." Rudeness and selfishness is evident everywhere—from airplane seats to restaurants to movie theaters. Radio talksters such as Howard Stern demonstrate daily the appeal of turning public discourse into trashy name-calling. Television talk shows aggressively promote confrontation between guests and audiences. Even U.S. Senators and Representatives are engaging in more hostile name-calling than ever before.

The adversarial culture bred by the litigation explosion has spread to every area of social life. Hostility has overtaken the workplace, where the rise in employment litigation has been called an "epidemic." Tensions in gender relations may be at an all-time high. Teachers and students are increasingly at odds. The media is becoming ever more predatory in their journalistic practices and confrontational in their entertainment programming. Race-horse journalism covers politics merely as a continual contest between the individual winners and losers. Television talk shows from "The McLaughlin Group" to "Crossfire" to "Meet the Press" rely on combat for their format, pitting conservatives against liberals, Republicans against Democrats. Even the political process has come to mirror the combativeness of the litigation arena.

THE EROSION OF DEMOCRATIC POLITICS
IN A LITIGATION AGE

As discussed in Chapter 5, the adversarial culture propagated by the litigation explosion is undermining the nation's democratic political culture. It is no coincidence that voting rates and political parties have declined in the litigation age. The two different cultures require and cultivate conflicting values and behavior. Democratic politics, on the one hand, require compromise, consensus, and the cooperative effort of individuals to reach common goals. Litigation, on the other hand, takes an adversarial stance. It encourages conflict and divisiveness. Consequently, as the litigation culture reigns, the democratic culture wanes, and the political process is undermined by the adversarial orientation of the litigation culture. Legislative gridlock, for instance, occurs more frequently and intensely—the by-product of an adversarial culture that rewards ideological combat. For in litigation-oriented politics, it is often more important to political interest groups to wage the spirited fight and to retain ideological purity than to compromise and reach mutually tolerable decisions.

As an adversarial culture has emerged, the rigid black-and-white outlook of litigation has replaced the more flexible gray approach of democratic politics. Between the extremes on political issues, the middle, or moderate, position is often a lonely and desolate place. The "us versus them" mentality of the courtroom has come to dominate political discourse. Voters have become accustomed to a familiar dialectic: advocates of political correctness versus the proponents of free speech, prolife versus prochoice, taxpayers versus welfare recipients, victims versus criminals, women versus men.

Following an adversarial model, the conduct of politics has become less and less civil. The unanimous verdict of retiring Senators and Representatives, regardless of party, is that the political process has come to resemble a bitter shouting match between combative litigants. Not only are programs and policies hotly contested, but also even individuals are subjected to brutal personal attacks. In Washington, politics during a litigation age has truly become a "blood sport."

As the litigation age has pushed aside the legislative age, the courts have increasingly become the forum for public policy. Not only is legislation routinely being "trumped" by judicial review, instigated by dissatisfied parties, but more and more political interest groups are bypassing the political process entirely and taking their agendas directly to the courts. Finding that the legislative process requires a consensus they cannot achieve, interest groups are instead adopting the litigation model and trying to gain their political goals through the securing of judicially awarded rights—rights that are safely off-limits to any future legislative action.

In connection with this shift in political focus from the legislative halls to the judicial courtrooms, the litigation culture has also affected notions of democratic equality. Historically, democracy meant that all citizens possessed political equality at the voting booth and in the legislative chambers. With fewer and fewer people voting, and with the legislative process increasingly gridlocked, however, the litigation culture is breeding a new sense of democratic equality. The new measure of equality is at the courthouse rather than the voting booth—and the issue is whether everyone is equal in his or her right to sue. As victimization erodes traditional majority rule, the most vehement social protests for equality are occurring at the courthouse, calling for their cases to be heard. And as the courts become ever more active, political interest groups are increasingly looking to the judicial branch as the venue in which to pursue their political agendas and shape public policy.

FUELING A CULTURE OF THE SELF

While transforming politics into a more adversarial, courtroom-oriented process, the litigation explosion has similarly influenced the evolution of America's cultural identity. In facilitating the "rights" revolution, it has entrenched the uncompromising, self-centered, individualistic culture that exists in contemporary America. Judicially awarded rights have been used to break down community authority and social cohesion; out of this breakdown has risen an indulgent culture of the self that has further eroded communal bonds, ignored individual responsibility, and weakened the web of social interdependency.

In eroding communal bonds and other traditional forms of social authority, the litigation explosion has also undermined nonjudicial methods of resolving disputes. It has drowned out a whole array of social customs that formerly regulated much of the country's cultural and social life. Matters that were once handled by families, churches, and communities are now addressed by the courts. Every disagreement, no matter how trivial, gets taken to court. Litigation has become the only cultural regulator, with "due process" the only standard for resolving disputes. Members of athletic teams cannot be suspended by coaches without getting their "due process." Employees cannot have their job assignments modified without "due process." Even the most routine activities of daily life are now being governed by litigation. Many cities and counties, for instance, have instituted so-called "harassment calendars" in their court systems, designed to deal with the numerous and petty personal type of disputes that judges say are not getting resolved outside of court—disputes that usually center around complaints about relationships turned sour, such as a woman whose boyfriend was withholding sex, or a golfer who claimed he had been left out of a game, or a hockey father who didn't think his son was getting enough playing time.[3]

LITIGATION IN AN AGE OF ENTITLEMENT

The litigation explosion also reflects and reinforces the American desire to create a perfect system of laws that will anticipate every dispute and eliminate any uncertainty. It strives to create a risk-free society. Yet it also mirrors the surge of disappointment in modern life. Economic downturns and persisting social problems have bred a rising sense of disappointment among Americans who have grown up in the age of entitlement, in which self-actualization and prosperity were not just goals but expectations. The frustration of those expectations is now seen as a great injustice, to be remedied by litigation. When it was discovered that corporate America could not fulfill all the expectations, that prosperity could not be uninterrupted, and that needs constantly seem to outrun incomes, Americans turned to the courts. Rejecting the limitations inherent in the human condition, individuals have looked to the courts to provide what life does not.

Perhaps the litigation culture is a natural outgrowth of the clash between the age of expectation and the inevitable disappointments and tragedies of human life, for in contemporary America, litigation has become the antidote to any tragedy or disappointment. In the litigation culture, the notion of tragedy has been rejected. Now, nothing unpleasant happens that isn't someone else's fault—someone who can be sued. Failure is grounds for a lawsuit; death is accompanied by depositions. For every hurt and loss, a legal cure is demanded.

THE RISE OF VICTIMIZATION

As a way of satisfying the expectations of the self, the litigation explosion has fueled the fires of victimization. A growing feature of modern life in the United States is the rush to identify one's self or one's group as a victim. The victim is becoming a sought-after social status; and the primary avenue for asserting victimization is through the courts, for in litigation, victims become victors. If one is a victim, then one can sue and recover damages—as did a man who was fired from his job after months of tardiness and repeated warnings. In his lawsuit, he claimed that he suffered from an ailment called "chronic lateness" and that he deserved reinstatement to his job. When another man was killed while driving a car he stole from a parking lot, his family sued the parking-lot owner for failing to take steps to prevent such thefts. A heavyset man in Chicago filed a complaint with the Minority

Rights Division of the U.S. Attorney's Office, alleging that his rights were being violated because the seats at McDonald's restaurants were too small for him. He was, the man said, being discriminated against no less than "blacks, Mexicans, Latins, Asians, or women." From a man ejected from a commercial airline, suing because of an alleged disorder that caused him to scream obscenities, to law students suing the trustees of their now-closed law school, arguing that they deserve a lifetime of earnings because they were not able to get their degree, to a woman claiming that her right to become a mother has been violated by an insurance company that refused to pay for continuing infertility treatments, to a child who sued her parents for allowance that was not paid during her adolescent years, the list of lawsuits asserting new kinds of victim status goes on and on, reflecting the constant escalation of personal grievances into legal lawsuits.

In providing the forum for Americans to assert their victimization, the litigation arena has also enabled the growth of America's therapeutic culture. A bridge of reinforcement has been built between the nation's lawyers and its psychologists, for as the psychologists discover more psychic and emotional victims, the lawyers receive more clients for lawsuits. And as more plaintiffs win large settlements for their emotional and psychological hurts, more people rush to therapists to discover their own victimhood.

As the therapeutic culture has encouraged Americans to dredge up psychological injuries from their past and to find someone or something to blame, the courts have made that endeavor economically rewarding. Litigation has become a vital treatment in the healing of emotional wounds. For only through suing those who have injured them can victims truly begin their healing process, or so claim both therapists and lawyers. In this way, the therapeutic and litigation cultures have combined to fuel the victimization trend in America.

This intermingling of the litigation and therapeutic cultures has also resulted in significant changes in how the individual is viewed. Seen as helplessly subject to the emotional and psychological traumas of their past, people are less and less held to the traditional standards of free will and rational choice. Despite the destructive or injurious acts individuals may commit, they might not be held responsible, because their actions are seen to be dictated by their psychological dysfunctions. Not surprisingly, as this view has gained popularity in the courts and in society at large, an intensifying political protest has complained about the modern-day erosion of personal responsibility.

THE EMPTY PROMISES OF THE LITIGATION EXPLOSION

The litigation culture, as shaped by the legal profession, has failed to deliver on its promises of a judicial system that diminishes conflict and propagates a set of consensual social values based on the ideals of truth and justice. Instead, as discussed in Chapter 10, the legal profession has institutionalized conflict in a way that proliferates more litigation. Lawyers have come to form a powerful business interest—one that has aggressively fueled the litigation explosion. Through organizations such as the American Trial Lawyers Association, lawyers target future areas of litigation. And contrary to the desires of public opinion, almost all legal-reform measures aimed at streamlining the litigation process get killed by the oppositional lobbying of lawyers.

If the condition and behavior of its leaders is any indication, the litigation culture is seriously flawed. According to all public surveys, lawyers neither command nor inspire trust or confidence. Even lawyers themselves are disillusioned with the litigation culture. Many lawyers have come to see themselves less as officers of the court than bitter adversaries bent on winning at any cost while inflicting maximum damage on the other side. The majority of lawyers would start new careers if they could; and lawyers, more than any other profession, suffer the most depression.

The dark side of America's litigation culture is also revealed by the failure of law to reform social behavior, particularly among lawyers. Clearly, with the highest legal literacy, lawyers should be model citizens in a litigation culture. Yet as the reach of law continually extends itself through the litigation explosion, lawyers are becoming anything but model citizens. With lawyers having as many legal troubles as everyone else, grave doubts exist as to the adequacy of litigation as the primary social regulator. Both criminal prosecutions and ethical complaints against lawyers have skyrocketed. Sexual harassment occurs as frequently in the nation's law offices as it does within the confines of corporate America. In a recent survey, 43 percent of women lawyers reported that they had experienced unwanted sexual harassment at the office. Furthermore, several states, responding to increasing complaints, have adopted rules prohibiting sexual relations between a lawyer and her client.

The greed and corruption that the law attempts to regulate within corporate America seems even more outrageously present among lawyers. Overbilling has become a widely known practice, even of the major firms. Predatory lawyers, seeking lucrative cases, prey on the vulnerabilities of disaster victims and their grieving families. The state of Texas, for example, because of widespread dissatisfaction with lawyers' "ambulance chasing," is considering a law that would outlaw lawyers' soliciting clients. The abuses in client solicitation were highlighted in 1989, when a school bus carrying 81 students in southern Texas was hit by a softdrink delivery truck and pushed into a water-filled pit. Twenty-one students were killed, attracting a swarm of attorneys, drawn by the deep pockets of the bottling company that owned the truck. One lawyer allegedly paid $10,000 to a go-between to refer him to the parents of a child who had died, while another offered a local woman $500 for each client she helped solicit, and yet another posed as a priest in an attempt to get at grieving families.

Although such catastrophic personal injury cases often show the most predatory side of lawyers, class-action lawsuits reveal the degree to which lawyers instigate and promote litigation primarily for their own benefit. In one suit, for instance, based on a 3-cent overcharge on the telephone bills of Chicago residents, the lawyers received a $750,000 fee for obtaining a 3-cent refund for each individual telephone customer. In the settlement of another class-action lawsuit brought against a manufacturer of dental adhesives, the 650 individual claimants received $7 each, while their lawyers pocketed fees amounting to $955,000.

LITIGATION AND THE PERPETUATION OF CONFLICT

The litigation explosion has detonated an array of problems that jeopardize America's cultural vitality and threaten social stability. Instead of providing a guide to society that helps to diminish future disputes, litigation is simply perpetuating social conflict. As with the much-publicized sexual harassment suit against Stroh's brewery by several female employees, who alleged that the company's ads featuring the "Swedish Bikini Team" constituted sexual harassment, litigation rarely provides answers or guidelines for society. With plaintiffs' lawyers proclaiming that they would break new ground in the field of sexual harassment law, the Stroh's suit was settled with a confidentiality clause prohibiting any of the parties from discussing the resolution.

Rather than teaching people to live harmoniously under some accepted social rules or codes of behavior, litigation is simply inviting them to join the fight. Indeed, the only cultural value litigation has produced, other than the universally held fear of being sued, is the ambiguous "right to choose." With its endless rules and procedures, and its lack of substantive values, litigation simply provides a battleground for society to fight its wars. Consequently, the litigation process is beginning to resemble the computer "Hal" in the movie *2001: A Space Odyssey*. Like Hal, the law is remaking society in its own image—an adversarial image. Ideally a tool with which a secular society can resolve its differences and reach common ground, the law has now grown to become in many ways an uncontrolled master of the society that once created it. The escalating litigation is drowning out other forms of social interaction and custom. Courts are becoming the only unifying social thread. Ultimately, everything gets "taken to court."

As evidenced by the nation's escalating litigiousness, the courthouse is becoming America's social gathering point. The act, or threat, of suing is shaping the way an increasingly fragmented and atomistic society gets along. Ingrained in the American mentality is the omnipresent fear of being sued. In a diverse nation of unpredictable social behavior, "going to court" is the one journey everyone can make. "Liability" is becoming the national buzzword, the one concern shared by all Americans. It is affecting the decisions and actions of millions of people and organizations that have never even been to court. Employees are hired in a way that fully contemplates future litigation. Schools decide whether to enlist community volunteers for extracurricular activities on the basis of potential liability. Every announcement of any contest or prize drawing is accompanied by a recitation of indecipherable legal jargon, intended solely as a defense to subsequent lawsuits filed by disgruntled contestants. And the nation's healthcare system often seems more of a system of liability mitigation than one of health maintenance.

Though the legal profession is often burdened with the responsibility of controlling the litigation explosion, it has proved unable to do so. The profession continually rejects attempts to streamline the litigation process, with its endless maze of rules and appeals. Even defense lawyers, whose clients include insurance companies determined to smother the litigation explosion have joined the opposition to legal-reform proposals frequently introduced in Congress. Moreover, through aggressive advertising, lawyers continually refuel the litigation explosion.

Not only do lawyers not have the desire to control America's litigiousness, but they also may not have the ability to do so. The litigation explosion has become a cultural problem, not just a legal problem. It has transformed various cultural and social values in ways that have realigned American society from the assimilation model of Ellis Island to the adversarial model of the courtroom. In so doing, the litigation explosion has had its most far-reaching and momentous effects. The litigation explosion has become too powerful for the nation's lawyers to control, but perhaps not for the nation's citizens.

CHAPTER 1

America's Litigation Obsession

THE LITIGATION EXPLOSION

The signs of the litigation explosion are ubiquitous. Litigation is increasing approximately seven times faster than the national population. The number of civil lawsuits commenced annually in the federal courts has quadrupled since 1960.[1] More than 37,000 lawsuits for civil rights violations alone were filed in 1994 by the country's prison inmates.[2] Estimates put the total number of cases filed each year in all the nation's courts at up to 30 million.[3] In the 7-year period from 1986 to 1993, the percentage of Americans having professional contact with a lawyer rose from 52 percent to 70 percent.[4] The present liability system in Illinois costs more than $1,000 per person per year.[5] And in California, the average jury award in cases brought by terminated employees is $1.3 million.[6] Even the President of the United States, besieged by litigation, cannot afford all his legal fees and has had to ask for donations to the Presidential Legal Expense Trust.

Along with the dramatic increase in litigation, the lawyer population is similarly swelling. With 5 percent of the world's population, America has more than 70 percent of the world's lawyers.[7] Since 1965, the number of lawyers, now at 864,000, has grown by 300 percent.[8] The ratio of lawyers to nonlawyers has nearly doubled: There is now one lawyer for every 350 people in America. And for every three janitors, there is one lawyer.[9] Meanwhile, more than 130,000 students are enrolled in American law schools each year.

The explosion in litigation has caused long delays and heavy backlogs in the nation's courts. In a New York federal court, for instance, litigants have been waiting for as long as 11 years for judges to reach their verdicts in nonjury trials.[10] A case filed in a Chicago court in 1979 by a woman who claimed she had been wrongfully forced out of her real estate business by a mortgage company was still unresolved in 1995, even though the mortgage company had gone out of business, and its parent company—a chief defendant in the case—had long since changed owners. Another lawsuit between a New York City apartment owner and his cooperative over the $909 cost of installing window metal bars lasted 7 years and generated total legal fees of $73,547.[11] And a California woman tied up her neighbor in court for 8 years over a dispute involving a backyard basketball hoop.

MEDIA FASCINATION WITH LITIGATION

The fallout from the litigation explosion extends well beyond the clogged court dockets and the growing lawyer population. It affects more than just the litigants themselves and the insurance companies that often end up paying the judgments. The litigation explosion has also served as a sponge on the social mind-set, increasingly soaking up the nation's attention. This growing obsession with litigation has further contributed to America's litigious mentality.

With more and more attention focused on the courts, even the nonlitigating segment of American society is swept into the litigation mind-set. Because of the intense media coverage of many trials, the public is virtually transported into the courtroom and drawn into the conflict–mind-set of the litigants. Such social involvement in the litigation process not only familiarizes Americans with the courts, but also subtly encourages them to someday take a more active role as litigants themselves. In publicizing prominent trials as it does, the media help to promote the glory and rewards of the litigation game.

A whole new subculture of legal media has grown up in the litigation age. Following in the legacy of "People's Court," Court TV now takes the viewing public inside the courtroom of real trials. Since its beginning in July of 1991, Court TV has covered more than 300 trials and now reaches over 14 million cable subscribers.[12] This success has been accomplished with, as of yet, a relatively bare-bones editorial product. During daytime hours, the channel shows live or prerecorded trial coverage, followed by its evening program "Prime-Time Justice," which provides highlights and commentary from the day's trials. Although the more salacious criminal cases have occasionally thrust Court TV into the midst of front-page news, the channel lives off of ordinary civil cases such as consumer liability and malpractice trials.

In addition to Court TV, the ESPN of the litigation world, television "tabloid" shows such as "Hard Copy" likewise rely on the courts as their programming staple. Cases involving sexual harassment, employment discrimination, and product liability complaints against large corporations are favorite topics. And with more and more celebrities embroiled in litigation (i.e., divorce, libel, and sexual harassment cases), courtroom news is never in short supply. Although Congressional sessions run for only part of the year, and foreign policy news only interests the American public for brief spells, news from the nation's courtrooms never ceases. Litigation illiteracy seems to pose no problem.

Litigation has become such a national obsession that it is becoming an increasingly popular subject for every type of medium. In a litigious society, hungry for the drama of conflict, litigants and their lawyers make ideal talk-show guests. Before a live audience and at the prompting of a confrontation-hungry host, litigants plead their case. On television news-magazine programs, lawyers argue to a viewing public, just as they would to a jury. In bookstores, judges and lawyers sign copies of the books that claim to tell the real story behind the trial. With increasing numbers of prominent lawsuits being publicized on Court TV and CNN, litigation is becoming somewhat of a spectator sport. Like athletic events, trials are now analyzed and dissected for the viewing public by a host of expert commentators and legal analysts. To provide this analysis, lawyer–commentators have emerged. They are retained by various television programs, ranging from "Larry King Live" to "Crossfire" to "Good Morning America," to provide running expert commentary on whatever trial is currently in the news headlines. Trial attorney Gerry Spence even has his own cable television talk show; and Barry Scheck, the DNA lawyer on the O. J. Simpson defense team, is developing a program for CBS.

Another indication of the public obsession with the judicial process is the plethora of novels, motion pictures, and television programs devoted to courtroom dramas. There seems to be nothing that interests Americans more. Lawyer–novelists such as John Grisham and Scott Turow attract audiences that crave both entertainment and a knowledge of courtroom law. A *New Yorker* article about a reporter's first-time jury service wound up in a bidding war between Hollywood producers who wanted to acquire the film rights.[13] And in a litigious society, there is plenty of real-life material on which to base all the movies and television shows. The program "L.A. Law," for instance, often portrayed fictional adaptations of real lawsuits. One episode, which depicted a man unable to speak without blurting obscenities and racial slurs at people, was modeled after a lawsuit filed by a couple who claimed to have such a disability, known as Tourette's syndrome. Conversely, in an example of fact mirroring fiction, an HIV-positive Philadelphia lawyer sued his law firm for discriminating against him. The firm tried to move the case to another city, hoping that jurors there would be less likely to think the case was the basis for the movie *Philadelphia*, which it was not.

THE PUBLIC'S ENTRY INTO THE JURY ROOM

All the publicity and public interest in trials is having a boomerang effect within the courthouse. Jurors, even before reaching a verdict, are beginning to consider the public reaction to their verdicts. This is a factor—the popularity factor—that is not supposed to enter the jury box; but in a litigious society, popular reaction is hard to ignore. The trial of the men accused of beating truck driver Reginald Denny during the 1992 Los Angeles riots illustrates this effect. As many analysts concluded, the jury's lenient treatment of the defendants was due to a fear within the jury room that an unpopular verdict could ignite a new round of violence.[14] In a litigious society in which the public claims to be the ultimate judge, the jury is no longer safe to freely conduct its deliberations without considering the wider social reactions to its verdict.

With the litigation explosion occurring in a media age, courtroom actors have attained a heightened, celebrity status. In addition to the litigants themselves, jurors and judges have now been thrust into the public spotlight. As a result of the public's craving for courtroom commentary, judges have begun appearing on such shows as "Rivera Live"—a television talk show largely devoted to trials. Instead of the jurors deliberating in sequestered isolation and then walking quietly away from the courthouse, as they were portrayed in *Twelve Angry Men*, they now leave the jury room for the studios of "Nightline" and "Inside Edition." Even those who would like to remain anonymous can quickly become the object of aggressive reporters. In one Minneapolis case, the judge had to dismiss a whole jury, because he felt that it had been tainted by news reports about one juror. A local television station had run a story about criminal charges that had once been brought against the juror. As the judge explained, "If they [jurors] think they're going to be on the evening news, we are never going to get jurors."[15]

This publicity factor can have a suffocating effect on potential jurors all across the nation. Because of all the juror interviews accompanying prominent trials in the past, potential jurors now know that their deliberations may well be a matter of media second-guessing and analysis. For some, this exposure may dampen their enthusiasm to serve or influence their final verdict. For others, the prospect of fame and financial gain from selling an inside account of the verdict deliberations is a tempting entice-ment to jury service. This lure, it is worried, may exert a distorting effect on jury deliberations.

Juror discussions, once a strictly confidential matter, have moved to the front page. Shortly after the acquittals in the 1992 trial of four Los Angeles police officers accused of beating Rodney King, jurors were inundated with media requests for interviews. Several appeared on "Nightline" and other television shows to explain their verdict. Newspaper and magazine stories followed, in which the deliberations were painstakingly reconstructed. Sim-ilarly, in recent trials involving Imelda Marcos, William Kennedy Smith, Leona Helmsley, Mike Tyson, and O. J. Simpson, stories on the juries' private discussions and petty rivalries appeared in the media within days of the decisions. Following the Simpson trial, a group of jurors demanded $100,000 for an appearance on "Inside Edition." One even posed for *Playboy* magazine.

The persistence of the media in dissecting jury deliberations worries some judges and scholars, who believe there may be dire consequences for the integrity of the justice system. If jurors know they may be publicly criticized because of news reports of their proceedings, these judges and scholars say, juries may be less likely to base their decisions on the facts and the law, and instead look to popular opinion. The main concern of some judges is that jurors, even in mundane trials, will be influenced by the highly visible roles they see "celebrity" jurors take—consequently, they will not feel safe speaking confidentially inside the jury room and will be less candid in their discussions.[16]

THE TRIAL AS PUBLICITY CAMPAIGN

With so much media attention devoted to courthouse trials, it is hardly surprising that publicity has become a significant litigation strategy of lawyers. As one Manhattan judge has observed, "Lawyers now feel it is the essence of their function to try the case in the public media."[17] News conferences are seen as basic duties of the modern courtroom lawyer. Although every lawyer claims a desire not to "try the case in the media," that is just what they do. Polls are even used to obtain the public's verdict on a particular case. "We used to have trial by combat, then trial by jury, and now trial by polls," says Tom W. Smith, director of the General Social Survey at the National Opinion Research Center.[18] Oftentimes, these polls are conducted even before a jury is assembled, with the respondents having little relevant information about the case.

In today's litigious society, generating publicity favorable to plaintiffs has become a well-planned legal strategy.[19] Seldom facing any opposition in this media context, litigants and their lawyers are able to present themselves as victims and their opponents as villains. Since the media interest is in the drama of the conflict, often only a one-sided version is presented. As a result, the trial, in terms of public judgment on the culpability and reputation of the parties, is held in the court of public opinion rather than in the legal courts.

Media reliance on litigation appears to be on the rise, especially as cable television channels proliferate. With dozens of talk shows in syndication and the networks scrambling to produce profitable news-magazine shows, there is a high demand for controversial subject matter that will attract audiences accustomed to a steady diet of dramatic conflict. The vast supply of litigant–combatants furnished by the litigation explosion fills this need. Trial lawyers and their clients are more than willing to satisfy the media's hunger for programming. In this way, the litigation explosion feeds off the growing media and vice versa.

One example of how litigants and the media feed off each other appeared in the lawsuit brought by a Florida widower, alleging that his wife died from a brain tumor caused by a cellular telephone. His only "evidence" was that his wife's tumor was located directly next to where the phone rested when she held it up to her ear. Despite this flimsy claim, and despite the fact that no scientific study has ever linked such phones to any kind of health problem, his lawsuit against the manufacturer was given news coverage on several network television shows, including ABC's "20/20" and CNN's "Larry King Live."

THE CROWDING-OUT EFFECT
OF A LITIGATION OBSESSION

With litigation becoming ever more consuming of social attentions, it can crowd out focus on other matters of public concern. All that dramatic action in the courthouse can divert attention from the less gripping but equally vital forums, such as state legislatures and Congressional hearing rooms. In newspaper articles discussing the 1994 elections in California, for instance, one headline read, "Simpson Trial Eclipses California Politics." Indeed, that year's primary elections attracted the lowest turnout of voters in the state's history. California politicians found that public attention was being increasingly dominated by the trial. Tony Miller, California's Acting Secretary of State, became so concerned about the trial's depressing effect on voter turnout that he asked the judge in the case not to hold court on Election Day. "There's no question the trial will have a huge effect on the campaign," predicted a spokesman for Governor Pete Wilson's campaign.[20] A leading California pollster acknowledged that the trial was "a depressant toward the motivation and desire of the public to vote."[21]

The litigation explosion also dominates public attention by instilling a continual fear of being slapped with a lawsuit. Ministers, teachers, coaches, and scoutmasters devote more and more of their time to protecting themselves against abuse lawsuits—time that would otherwise be directed to the children under their care and tutelage. Fear of abuse allegations has made it harder to find qualified volunteers to work with children, says Richard Walker, national spokesman for the Boy Scouts of America.[22] In the business world, fear of litigation often impedes the sharing and transmittal of valuable information. Employers are hesitant to provide any information regarding the performance of former employees.

And because of the threat of strike suits—lawsuits initiated by disgruntled shareholders when a company's stock price declines—more than half of the companies responding to a 1994 American Stock Exchange survey said that the prospect of shareholder litigation inhibited them from disseminating forward-looking information.[23] Even the cherished doctor–patient relationship is colored with fear. A Manhattan hospital, for instance, has estimated that up to 25 percent of its services are unnecessary and done solely for defense in potential lawsuits.[24]

America's litigation obsession, as well as the prominence of trials and lawsuits in the media, shows just how far the litigation explosion has come. It has overtaken not only the courthouses, but also the social mind-set. Lawsuits are constantly in the news. Lawyers are better known than members of Congress. Legal strategies are dissected more than the negotiations over major legislative programs. In a litigious society, the courts have become the focal point of society's attentions. For a democratic society, however, this is an ominous sign.

CHAPTER 2

Pioneering on the Litigation Frontier

THE COURTROOM AS THE MODERN FRONTIER

Litigation has become the new American frontier. Litigious pioneers are continually exploring new kinds of cases and going after new types of defendants. Areas of American life that were once quite insulated from lawyers' offices and courtroom scrutiny have been invaded by litigants. Matters that were once privately handled by nonjudicial practices and institutions are now fought over in the courtroom. Because of the litigation explosion, practically no area of individual or social life has remained untouched by its tremors.

Few cultural symbols or myths carry as much importance to Americans as does the myth of the frontier. Throughout history, the frontier has always symbolized the promise and future of America. At first, it was the Western frontier, with its powerful allure to immigrants and urban dwellers looking for a new start in life. When that frontier closed, Americans looked to the urban–industrial frontier to provide opportunities for individuals. Then came the overseas frontier, followed by the technological frontier.

Now it is the litigation frontier that is attracting individuals' pioneering spirit.

Americans have always thought of their country and future in terms of frontiers, for it is on the frontier that the creative individual looks for opportunity and wealth; and it is on the frontier that individuals look to make their mark on society. The frontier, according to historian David Wrobel, "has become a metaphor for promise and ingenuity."[1] It is where individuals compete for a piece of the American dream.

With the litigation explosion, the frontier has moved to the courthouse, where the litigant pioneers rush to claim their fame and fortune. Just as once did the Western frontier, the litigation frontier now serves as the safety valve of a tense nation—where individuals get one more chance. And like the Western frontier, the litigation frontier encompasses the battleground where America's cultural colonizing is taking place.

On the litigation frontier, innovative explorers are continually discovering new territory. In an atmosphere of litigious hysteria, there seems to be a contest to see who can be the first pioneer to litigate a new kind of case. This frenzied contest resembles the great land rushes of the 19th century, when everyone rushed to stake the first claim on the open lands of the West. And just as those open lands eventually got settled, almost every area of American life is getting litigated. Even President Clinton, besieged by litigation, has established a legal defense fund to pay lawyers' bills. No other president has ever faced such a reality.

Not only is the litigation frontier a source of opportunity for individual fame and fortune, but it is where people duke out their differences, just as they might have once done on the dusty streets of the Old West. For instance, an Ohio man was sued in 1991 for blowing smoke in the plaintiff's face. According to the complaint, the smoke caused physical discomfort, humiliation, and distress. Whereas the matter might once have been settled with shoves and pushes, or a volley of angry words, on the litigation frontier it is handled with a lawsuit.

With the rush to break new legal ground, any boundaries to the spread of litigation have all but disappeared. In a litigious society, the great issue of the day is access to the courthouse—the gateway to the frontier. Not access to the voting booth or to the printing presses, but access to the courts is the demand so often heard on the evening news. Paula Jones, the woman suing President Clinton for sexual harassment, wants access to sue the president. Students want access to sue their teachers, and parents want access to sue their children's therapists.

This rush to the courts sometimes results in cases that ask judges to resolve technical or scientific questions over which even the technicians and scientists cannot agree. For instance, increasing numbers of employees are demanding workers' compensation benefits for a condition called "multiple chemical sensitivity" (MCS). This condition is allegedly caused by too much chemical exposure in the workplace and can subsequently result in severe reactions if the sufferer comes in contact with even the trace amounts of chemicals in perfumes or carpets. Although the New Hampshire Supreme Court ruled in 1994 that MCS is a qualification for workers' compensation, and regulators in 1991 declared that MCS can be a disability under the Americans with Disabilities Act, scientists and doctors are still debating whether MCS even exists. And even the doctors who diagnose MCS cases agree that it is a fuzzily defined disease. Yet while the scientific debate over this disease remains unresolved, the litigation of it moves ahead.

LITIGATION AS AN ARENA
FOR INDIVIDUAL OPPORTUNITY

Going to court is one of the few remaining endeavors that individuals, regardless of their educational or social or economic standing, can do on their own. It is like investing in a high-risk business venture or gambling on a bet. "Litigation is a bit more expensive than the lottery," explained one Connecticut lawyer, "but [the] chances of hitting are better."[2] Of course, like everything else, gambling has become an area ripe for lawsuits. One New York Lottery winner, Daisy Fernandez, was sued by her son's teenage friend, whom Ms. Fernandez had previously asked to pray for her and for her chances of winning the lottery. When she did win, the teenage boy claimed half of the jackpot. The case went before a panel of five State Supreme Court judges, who ruled against the boy, declaring soberly that in a modern court there was no way to prove the efficacy of prayer.

As with the Western frontier before it, the litigation frontier offers to the poor and dispossessed a shot at the economic rewards that have previously eluded them. Personal injury lawsuits, for instance, are one way in which modern litigation pioneers might replicate the economic achievements of the more fortunate 19th-century homesteaders on the Western frontier. Fender-benders and slip-and-falls provide a chance to squeeze out a settlement for whiplash or wrenched back from a cash-laden insurance company. Indeed, to many people, the site of an accident is the sight of a cash windfall. Mass transit operators, for instance, have long worried about the growing phenomenon of ghost riders—people who file insurance claims for injuries they never sustained in public transit accidents. When there is a bus or train accident, bystanders often race on board and claim they were victims. Concerned about this problem, New Jersey set up and filmed a sting operation by staging more than ten accidents around the state. Then, it watched the claims pour in. In one accident, a bus carrying 15 passengers, all participating in the sting, was hit from behind by a car going less than 10 miles per hour. Video cameras filmed 17 people scrambling onto the bus before the police arrived. All later claimed to be injured in the accident. Another two people who were never even on the bus also filed claims. Although, in this case, evidence of the fabricated claims was incontrovertible, insurance fraud is generally quite hard to prove. Transit operators—both public and private—estimate that such fraud may add up to hundreds of millions of dollars annually.[3]

Another gold mine of the litigation frontier lies in the rich reward of punitive damages. If a plaintiff can garner enough sympathy from a jury and convince that jury that the defendant should be punished for its acts, then the possibility exists for an award of punitive damages, in addition to whatever actual damages the plaintiff might have incurred. In June of 1996, an Alabama jury gave an individual plaintiff $100 million in punitive damages against General Motors. According to Steve Bokat, Vice President of the U.S. Chamber of Commerce, the verdict illustrated "the candy store approach to tort litigation in which you have a sympathetic plaintiff and a corporation that is perceived as having a lot of money."[4] Just like the promise of gold in California in 1849, the ever-present chance at punitive damages makes litigation a modern frontier of opportunity.

Plaintiffs on the litigation frontier strive to direct their lawsuits to the deep-pocket defendants—individuals and corporations wealthy enough to pay any judgment the plaintiff obtains. Because of this deep-pocket strategy, people and corporations who appear to have little immediate connection to the plaintiff's injuries are sued. For instance, when a person negligently runs a stoplight and injures another, the lawsuit will most likely focus on the municipality charged with erecting and operating the stoplight. The complaint will allege that the light was not working properly, or that it was not properly located in the intersection.

NEW TERRITORIES BEING SETTLED
BY PIONEERING LITIGANTS

On the litigation frontier, practically any dispute over any matter can now have its day in court. An author sued the *New York Times Book Review* for $10 million because of a harsh review in which it charged the author with "sloppy journalism."[5] A Little Rock, Arkansas, family was sued for the Christmas lights displayed outside their home. Injured during a collision at home plate in a Sunday-afternoon softball game, a player sued his colliding opponent—a longtime friend who had broken the "unwritten rule against sliding in their weekly pickup game."[6] A Davis, California, woman sued the city after police came to her door to investigate noise complaints from neighbors—noise that, as it turned out, was made by the woman's loud snoring. In another California case, a disgruntled homeowner sued the builder not only for the cost of repairs to the house, but also for the emotional distress she suffered when she was too embarrassed to entertain guests at her less-than-perfect dream home. A Minneapolis couple sued a church for refusing to marry them. And a monk sued his religious superiors for transferring him to an undesired location.

The litigation explosion has not only intruded into the most petty, mundane, and ridiculous matters of everyday life, but it has also entered the most private and previously unlitigated areas of life. Five such areas include religion, family life and child raising, sexual and romantic relations, death, and the educational environment at schools. The reach of litigation into these areas reveals that, in the litigation age, no aspect of American life is free from the purview of the courtroom.

Litigating Religion

In one of the areas of American life most traditionally immune from litigation, the courts are increasingly being forced to resolve disputes involving religious matters. The continuing struggle for America's religious soul has taken a decidedly litigious turn in recent years. Angered by the rout of prayer from schools, the advance of gay rights, and the legalization of abortion, conservative Christians who once disdained legal remedies as too worldly have decided to fight from the bar as well as the pulpit.

To wage this fight, the number of Christian-oriented legal-aid groups has grown significantly. The American Center for Law and Justice, founded in 1990 by televangelist Pat Robertson, has already represented clients in nine cases before the Supreme Court and boasts of legal "SWAT teams" ready to descend on schools that deny students the right to pray at high school graduations. Yet another legal organization, the Christian Educators Association, holds seminars in which teachers are taught legal ways to introduce religion in classroom discussion. One of its workshops is called, for example, "The First Amendment: How to Share Judeo-Christian Perspective without Being Sued."[7]

Perhaps the most currently active of the Christian legal groups is the Rutherford Institute in Charlottesville, Virginia.

Rutherford receives about 2000 requests each month for legal help regarding religious-freedom issues.[8] It has assisted a pupil who was admonished for writing "I love Jesus" on a valentine card, another who was prohibited from bringing a church keepsake to show-and-tell, and yet another who was prohibited from writing a research paper on Christ as a historic figure. The institute has also intervened in hundreds of cases in which students were denied use of school property for Bible clubs when other noncurricular clubs were allowed.

In the litigation age, religious activists have waged their crusades in the courtroom, as well as in their churches. Whereas they once shunned any involvement in the legal system, they are now embracing it. The rapidly growing network of Christian legal organizations around the country has adopted the techniques of legal activism developed by such groups as the ACLU and the NAACP Legal Defense Fund. These organizations are fed by a small number of law schools that teach a religious jurisprudence. The Regent Law School, which opened in 1987, is the largest. Its more than 300 students are being trained in what the catalog describes as "God's perspective on law."[9] According to Keith Fournier, executive director of the legal foundation run by the Regent Law School, "We have learned a lot from watching the public interest groups utilize the courts."[10]

Another front in the new religious litigation war is the crusade of Life Dynamics, Inc., a Christian antiabortion organization located in Denton, Texas. Whereas other groups provide free representation to clinic demonstrators or help states draft antiabortion laws, Life Dynamics has developed a new strategy encouraging patients to file lawsuits against abortion providers. Life Dynamics claims to have a network of more than 600 lawyers ready to file such cases and has been recruiting more with the distribution to thousands of personal injury lawyers of a how-to video and a brochure promising that "abortion malpractice is poised to become the most prolific litigation opportunity of a decade."[11]

Not all litigation over religion, however, is initiated by religious groups. For years, civil libertarian groups have been suing schools to prevent the use of Bibles or other religion-oriented materials in the classroom. Cities have been sued for erecting creches during the Christmas season. Even a nongovernmental organization such as the Boy Scouts was sued by two 9-year-old atheists who were excluded from a Cub Scout pack because they would not pledge duty to God.

Family Relations in the Courtroom

Just as religion has gone litigious, so too has another traditionally private institution and activity—the family and the raising of children. The nation's family law courts have witnessed some of the highest increases in caseloads in recent years. These courts are where Americans go to get divorced, divide household goods, obtain custody of their kids, deal with domestic abuse charges, and claim paternity. Just in the area of child abuse and neglect, a new case was filed every 10 seconds in the United States in 1993, according to the National Committee to Prevent Child Abuse.[12]

In addition to the traditional family-law matters, there are also new kinds of cases and legal theories appearing. For instance, estranged husbands and wives can now sue for damages, in addition to divorce. Under a developing legal specialty known as "domestic torts," aggrieved spouses can sue each other for wrongful marital conduct and recover sizable awards for such offenses as fraud and intentional infliction of emotional distress. The result has been "an explosion of civil damage suits."[13] Just a decade ago, such civil damage claims were virtually unheard of in matrimonial law, but now they have become "really hot stuff," says Lee Rosen, a committee chairwoman of the family-law section of the American Bar Association.[14] "Some of the appellate courts around the country are beginning to recognize these creative causes of action," she notes.[15] Lawyers are also beginning to explore new avenues of recovery in this emerging domestic torts field, particularly under homeowner insurance policies.

After the divorce, of course, comes the child-custody battles. In recent years, however, these battles have taken a new twist.

Custody awards have been reconsidered or reversed when one parent alleges that the other's "parenting time" has been altered by work demands. This issue arose with Marcia Clark, the chief prosecutor in the O. J. Simpson murder trial, who had been awarded primary custody in the divorce decree ending her 13 years of marriage to Gordon Clark. Months into the Simpson trial, however, Ms. Clark's ex-husband filed for primary custody of their two children, arguing in his petition that the trial was taking too much of her time away from their two boys. Gordon Clark alleged in court papers that "on most nights, [Marcia] does not arrive home until 10 P.M., and even when she is home, she is working."[16] Not only are custody rulings being increasingly challenged by men, but the Clark case demonstrates that such rulings can be reconsidered months or years later, forcing judges to delve into the intricate details of family life.

Some custody cases have involved private details of family life that have never before warranted judicial intrusion. In one Texas case, for instance, the judge reprimanded the mother for speaking only Spanish to her child. The judge told the mother she "was abusing her child," whereas the mother claimed she was being denied her right to speak her native language.[17]

Child custody and visitation have always been a litigated matter, but now the cases are expanding beyond just the biological parents. Lawsuits have been filed over the issue of whether grandparents can have visitation rights, even if their children object. These cases have led to the organization of grandparents' rights advocacy groups. Rising numbers of custody and adoption lawsuits are also increasingly being brought by gay and lesbian couples, especially in the wake of such court rulings as that of the Florida Supreme Court in April 1995, which opened the door to a constitutional challenge of that state's ban on adoptions by homosexuals.[18]

Another new type of dispute, exemplified by the "Baby Richard" case, involves custody battles between the child's adoptive and biological parents. Considering a petition by a 4-year-old boy's biological father who wanted to win custody of the boy from his adoptive parents, the Illinois Supreme Court, in 1995, in the

"Baby Richard" case found that the biological father's rights had been improperly terminated. As a result, the court removed the boy from the only home he had ever known. In making its decision, the court articulated and weighed three different sets of rights: those of the biological parents, the adoptive parents, and the child. Thus, in a litigious society, child custody is a matter of balancing objective legal rights.

In addition to custody disputes, hundreds of thousands of child abuse cases are filed each year.[19] These cases involve everything from child beating to having a filthy house, to leaving children alone, to spanking as a means of discipline. Consequently, the standards for acceptable parental behavior are increasingly being set in the courts.

Nonfamily child-care providers are also facing legal barrages. Teachers and day-care centers find themselves increasingly being hauled into court on child-abuse charges. Court dockets across the country have become congested with emotionally devastating and legally perplexing cases in which there is little or no physical evidence and the primary witnesses are children. Contributing to the plentitude of these cases is the fact that they can proceed even when the children deny that anything improper occurred. As a psychiatrist in one such abuse case argued, a child's denial of sexual abuse can be evidence that the abuse actually occurred. This is called the child sexual abuse accommodation syndrome, and it has been successfully used in court. It is also another example of how America is developing a cultural bias in a litigation age toward stories of abuse, and how responsibility for child welfare has been transferred from the family to the courts.

Litigating the Libido

A third previously private area into which litigation has intruded is sex. Sexual harassment cases are among the fastest growing areas of litigation, with men now having joined the plaintiffs' ranks. Instances of men alleging sexual harassment are no longer just the material for fiction, as in the best-selling novel *Disclosure* and the movie based upon it. A male employee of the

Federal Aviation Administration, for instance, filed a sexual harassment lawsuit against the agency, alleging that he had been groped and verbally harassed by female co-workers as part of a cultural diversity training workshop sponsored by the agency. And a male aide to a female St. Paul, Minnesota, city council member won a settlement in his suit for sexual harassment against his boss.

Law has even entered the field of romance. Detailed sexual conduct codes have been adopted at colleges such as Antioch College. The Antioch code requires for "each new level of physical and/or sexual contact/conduct" a clear and verbal "yes": "yes" to a kiss, then "yes" to a touch, then "yes" to unzipping. "Asking 'Do you want to have sex with me?' is not enough," the code warns.[20] A generation ago, colleges were retreating from students' social lives and eliminating curfews and rules about who could be in whose dorm and when. But as the Antioch code demonstrates, colleges are now stepping back in to explicitly regulate their students' sexual lives.

In the litigation of sexual behavior, new types of cases are continually appearing. A Michigan case involved the issue of whether a man's persistent E-mail messages of love—messages such as, "If you let me, I would be the best lover you ever could have"—amounted to stalking or innocent courtship.[21] Street construction workers in Minneapolis have been prohibited from "visual harassment"—the staring at female pedestrians.[22] On the campus of Swarthmore College, a male student who continually tried to "date" a woman, despite being told that she was involved with someone else, was found guilty of sexual intimidation (but not harassment). And a professor from Northwestern University School of Law has proposed that the courts recognize a new kind of lawsuit for sexual fraud. Such cases, for instance, could be brought by persons who find out that their sexual partner lied about being unmarried, or by someone whose partner lied about sterility or using birth control, or even by a person who had been sexually rejected.[23]

Besides the growing litigation over the sexual behavior of heterosexuals, there has also been a rising litigiousness over the

rights and activities of homosexuals. Just as are the sexual relations between men and women in a litigious society, the sexual
activities and rights of gays and lesbians are being increasingly
regulated by the courts.[24] The passage and subsequent legal trial
of Colorado's anti–gay rights amendment is one example. Another is the lawsuit filed against the state of Hawaii that aims to
force the state to legally recognize gay marriages. If just one state
legally recognizes same-sex marriage, according to a Hawaii assistant attorney general, "We will have literally a state-by-state litigation explosion over the question."[25]

Across the country, corporations and municipalities have
been sued because they have not bestowed the same financial
benefits on homosexual couples as they do on married heterosexual couples. In one lawsuit, a lesbian couple sued a doctor who
told them she was "uncomfortable" performing an artificial insemination procedure and advised them to go elsewhere. The
couple said they "were so emotionally distraught over the decision that one of them ran out of the examining room in tears."[26]
Their lawsuit alleged discrimination, even though artificial insemination is considered an optional medical procedure, and doctors
are legally required to give medical treatment only in emergency
situations.

Dying and Suing

Like sex, death has also become a litigated event. The ordeal
of Jamie Butcher illustrates the legal maze that must be trans-
versed before nature can take its course. In 1977, a car accident left
Jamie, a high school track star and straight-A student, in a coma,
kept alive only by machines. In 1993, his parents decided they did
not want their son to remain in a vegetative state any longer and
began making plans to take him out of the nursing facility so that
he could die at home. But an advocacy group representing disabled people filed a motion to stop them. A spokesperson for the
group said that "people with disabilities deserve their day in
court."[27] The group wanted a legally appointed guardian, not the

parents, to make all decisions regarding Jamie's future. After a year-long court battle, however, the parents finally won and took Jamie home. It was a long litigation struggle just to let their son end his 17-year vegetative coma and die at home. Even when patients have given advance instructions about what to do in the event they become incapacitated or dependent on external life support systems, disputes arise that lead to litigation. The medical staff, afraid of malpractice suits if they do not do everything in their power to save a life, is in no rush to let a patient die. Furthermore, doctors oftentimes do not know how disabled a patient might become or whether a particular treatment will work. The patient or the family, on the other hand, is often confused and fails to give clear directions in an emergency. Moreover, as doctors argue, advance directives "do not always resolve what to do in an emergency both because patients and families often waver when confronted with imminent death and because it is often hard to predict whether an emergency intervention will improve the patient's quality of life."[28] As a result of these factors, a new wave of lawsuits is seeking to hold medical personnel liable for ignoring advance directives. Increasingly, lawyers are arguing that treatment contravening such directives constitutes battery— an illegal attack on the patient's body.

Taking the Classroom to the Courtroom

A final area of American life that has become riddled with litigation is its educational system and the teacher–student relationship. Schools are getting sued if students get denied scholarships or receive low grades. In 1996, a New York City high school senior sued her school in a dispute over who was to be named as class valedictorian. Teachers get sued if they discipline some students or get too friendly toward others. Coaches have been sued if certain children do not get picked for a sports team, or if once picked, they have not been chosen for certain honors. Parents have been sued by teachers who claimed they were being harassed, whereas teachers have been sued by parents claiming a right to participate in their children's classroom education. And even when students have been expelled for such reasons as carrying a knife, school administrators have been sued.

In 1992, the Supreme Court ruled that students could sue their schools for sexual harassment or sex discrimination. Since then, complaints of sexual harassment at schools have skyrocketed. The number of such complaints to the Department of Education's Office of Civil Rights jumped by almost 400 percent from 1992 to 1994.[29] As one lawyer predicted, "There's going to be a lot of litigation over the next five years."[30] Some of that litigation will be directed at teachers who are perceived to treat their male and female students differently. Such was the 1994 case filed by a 12-year-old girl in an Albany, New York, federal court. In her complaint, she asserted that her entire sixth-grade year was ruined by a teacher who segregated some class projects by sex and allowed boys to engage in offensive sexual behavior toward the girls. According to the girl's complaint, the teacher provided plenty of materials and assistance to the boys, but gave little help to the girls on their projects.

A growing subject of litigation involving schools is the sexual behavior among and between students. A 7-year-old girl who accused boys of sexually harassing her on the school bus won a settlement of her civil rights lawsuit against the school district. In her suit, she alleged that the school district failed to respond properly to a sexually hostile environment that upset her. Another lawsuit filed by a California junior high school girl accused her school of not protecting her from the sexual teasing of her male classmates. She sued her school, rather than the offending boys, for money damages. The parents of a Georgia fifth-grade girl sued their school district for the vulgar language and attempted groping of a boy who sat next to her.

In a case described by a gay-rights lawyer as "the first wave" of such litigation, a 19-year-old gay man sued his former high school in Ashland, Wisconsin, alleging that his principal and teachers had failed to ensure a safe and nondiscriminatory learning environment. The man's lawyer argued that the taunting by his classmates and the school's failure to stop it "forced [the plaintiff] into forfeiting what should have been the happiest times of his life."[31]

These kinds of lawsuits have raised the questions of whether legal action, rather than counseling and education, should be used to socialize young people. They have also caused educators to ponder the impact of attaching an adversarial adult label such as "sexual harassment" to broad categories of childhood behavior. Unquestionably, there is much inappropriate sexual behavior among children. First graders on a bus in Minnesota shout about sexual acts they couldn't possibly understand. Fifth graders in Missouri rub their penises through their pants to embarrass the girls. In Maryland, elementary-school girls try to kiss boys' genitals; the boys, in turn, jump on the girls' backs, crotches pressed against the girls' buttocks, in a stunt called "nutting." Teenagers at an elite Los Angeles high school use their computers to publish a newsletter filled with lurid descriptions of the supposed sexual habits of the popular female clique.

In a 1993 survey of 8th–11th grade students by the American Association of University Women, 81 percent of all students— boys and girls—reported that they had experienced sexual harassment at least once in their school experience.[32] The problem, however, is applying the adult legal standard of sexual harassment to child and adolescent behavior. As a lawyer for the National Organization for Women (NOW) Legal Defense and Education Fund explained, "The way we establish the rules and lines of behavior is by litigation."[33] This has become the instinctive approach in the litigation age. Judgment calls are taken out of the hands of educators and put into the adversarial arena of litigation, which often cannot distinguish between the name-calling of an elementary-schooler and the breast-grabbing by a high-schooler. With the sexual liberation of the 1960s having eliminated the old rules of etiquette between the sexes, however, the courts have now become America's sexual arbiters.

Student-on-student sexual harassment presents a particularly murky area for educators. Schools are increasingly perplexed about what they must do to prevent such claims. And they are uncertain about what must be done, from a legal standpoint, to ensure that they are not maintaining a "sexually hostile educational environment." Although the thrust of the last 25 years has been for schools to withdraw from a parental role and leave students on their own, the current litigation environment requires schools to be responsible for how students treat each other. Certainly, in terms of sexual behavior, educators in the future will have to become trained in the ways of the litigation process. But as one college student accused of sexual harassment said when he was asked whether he would fight a lawsuit filed by another student to keep him from returning to campus, "When you're trying to get an education, you don't want to spend all your time litigating."[34]

Even the content of class lectures and study materials have become subjects of litigation. A University of New Hampshire communications professor was suspended without pay in April of 1993, after several female students charged him with verbal sexual harassment for remarks made in class. The professor, in an attempt to illustrate vivid language, had cited a belly-dancer's description of her craft as akin to "Jello on a plate with a vibrator under the plate."[35] After his suspension, the professor sued and obtained reinstatement. The federal court's ruling also permitted him to sue university officials for money damages resulting from his suspension.

Men have not been the only ones sued for their classroom lectures. A California State University professor and lesbian activist was sued by a male student for her lecture in a Psychology 100 class aimed at one of her life's goals: to empower women to masturbate so they can overcome the "hardship" of sex with men. The lecture included personal sex tales, how-to tips and close-up slides of women and girls' genitals, along with flippant remarks about male genitalia. Although the professor's lawyer dismissed the plaintiff as a prude and his complaint as "fundamentalist Christian McCarthyism," the plaintiff's lawyer accused the university of having a politically correct double standard: It was unimaginable, the lawyer argued, that a male professor delivering the same lecture while demeaning women would not have been punished.[36]

As has happened with religion, sexual behavior, death, and family life, education has been overrun with litigation. Schools have had to battle litigation on countless fronts. In embracing dress codes to protect students from clothing-conscious gangs who have gunned down kids for a jacket or a pair of sneakers, for instance, schools have been sued by various legal-rights groups. Even when schools seek to close down, they find themselves mired in litigation. When the Commonwealth School of Law in Lowell, Massachusetts, shut down, four students sued the board of trustees. They asked for damages of $14 million to cover a lifetime of earnings that they claimed they would have received if they had been permitted to get their degrees and become lawyers. Although the figure seems quite high, perhaps it is not that outrageous in a litigation age.

The litigation explosion is not just producing more lawsuits, but it is also forcing the courts to govern ever more aspects of individual and social life. And as the explosion continues, more people more often will be going to court for more and more matters.

CHAPTER 3

Cultural Foundations of America's Litigation Explosion

FILLING THE CULTURAL VOID

The litigation explosion cannot simply be explained from a legal or judicial point of view. It cannot be traced, as legal critics so often do, exclusively to features of the American judicial system that encourage the filing of lawsuits, nor can it be attributed simply to the number of lawyers or to the all-encompassing American belief in individual rights. The litigation explosion has, more broadly, arisen from the kind of culture and society that America has become in the late 20th century.

American culture has evolved in a way that promotes litigation. The social and cultural forces that once may have inhibited litigation, or that inhibit it in other countries, have eroded in contemporary America. These forces formerly served as cultural regulators: shaping social behavior and resolving conflicts before they wound up in court, thereby relieving courts of the burden of being the primary social arbiter.

One of the cultural developments contributing to the litigation explosion has been the decline of such a widely accepted set of social values. In modern American society, most consensual social values, along with many traditional behavioral standards, have practically disappeared. As young people are taught to tolerate no restrictions on their right to express themselves, the authority of any elders is undermined. With moral judgments of right versus wrong seen as symptoms of an intolerant, repressive, and outdated attitude, any nonlegal guidelines to social and individual behavior virtually evaporate. The relaxation of the social, cultural, and moral stigma against out-of-wedlock births, for instance, has resulted in a 419 percent increase in illegitimate births since 1960.[1] In the same time period, violent crime has increased 560 percent, and divorce rates have quadrupled. To combat the growing social breakdown, President Clinton, in unusually blunt language during a 1994 speech, urged Americans to adopt a new and less tolerant attitude toward illegitimacy, abortion, and single parenthood.[2] Such a new attitude would obviously differ from the approach used by Planned Parenthood of Leadville, Colorado, to fight teen pregnancies—it pays teenage girls $1 for each day they avoid getting pregnant.[3]

President Clinton's message on values mirrored the attitudes of the American public. In a January 1994 *Time* magazine poll, the lack of values/morals was cited as the second most important problem facing the country, just behind crime.[4] A 1994 *Newsweek* survey showed that 76 percent of Americans thought their country was in a spiritual and moral decline. The popularity of William Bennett's *The Book of Virtues* also revealed a public hungry for a revival of civic values.[5] Whereas the more traditional society of the past supported and maintained a set of virtues, Bennett argues, America's modern society has subsided into a psychology of grievance and entitlement. And whereas some of the most important virtues (self-discipline, courage, responsibility) require self-abnegation, the modern age regards self-abnegation as an offense against self-fulfillment—the pervasive pseudovirtue so powerful in America's contemporary litigation culture.

Bennett, the former Secretary of Education, is not the only prominent social critic to focus on the decline of values. As social critic Christopher Lasch argues in *The Revolt of the Elites*, social elites have abandoned the Western values that shaped American development and history.[6] Consequently these elites, the social leaders, have undermined the existence and potency of any American shared value system. In *The Rise of Selfishness in America*, the social critic James Lincoln Collier attributes most of the nation's social ills to the demise of the Victorian belief system and its replacement by the new ethic of the self.[7] Likewise, in *The Moral Sense*, James Q. Wilson claims that American society is morally confused, reluctant to make any judgments about what is right or wrong.[8] It is in this values void that litigation has so pervasively taken hold of society, providing the primary, if not only, guide for social behavior.

In one of the most debated books outlining America's values decline, historian Gertrude Himmelfarb in *The De-Moralization of Society* argues that the nation's problem is not that it has the wrong morality but that it does not have any morality at all.[9] By taking a thoroughly relativistic approach, in which people are constantly urged to be nonjudgmental, American society is left with no standards other than law to govern sex, marriage, divorce, children, and crime. The great Victorian achievement, as Ms. Himmelfarb sees it, was a moral reformation that allowed Britain to achieve a civility that became the envy of the rest of the world. In devaluing middle-class Victorian virtues—the only set of values or standards it had—American society has experienced soaring rates of sexual harassment, divorce, domestic and child care abuse, violent crime, and, not surprisingly, litigation. For without a moral force or defining social standards, society loses any cultural rudder other than its courts.

The distancing of religion from America's public life has also contributed to the decline of values. Through a series of court cases, a Berlin Wall of separation has been built up between church and state—a separation that greatly differs from the American experience up to the 1970s, when such national crusades such as abolitionism, child labor laws, New Deal reforms, and civil rights were inspired by religious ideals and leaders. To individuals who wish to publicly express their beliefs and values, the threat of a lawsuit constantly looms. Prayer and religious symbols have been banished from the public sphere. And the denial of any mention of religious values in the course of political debate has effectively eliminated any consideration of personal and social morality standards from the public realm.

The legal assault on the presence of American religious values in the public arena greatly erodes one of the traditional mechanisms for regulating social behavior outside of the courts. Yet, even apart from religious or moral values, American society possesses no other set of social or cultural standards that might dictate and shape social behavior in ways that would minimize litigation. It is because of this lack of consensual public values that the United States will never be able to achieve, nor probably even want to achieve, the low rates of litigation characteristic of a nation such as Japan—a country whose relatively minimal litigation is often, but mistakenly, held out as a role model for America.

AN UNATTAINABLE ALTERNATIVE

As a homogenous, hierarchical, tightly knit and rigidly con- trolled society, Japan possesses a culture that promotes a host of values that significantly deter and discourage litigation. Although, of course, this comes at a price—individual freedom in Japan is not what it is in the United States. Japan is a society committed to social harmony. Individualism, so important in the United States, is muted in favor of social order. Japanese identity derives not from the individual but from membership in a larger social group. In Japan, the welfare of the group depends on unanimous conformity.[10]

Japanese-style democracy might be defined as a system in which individuals are assured a secure life in exchange for bury- ing themselves in the group. There is no room in the system for the concept of individual rights. Similarly, in the economic sphere, Japanese corporations still hew to the tradition of providing workers with jobs for life. Nippon Steel, the world's largest steel- maker, kept a factory operating long after it became unprofitable and closed it only gradually, transferring workers to other plants.[11]

When it could no longer transfer workers, the company scrambled to create almost any business it could to employ the former steelworkers, including an ill-fated attempt at growing mushrooms. Loyalty and cohesion are the rule in Japanese society. Toyota's anthem, played at the end of each working day, reflects this social conformity: "With a global wisdom and a dream of plentiful technology, we lead history for a bright future, we get together, and head for new steps. Oh! our Toyota." At every turn in Japanese life, people are geared toward conformity. A authoritative mix of bureaucracy and convention ensures this conformity. For instance, everyday at 5:00 P.M., loudspeakers mounted on lampposts all over the country remind mothers to go home and look after their children. And because mothers at home mean there are no latchkey children, juvenile delinquency is rare.

Japanese schools are social assembly lines that mold students into the same shape and constantly remind them that they are members of a larger community. Rules are ubiquitous, and the atmosphere even at public schools is a bit like that of an American military academy. Not only do schools stipulate the uniform, but also they often ban wristwatches, hair ribbons, curled hair, bleached hair, perfume, scented deodorant, earrings, makeup, money, or anything else that could set one student apart from another. Even outside of the classroom, Japanese schools freely set standards for students at home and during summer vacation. The idea is that schools not only teach students but also train them on how to fit into society. Junior high schools, for instance, bar students from stopping anywhere on their way home from school, even at a store to buy a beverage.[12] On vacation, students are not allowed to visit *karaoke* restaurants, coffee houses, or arcades. Even romances are scrutinized, with teachers keeping a careful eye on boyfriends and girlfriends.

The values that dominate Japanese society are inculcated in the schools. Hierarchical authority is one such value, as are social harmony and a belief in reciprocal obligations. And along with this social harmony comes social trust. For instance, anyone can go to a police station and, without showing identification, borrow the equivalent of $10 or $20 for transportation home. Of course, this trust is understandable, given the low crime rates in Japan. It has only 1/8th as many thefts and burglaries as America. And with 48 percent of the population of the United States, Japan has 1/20th as many killings, 1/70th as many arson cases and 1/300th as many robberies. But the endurance of social trust arises not just because of low crime rates but also from a pervasive social stigma against reneging on one's promises. Consequently, contracts are rarely broken, whereas in the United States, it is perfectly acceptable to breach a contract so long as one is willing to pay the damages.

Strong sanctions, such as communal condemnation and rejection, discourage the Japanese from acting against the common values of society. For instance, only 1.1 percent of Japanese children are born to unmarried mothers, whereas in the United States the figure is 30.1 percent.[13] Because of their strong sense of harmony and social cohesion, the Japanese also hesitate to use litigation. Consequently, the amount of litigation is marginal as compared to other industrialized nations, especially the United States. Not only is there a reluctance to litigate, but there is even a hesitancy to consult a lawyer. Whereas Japan has one attorney for every 10,000 people, the United States has one lawyer for every 360 people, and only 3 percent as many lawyers exist in Japan as in the United States.[14] Not surprisingly, Japan has been described as "a nation in which the formal system of justice, so eagerly embraced in the U.S., is shunned."[15]

Due to the desire to avoid the harmony-destroying bitterness that might develop in an adversarial type of adjudication, the great majority of social conflicts find their solutions outside the courts. Even when conflicts do arise, they are put into less confrontational terms. Turning to legal help is like admitting failure. When a Japanese man calls his lawyer, he is sadly admitting that, in his case, his social system has broken down.[16]

LITIGATION IN A CULTURE OF THE SELF

The social homogeneity and conformity of Japanese society could never be transplanted to the United States, nor would the vast majority of Americans desire such a result. But a comparison with Japanese culture does demonstrate why litigation is so much more prominent in the individualistic culture of America.

Whereas the structure and values of Japanese society greatly inhibit and discourage litigation in that country, the "culture of the self" existing in the United States provides much fuel to its litigation explosion. A culture of the self is an individualistic culture exalting self-fulfillment and self-gratification. It is a culture that sees no boundaries or limitations to self-expectations. In such a culture, litigation thrives, as it is an act predicated upon the individual's self-asserted freedom from the communal constraints against which he or she is complaining. Individual plaintiffs can pursue their judicial agendas alone. Whereas most other social institutions, such as schools and churches, are aimed at groups and communities, the courts are geared to the individual. The judiciary is the social institution geared primarily to individual demands and grievances, open to any person who possesses a complaint against the community.

In America, litigation allows individuals to break away from the authority of their larger community. Whereas legislatures require a majority-building process, the courts permit individuals to go it alone. Through litigation, an individual can not only break away from communal life and values, but also he or she can even take an adversarial approach to the community. He or she can prevent a minister from speaking at a community event, halt a school program, stop a public meeting, or prevent regulations from being enforced—all through the filing of a lawsuit.

The courts permit the individual to define her identity and objectives totally in terms of the self. Courts also provide a forum for remedying the failed expectations of the self. When an investment does not turn out to be what was expected, a lawsuit provides a remedy for the disappointment. When one's business partners don't live up to expectations, a lawsuit might gain what the partnership failed to achieve. When one's job doesn't furnish the material rewards expected, a lawsuit might do so. Litigation is the means by which the individual has a second chance to fulfill his or her expectations, to satisfy his or her desires—a second chance to achieve self-gratification.

The values promoted by a culture of the self also contribute to the litigation explosion. In glorifying the unrestrained self, America's modern culture has discarded values such as social order, self-discipline, delayed gratification, and individual restraint. Such a culture does not encourage people to be modest or self-effacing, nor to submerge their egos or sacrifice their personal desires for some higher cause. Such a culture encourages lawsuits such as that of Carol and Jim Harris, who sued Mothers against Drunk Driving (MADD) after being barred from the organization. The Harrises claimed that MADD violated their civil rights, that they were "victims of personality bias because other members of the organization found [them] unpleasant."[17] Although once vertical, imposing order and rules, social authority has greatly eroded in a litigation culture that disdains hierarchy and indulges the desires of the individual. In California, for instance, antidiscrimination laws have been used to extend special privileges to motorcycle-club members and unconventional dressers. "To me, discrimination occurs anytime everyone isn't treated exactly equal," argues Kenneth Lipton, a California lawyer who has specialized in civil rights law since winning a "nerd-bias" case against a nightclub.[18]

Litigation has followed this breakdown of vertical authority and has, in fact, contributed to it, for litigation entails an approach adversarial to the community—an opportunity to avoid communal authority while still enjoying communal benefits. Obviously, when one compares the social structure of Japan, the values promoted by America's culture of the self encourage rather than discourage litigation. In return, the litigation explosion further solidifies the individualistic culture of the United States.

The proliferation of libel lawsuits, for instance, follows from a culture of the self, for in such a culture, individual image is vitally important, and libel lawsuits seek to vindicate and uplift that image. Such lawsuits have become standard strategies in the arsenals of famous people who seek to create a particular image—any criticism is met with a lawsuit. But not just the rich and famous resort to libel lawsuits. In 1994, Carol Publishing agreed to settle a lawsuit brought by a convicted killer alleging that a book described him as a serial killer, when, in fact, he was a multiple killer. Not only does American individualism actively promote litigation, but its flip side also provides an additional, albeit more passive, support to the litigation explosion. By weakening social trust, a culture of the self further contributes to litigiousness. During the litigation age, Americans have become significantly less trusting of each other. The proportion of Americans saying that most people can be trusted fell by more than one-third between 1960, when 58 percent chose that alternative, and 1993, when only 37 percent did.[19] This decline in trust not only contributes to the rise in litigation, since an adversarial posture obviously presumes lack of trust, but has also followed from the litigation explosion, since the more litigation, and the more its message of mistrust is conveyed, the less trust is likely to exist.

LITIGATION AND THE EROSION OF COMMUNITY

Along with the decline of social trust has occurred an even larger cultural development that further contributes to litigious behavior. Over the last several decades, America has become more of a mobile and noncommunal society. And as this trend continues, litigation will likewise continue to increase, for litigation provides an essential social glue for an impersonal, mobile society. The knowledge that one can sue is a substitute for personal trust or acquaintance (e.g., contracts can be entered into with unknown parties; unfamiliar doctors can be consulted; houses can be bought in strange locations; business partnerships with unknown persons can be formed), because if things do not work out, one can always sue. Moreover, as communal bonds diminish, the social values and forces working to lessen individual and social disputes are similarly weakened.

America has always been a mobile society, but during the litigation age, many long-established communal ties have declined. Since 1973, for instance, the number of Americans reporting that in the past year they have attended a public meeting on town or school affairs has fallen by more than one-third.[20] Similar declines are evident in responses to questions about attending a political rally or serving on a committee of some local organization. By almost every measure, public engagement in politics and government has fallen steadily and sharply over the last generation. Participation in parent–teacher organizations has dropped from more than 12 million in 1964 to 7 million in 1994. The same pattern exists for civic and fraternal organizations. Membership in the League of Women Voters is down 42 percent since 1969, as is membership in mainline civic organizations such as the Boy Scouts (down 26 percent) and the Red Cross (down 61 percent). Labor Department surveys have shown that "regular" (as opposed to occasional or "drop-by") volunteering declined by almost 20 percent from 1974 to 1989. Finally, in his study of American civic engagement, Harvard professor Robert Putnam has uncovered a curious, but startling, bit of evidence of social disengagement in contemporary America.[21] He found that although more Americans are bowling today than ever before, bowling in organized leagues has plummeted. Between 1980 and 1993, the total number of bowlers increased by 10 percent, whereas league bowling deceased by 40 percent. (Not wanting this to be thought a wholly trivial example, Putnam points out that 80 million Americans went bowling at least once during 1993—nearly one-third more than voted in the 1994 Congressional elections and roughly the same number as claim to attend church regularly.)

This breakdown of community, along with the erosion of American social values and the rise of a culture of the self, contributes to the American tendency to litigate. Without community structures, there is little left to mitigate the kinds of social conflicts that eventually lead to litigation. At the same time, the litigation explosion further erodes community and social authority. Take, for instance, developments in the nation's schools. As a result of procedural rights gained through litigation by students, schools have much greater difficulty in expelling or disciplining disruptive students. The right to challenge the authority and judgment of teachers has altered the attitude of many students. It has helped to equalize the status of students and teachers, creating a sense of invulnerability among students and encouraging defiance.

A LITIGIOUS CULTURAL MIND-SET

With the decline of the community, a growing litigation mentality has become a substitute for any other consensual social or cultural values. Litigation, in a sense, has become the American social mind-set. It is one of the few unifying national beliefs or activities. And as this mentality has become more ingrained in the public consciousness, it further fuels the litigation explosion.

Litigation has both followed from and contributed to a social mind-set in America that looks to create a perfect system of law. This mind-set seeks to establish an American legal system that anticipates and covers every eventuality—a legal system that is the perfect regulator, the all-wise and all-protective parent.[22] It is as though the American mind looks to the law as the sole expression of society, as if a perfect law will lead automatically to a perfect America and a perfect life. If such a legal system is established, one that eliminates all uncertainty, contemporary American society will have reached its zenith—a risk-free society. Consequently, through the litigation explosion, a perfect body of law is sought, one in which all tragedy and disappointment and risk will be eradicated. By fine-tuning every kink or uncertainty in modern life, the courts, in effect, strive to create through their case law an overwhelming and omnipotent instruction manual for American social life.

The drive to make rules and laws so specific that they will cover any circumstance or conflict arising in daily life has intensified the litigation urge. The thousands of Occupational Safety and Health Administration (OSHA) regulations governing safety in the workplace, for instance, have spawned hundreds of thousands of court cases addressing their meaning and application.[23] The linchpin connecting the desire for an all-protective legal system with the litigation explosion has been the ever-expanding notion of *liability*—a word that has become a staple of American vocabulary and conversation. As the detonator of the litigation explosion, liability has become the all-encompassing governor of American society. Nearly every aspect of modern social life in some way entails a consideration of the existence or threat of liability. Workplace personnel decisions take into account liability potential almost as much as they do productivity potential. Schools and public buildings open or close their doors to after-hours community activities depending on the liability risks. Parties are planned according to the rumors of liability and lawsuits that have spread through the neighborhood. The intricacies of liability have even become the new directional force behind architectural design. Every stairway, every walkpath, every corner is gauged in terms of its liability potential. Plexiglas™ shields are installed on balconies to prevent suicides.

Because of the threat of liability, society no longer expects people to think for themselves and to be responsible for the risks they take. Little is left to human discretion or imagination. Endless legions of mindless warnings constantly parade through daily life. Power saws carry warnings that fingers should not be placed in the path of the whirling blade—but if consumers are really that dense, perhaps they should not be allowed to buy such tools. Beer bottles are stamped with warnings against drinking and driving, even though no instance has ever been found of a person who, after guzzling a bottle of beer, suddenly stops to read the warning and becomes newly enlightened to the risks of driving after drinking. Just to be safe, from litigation, that is, signs warning about the danger of skating on thin ice are left up all winter long on the edge of ponds frozen with ice so thick it could support a truck. People cannot be trusted to reason that if the ice is thin, skating on it could be dangerous. Yet, even though a litigious society seeks to eliminate all risk of danger, it may, in fact, achieve the opposite. By not encouraging its people to think for themselves and to learn *how* to take risks, such a society makes the world more dangerous.

Aside from the questions of whether a society can ever really eliminate risk, any such effort unquestionably requires an almost endless chain of litigation. To strive for a perfect body of law that eliminates all risk and uncertainty is to sanction an ever-escalating litigation explosion. That is because the risk of failure is inherent in every endeavor. Consider the lawsuit filed by a group of mountain climbers. In July of 1993, five teenage boys and three adult leaders from a Mormon youth group rappeled into a 65-foot sandstone canyon in southern Utah. At the bottom, the group was swept away by a swift, chilly current—the spring runoff from the Rocky Mountains. One boy and a counselor died in the torrent; the rest of the group had neither the skills nor the equipment to climb back up. They clung to canyon walls until a Park Service helicopter rescued them, at a cost of $60,000. But the angry survivors sued the Park Service, alleging that they should have been warned of the danger, despite the fact that they were told to expect high, cold water. Their lawsuit condemned the very risk that led them to their adventure in the beginning. Or consider the dilemma of a California parks supervisor. On one hand, he tried to close playgrounds after a lawsuit was filed by the parent of a child who had been hurt by an animal swing that had been in the playgrounds for decades. On the other hand, community groups were outraged by the dismantling of popular playground equipment. To further complicate matters, budget considerations greatly favored use of the durable and vandal-resistent swings, but because of that durability, the swings no longer met all the current safety regulations and therefore exposed the city to litigation risks. In yet another case of the litigation quandary imposed by a no-risk social mentality, a Texas launderette company was sued for millions of dollars by survivors of a man shot to death near the entrance of one of the company's launderettes. The plaintiffs' attorney claimed that the launderette should not have been open that late at night, but the late hours were exactly what attracted patrons to the self-service launderette.

American litigiousness is fed by a social mind-set that not only looks to create a perfect law, but also yearns for that law to be the provider of social meaning and identity. In advocating her vision of a "politics of meaning," for instance, First Lady Hillary Rodham Clinton called for law to provide the kind of deeper social and personal meaning that was once furnished by religion and philosophy. Probably more than any other country, the United States throws its entire being into the legal arena—its gender wars and values debates, its failed hopes and hopeful dreams. Americans expect the legal system to solve problems that other societies believe are better left at the dinner table. In the European view, for instance, law is about social order. But to many Americans, law is about the character of life.

Similarly, such political approaches as "the personal as political" see every issue in private life as inherently legal. Dress codes at work become a matter of legal conflict. The allocation of child care burdens between two parents rises to a matter of law. A person's private sexual life is litigated. Every personal action or decision has the potential of becoming a legal issue. The courtroom becomes the forum for the vindication and legitimization of personal and moral beliefs. It becomes the gladiatorial arena in which the battle of "values" is fought. Unmarried lovers seek retribution from devoutly religious landlords who refuse to rent to them. Lesbian couples sue to force a doctor to perform artificial insemination on one of them. Students litigate their desire to pray in school.

The techniques of law have become a kind of civic religion, according to Robert Nagel, a professor of law at the University of Colorado. "From the deepest political dispute to the smallest misunderstanding at the office water cooler, Americans discuss every disagreement in the clumsy jargon of rights," he argues.[24] Any beliefs about right or wrong, moral or immoral, are quickly translated into arguments about legal rights. Consequently, legalistic thinking drowns out any other set of social standards or cultural values. When Hillary Rodham Clinton called her healthcare legislation a "moral issue," just as religious fundamentalists call school prayer a moral issue, she, in effect, eliminated any difference between law and morality.[25] However, by assigning the law to also perform the role of morality is to give it an unending task—a task that requires unending litigation.

The wrestling with unending personal issues—seen as political and legal issues—leads inevitably to more and more litigation. Indeed, under such an approach, in which law supersedes every other source of meaning and direction in life, litigation becomes just another exercise in the search for personal growth. And the path to this growth is through the acquisition and assertion of rights.

The litigation explosion has both resulted from and triggered a corresponding rights explosion. In a litigious culture of the self, rights become the social currency. Their power is supreme, and they trump all other social considerations. Not surprisingly, if rights trump every other moral claim, or if every major issue of public policy is framed in the absolutist terms of unconditional rights, then litigation will continue unabated. But this approach considers that just the right kind of laws are sufficient to make a democratic society work. With the right legal system, so the thinking goes, democracy can dispense with civic virtue. And the way to build such a system is through unhindered litigation, for only litigation can create and assert rights.

The legal mind-set that expects law to subsume all other sources of civic virtue and personal responsibility will turn litigation into a moral crusade. By allowing legal rights to drown out everything else, the litigation explosion will escalate even further, for in a culture of legal rights, litigation is inevitable and unending. In a culture that defines child custody and visitation in terms of "men's rights" versus "women's rights," litigation encompasses every matter.

CHAPTER 4

The Breeding of
an Adversarial Culture

THE COURTROOM AS AMERICA'S
MODERN-DAY ELLIS ISLAND

American society has always had its cultural myths. From the 17th-century Puritan "City on a Hill" to the rugged individualism of the Western frontier, certain cultural models have been used to characterize and describe American society. Perhaps the most enduring social model and cultural myth has been that of the melting pot. Symbolized by the Statue of Liberty and Ellis Island, the melting pot model described America as a country where immigrants from different corners of the world came to start a new life by stepping out of their previous ethnic identities and into the American melting pot. It was this melting pot in which they were all transformed into the ingredients of one and the same national brew.

The melting pot model relied on assimilation, in that being an American meant giving up individual differences and becoming part of a harmonious and unified new society. America in the 1990s, however, no longer follows the melting pot model. Divisiveness has replaced assimilation as the defining social trait. Social fragmentation is occurring on many levels: race, gender, religion, immigration, age, education, crime. Even single issues, such as child care or abortion, have sharply polarized people into opposing camps.

With the rise of multiculturalism and the increasing value put on diversity, the melting pot or assimilation model has been cast aside. In its place, the multicultural model has been used to portray America as a mosaic, with all of its people retaining their own ethnic, racial, and cultural identities. Although the multicultural model describes the diversity of America, it does not serve as a model for the dynamics of American society. Multiculturalism may provide a static picture of America's residents, but it does not supply a working model of how those residents interact with each other in society. The multicultural model focuses on demographics— the racial and ethnic makeup of American society, but it does not address how social relations within or between those groups are being conducted. For this purpose, the litigation model, with its adversarial process, is needed.

Just as the immigrant explosion into Ellis Island once taught Americans to assimilate, the litigation explosion now teaches Americans to be adversaries. In a direct contradiction to the assimilation model, American society and culture is realigning toward the adversarial process of the courtroom, with litigation serving as the guidepost for social relations. Consequently, the adversarial model of the litigation process now best exemplifies, as the assimilation model once may have, the dynamics of contemporary American society.

Modern America has often been described as a society at war, one that has gone from melting pot to boiling point. A growing adversarial culture has greatly eroded any sense of shared community, common values, and national identity. Ideological polarization has become locked into society and politics: the religious right versus the politically correct liberals; religious fundamentalists versus secular humanists; conservatives as greedy capitalists versus liberals as whiny do-gooders; taxpayers versus welfare recipients; prolife versus prochoice; gay rights versus family values. According to Robert Hughes, the longtime art critic for

Time, this conflict has weakened and, in some areas, broken the traditional American genius for consensus.[1] The constant ideological conflict, as reflected in the "culture wars," has annihilated the compromises necessary for social harmony.

This fragmentation and ideological conflict is not necessarily a result of a multicultural society. America, whether recognized or not, has always been a diverse and multicultural society. There have always been tensions between racial and ethnic groups in America, but what has now happened is that social relations in the litigation age have begun following the adversarial model of the courtroom rather than the assimilation model. It is the adversarial model, after all, that describes even the conflict that is presently occurring within racial and ethnic groups in America. Social breakdown is occurring along nonracial and nonethnic lines, just as it is between the different racial and ethnic groups.

Because the litigation process rests on an adversarial model, the litigation explosion has injected a heightened adversariness into American society. The consensus of the assimilation model, upon which the legislative process is based, has been eclipsed by the combative nature of the adversarial model. Consequently, in the United States at the close of the 20th century, citizens are acting more like litigants in court than like partners and negotiators at the table of political compromise. The litigation model, however, is not alone in turning America into an adversarial society. Reinforcing the message of the litigation process is the increasingly pervasive example of America's sports culture—a culture that has likewise become quite adversarial and obviously celebrates the process of conflict. In this way, athlete celebrities have joined lawyers in shaping the adversarial nature of contemporary American society.

THE MODELS FOR A CULTURE OF CONFLICT: SPORTS AND LITIGATION

If there is anything as popular as litigation in America, it is sports. And because they are providing the role models for society, both litigation and sports cultures reflect and influence what is happening in American society as a whole.

Just as litigation requires a combat of litigants, sports demands a battle of athletes. As one of the most revered activities in contemporary America, sports has helped foster a model of social behavior that emphasizes conflict between adversaries. A litigious society, increasingly awestruck with a glorified sports culture, is learning that combat and victory is the model for social life, and that for every winner there must be a loser. From Court TV to ESPN, from Judge Wopner to the artificial wars of "Monday Night Football," the message to Americans is that conflict and combat is the only way to live. As in televised sports, televised trials, with their entourage of network commentators who speculate daily about the courtroom winners and losers, pull their huge audiences into the drama of conflict.

Sports has become an $80 billion per year industry—an industry bigger than the auto, petroleum, lumber and air transportation sectors of the economy.[2] Thirteen billion dollars of licensed sports merchandise—such as shirts, hats and jackets all displaying the names and logos of sports teams—are sold each year. In 1972, ABC paid $7.5 million to televise the Summer Olympic Games, whereas NBC paid more than $400 million for the same opportunity 20 years later. In 1973, the average baseball salary was $36,566, and baseball's highest-paid player was Dick Allen of the Chicago White Sox (earning $225,000); in 1993, Bobby Bonilla of the New York Mets earned $6.2 million. Corporate spending on sponsorship of sporting events reached $2.85 billion in 1994, a figure more than ten times the amount companies spend on sponsorship of the arts.[3]

With more and more cable channels devoted to sports coverage, television audiences have grown tremendously. There is "an insatiable public appetite for sports," according to John Mansell, a media consultant.[4] As ESPN executive vice president Ed Durso notes, "We are very encouraged by the appetite of the sports viewer."[5]

Sports figures have become more than accomplished athletes: They are now celebrity spokespersons who have become cultural role models. In commercials, Deion Sanders proudly proclaims he wants, and gets, it all. Dennis Rodman has become a celebrity in part by hitting referees and taunting fans. The superstars in Nike commercials tell their audiences to "Just do it." Countless others brashly brag of their ability to squash an opponent.

It is not, however, just the overwhelming popularity of sports and the godlike status of sports celebrities that is reinforcing an adversarial model for society—it is also the way in which sports are now played. Gone are the days when the standard of good sportsmanship ruled. Gone are the days when the values of sport—honoring boundaries, playing by the rules, working together for a common goal, submitting to authority—were the same values that shaped the national character. Now the football field and the basketball court are the site of rude and contentious behavior. In playground ball, half the game lies in the art of mercilessly taunting one's opponents during the game, then rubbing their faces in the ashes of defeat afterward. "Victory is not enough; you have to humiliate," observes Frank Deford, who devoted a weekly sports commentary on National Public Radio to the decline of civility. Trash talking, finger pointing, and dancing over fallen opponents is commonplace. Prizefighters learn how to demean a man before they have mastered the uppercut. Basketball players make choke signs and spew out a torrent of trash talk. No football player seems able to carry a ball for a touchdown or tackle an opposing ball carrier without following up with some taunting dance. Not just beating, but also antagonizing the opponent has become a necessary part of the performance. "It's becoming fashionable to be on the attack," says Hubie Brown, a former NBA coach.[6]

This contentiousness, however, is not confined to professional sports. Both athletes and coaches around Los Angeles say sporting contests have become more bitter at all levels in recent years. According to the California Interscholastic Federation, 15 to 20 incidents of unsportsmanlike behavior occurred 10 years ago in basketball. Today the figure is over 200.[7] Even on the most remote high school baseball field, mean-spirited combat is replacing sportsmanlike competition. In the communities of Ventura County in southern California, for instance, the handshake—the universal symbol of good will and good sportsmanship—was banned at the close of sporting events in 1994 for fear that fistfights might ensue.[8] One high school athletic director said the death of the custom reflected the way high school and college athletics were taking on the high stakes aggressiveness of professional sports. But more importantly, this handshake ban, like the daily combat of litigants, has come to symbolize a spreading social warfare that goes well beyond sports.

There have been so many fights between rival fans at two Los Angeles Catholic schools that officials banned spectators for 2 years from attending any sporting event between the two teams. When the two football teams played for the league championship in 1993, the game was held in secrecy at a neutral site in an empty stadium on a Thursday afternoon. Likewise, in Philadelphia, the threat of violence has forced some schools to schedule all their athletic events during the day. During one argument-turned-fight between two rival North Carolina youth-league baseball coaches, one coach had his throat slashed and required 50 stitches. A Beaumont, Texas, senior who was the mascot for her high school football team ceased wearing her costume because she was afraid "it would make her a target" at the games. Indeed, high school football has come to generate such passions in Texas that, in recent years, bloody scuffles in stadium parking lots have become commonplace.

Caught in the middle of this overaggressive sports behavior are the umpires. Fed up with being the target of punches and kicks, referees and umpires are taking abusive fans and coaches to court.[9] Not only are more and more officials going to court, but in the first 6 months of 1994 alone, legislatures in California, Massachusetts, Iowa, Illinois, and New Jersey all considered bills that would stiffen the penalties for attacks on umpires and referees. There have been so many incidents of assaults on referees that *Referee* magazine, a trade publication, temporarily stopped running news items about attacks on sports officials. The editors felt the constant onslaught was demoralizing to its readers.

The win–lose, opponent-trashing mind-set of sports is becoming the national mentality. It carries over to every aspect of society. Musicians, authors, and film producers are judged like sports teams, with their newest recordings, books, and movies instantly ranked as wins or losses. On weekly television shows such as "The McLaughlin Group" and "The Capitol Gang," the primary political question is "Who won the week?" Even academic achievement is becoming an adversarial contest. The number of elementary and high school academic competitions have increased dramatically—since 1983, the number of students participating has grown by 6,250 percent—setting off a frenzy of cutthroat contests for medals, trophies, and scholarships.[10]

The sports mentality has become so pervasive that there are now many opportunities for the nontraditional athlete to achieve media glory through defeat of one's adversary. Such opportunities offer the chance, however fleeting, to emulate professional-athlete heroes. The television show "American Gladiators," for instance, attempts to duplicate for nonprofessional athletes the glory of televised conflict. It is another example of the increasing glorification of the win–lose conflicts dramatized by professional sports.

Even though America's growing addiction to sports has fueled an increasingly adversarial model for society, not everyone can compete in athletic contests. In fact, only a small fraction of Americans will ever have their athletic skills shown on television. Although most people can't be sports heroes, they can participate in the litigation battle and triumph as victorious litigants. Suing is a game every person can play, and litigation is the competition that is most universal in its accessibility. In a sports-minded world, litigation offers all nonathletes the arena and the opportunity to triumph over their adversary. As Massachusetts Superior Court Judge Hiller Zobel has observed, "Lawsuits have always furnished us with ... the vicarious triumph and defeat of an athletic contest."[11]

Both the sports and litigation explosions are reinforcing the adversarial model for society—a model that encourages a society of combatants. As the adversarial mode gains strength in the continuing litigation explosion, every aspect of American society has followed its lead and become more adversarial.

SYMPTOMS OF AN ADVERSARIAL SOCIETY

The Decline of Civility

The adversarial style so characteristic of the litigation process is showing up in a wide array of social relations. People increasingly treat others with more adverseness and rudeness than courtesy and accommodation. The decline of civility is one notorious trademark of the growing contentiousness of American society. According to polls, nine out of ten Americans think incivility is a serious problem, and 78 percent say the problem has worsened from 1986 to 1996.[12]

Symptomatic of America's rising incivility is, as social scientist Elijah Anderson theorizes, a growing urban oppositional culture.[13] The code of the nation's streets, argues Anderson, commands the youth to compete for respect and status by "dissing" or "messing with" each other. The extent to which persons can raise themselves up depends on their ability to put another person down. Disputes are settled through cursing and abusive talk, if not aggression and outright violence. This "oppositional culture," according to Anderson, is not confined to the inner city.[14] It reverberates throughout American society and at the same time reflects the attitudes of the wider society. Consider, for instance, the Chevrolet television advertisement showing a frustrated woman in a Camaro passing a leering trucker. As the narrative expresses her angry thoughts about her boss, her ex-husband, and an incompetent waitress, she thrusts a blurred arm in the air at the truck driver. Despite the blur, the gesture strongly suggests the kind of hand signal that accompanied it.

As Pete Hamill wrote in *Esquire*, American society "is becoming swept away by a poisonous floodtide of confrontation, vulgarity and flat-out, old-fashioned hatred."[15] Present-day incivility occurs everywhere in society: from the football field, to the highway, to the political arena. The guy in the next airplane seat thinks nothing of pulling out his cellular phone for a loud conversation or of cramming his unchecked bags under someone else's seat. Persons at the beach are apt to plant their boomboxes 10 inches from your ear. Noisy audiences have become the norm at theaters and movie houses. Restaurants are plagued with broken reservations and ill-mannered patrons. The media, through such television programs as "The Simpsons," "The McLaughlin Group," and MTV's "Beavis and Butt Head," reflect this vulgarity and rudeness. Popular music has become increasingly ugly and antisocial.[16] From gangsta rappers and skinhead rockers, the only acceptable human emotion is rage—there is no room for lyricism, melody, or wit. A growing body of contemporary art, as reflected in the works of Andres Serrano and Robert Mapplethorpe, has been described as tough art—art that is combative and confrontational. One exhibit that began touring U.S. museums in 1994 featured an American flag made of dried strips of human skin, a flag stuffed into a toilet bowl, and a flag spread out on the floor for visitors to walk or stomp on.[17]

In a country that coined the term "Have a nice day," citizens now wear sweatshirts that scream "Back off" and "Outta my face." Even President Clinton, in an off-the-cuff response to a heckler, said: "I might say this is another thing wrong with this country. There's not enough civility in how we treat each other."[18] This growing incivility arises from a society that values a win–lose, all-or-nothing mentality that tends to narrow people's chances for settling disputes peacefully. In an adversarial society, people feel that being polite doesn't get them anywhere, that it's a sign of weakness. Social relations are increasingly being modeled after the "in your face" style of sports, a style that is loud and boastful, and that is being increasingly adopted by politicians, business executives, and educators.

Even New Yorkers have noticed a decline of civility. "New Yorkers have never been terribly civil, but it never had an ideological edge, which it now has," according to Fred Siegel, a professor of humanities at Cooper Union in New York.[19] A nonprofit group called New York Pride was set up in 1990, and one of its first projects was a campaign to reduce rudeness. But the group didn't even last 3 years. Yet another community tried a different approach to the battle against rudeness. The New Jersey town of Raritan has prohibited "rude or indecent behavior," including profanity or "making insulting remarks or comments to others" on the borough's quaint and quiet streets.

The decline of civility reflects and flows from an increasingly litigious society, as courtesy and sensitivity are not thought to be useful traits in the waging of litigation combat. But rudeness also feeds the litigation explosion, as rude people are more prone to sue and be sued. According to a study done by doctors from Vanderbilt University, for instance, physicians are more likely to be sued if patients feel they are rude, insensitive, and uncommunicative.[20]

The adversarial social attitudes showing up in the decline of civility, however, have spread well beyond the courtroom. They now appear in nearly every aspect of American social life.

Conflict in the Classroom

Adversity is increasingly characterizing American education. A slew of recent books have documented the increasing conflict within higher education: Gerald Graff's *Beyond the Culture Wars*; Charles Sykes's *Prof Scam*; Roger Kimball's *Tenured Radicals*; Dinesh D'Souza's *Illiberal Education*; Allen Bloom's *Closing of the American Mind*; Martin Anderson's *Imposters in the Temple*; and Richard Bernstein's *Dictatorship of Virtue*. The battles over political correctness, for instance, reflect a bitter warfare going on in the university. As one dean of a humanities department proclaimed: "I see my scholarship as an extension of my political activism."[21] Furthermore, the proliferation of speech codes show that even speech has become a casualty of the war over political correctness.

Curriculum battles over what will be taught and who will teach it present another front in the education warfare. The prolonged and bitter battles at such schools as UCLA and the University of Texas exemplify this warfare. In *Beyond the Culture Wars*, University of Chicago literature professor Gerald Graff writes: "The curriculum is already a shouting match, and one that will only become more angry and polarized if ways are not found to exploit rather than avoid its philosophical differences."[22] Likewise, in *The Western Canon*, Harold Bloom—one of the world's most influential critic–scholar–theorists—similarly notes "the balkanization of literary studies."[23] In *Dictatorship of Virtue*, Richard Bernstein reveals how a heavy yoke of mistrust, intolerance, and combativeness is hanging over the American liberal arts academy.[24]

The climate of ideological warfare at the university not only discourages any middle ground, but it also sharply divides students and faculty into opposing camps that revel in their conflict with each other. According to Richard Rorty, professor of humanities at the University of Virginia, the conflicts within the university result from the "politics of difference" that "repudiates the idea of a national identity."[25] At the University of Pennsylvania in 1993, black students who disliked a student's columns challenging affirmative action stole 14,000 copies of the student newspaper and claimed they were fighting institutional racism. At Duke University, gays who disagreed with a student columnist's opinions blocked his way to class and shouted epithets. Yet at neither school were the perpetrators disciplined. During a 1996 visit to the University of Illinois at Urbana for a debate in which she was to argue against affirmative action, columnist Linda Chavez was jeered as a fake Latino and needed a police escort to get to her room. Even homecoming festivities have caused rancor and conflict on college campuses. Fights over the selection of a homecoming queen have resulted in boycotts and protest marches at the Universities of Georgia and North Carolina.

The explosion of sexual harassment battles marks another front in educational warfare. At the University of Nebraska, a graduate student displayed a desktop photograph of his wife wearing a bikini, until two female co-workers complained that it constituted sexual harassment and got the department chair to order it removed. Several colleges, in an attempt to end sexual harassment of students by faculty, have enacted policies prohibiting certain faculty members from "dating" certain students. Other schools have employed monitors to sit in on classes to make sure that teachers do not say anything sexually offensive. One such case involved Graydon Snyder, a 63-year-old religion professor at the Chicago Theological Seminary. In a discussion of the role of intent in sin, Snyder recited a story from the Talmud, the writings

that make up Jewish civil and religious law, about a man who falls
off a roof, lands on a woman, and accidentally has intercourse
with her. The Talmud says he is innocent of sin, Snyder lectured,
because the act was unintentional. But a woman in the class was
offended, because she believed the story justified brutality toward
women. She filed a complaint against Snyder, an ordained minister who had used the Talmudic lesson in the classroom for more
than 30 years. The university issued a formal reprimand and put
notices in the mailboxes of every student and teacher at the school,
telling them that Snyder had "engaged in verbal conduct of a
sexual nature" that had the effect of "creating an intimidating,
hostile or offensive" environment. The professor, contending that
his reputation was unjustly tarnished, sued the seminary for defamation. Scholars watching this case have argued that the specter
of sexual harassment charges is having a chilling effect on intellectual discourse in U.S. colleges. According to a spokeswoman for
the American Association of University Professors, universities
have seen a sharp increase in the number of sexual harassment
charges that focus on the content of classroom lectures or reading
materials.[26]

Gender conflict in the university has also appeared within the
women's studies programs. According to critics, even feminist
critics, many programs have grown increasingly dogmatic and
intolerant of deviant beliefs, with departments disintegrating into
competing ideological cells. The programs, argue Daphne Patai
and Noretta Koertge in *Professing Feminism: Cautionary Tales from
Inside the Strange World of Women's Studies*, tend to evince a bunker
mentality that regards the outside world with a mixture of hostility and disdain. Patai and Koertge cite an "art project" at the
University of Maryland that "listed as 'potential rapists' male
names pulled randomly from a student directory."[27] The contentious nature of women's studies programs often arise, according
to Patai and Koertge, because teachers use "their classrooms as
sites for the recruiting and training of students to be feminist
activists."[28]

Tension and conflict in the university, however, is not confined to racial or gender disputes. As activist academics have

increasingly tied their scholarly pursuits to political agendas, university departments have disintegrated into combative ideological factions. Within the ranks of faculty, according to many academics, professional nastiness has never been more vicious than it is today. This nastiness is often expressed in departmental meetings and in peer reviews of books and articles written by academics. It is heightened in the battles over salaries and tenure. In their recent critique of higher education, *Up the University*, Robert and Jon Solomon declare that "the level of mutual respect in academia is probably the lowest of any job or profession in America, except perhaps for professional wrestlers."[29]

Even the works of academicians have taken an adversarial turn. The art of biography, for instance, has recently been described as "blood sport."[30] Biographies written by scholars and academics have become increasingly negative and accusatory toward their subjects. Biographies of President John F. Kennedy, Pablo Picasso, and Jackson Pollack have focused more on the subjects' philandering, destructive relationships with women, and dysfunctional childhoods than on their political and artistic accomplishments. As the historian Ronald Steel has observed, "The current trend in biography, corresponding to the public fascination with gossip and disenthronement, is one of unmasking the misdeeds of the mighty."[31] The readers of such biographies learn very little of the subject's accomplishments, only a depressing expose of a dysfunctional human being gripped with scandalous vices.

As these examples demonstrate, the American university is becoming more like the combative litigation arena. It is becoming a place where students do more fighting than learning. But the conflicts in education are not confined to the university. The battles likewise rage in the primary and secondary schools.

The conflicts over textbooks in the nation's public school systems reflect this growing ideological combat. Religious conservatives oppose the teaching of evolution and secular humanism. At the other end of the ideological spectrum, gay and lesbian groups push for an acceptable recognition of homosexuality in the classroom. African Americans object to the use of such books as

The Adventures of Huckleberry Finn because of their derogatory depictions of blacks. And feminists oppose books that contain sexist references or cast women in stereotyped roles.

One of the most vicious battles is over the teaching of AIDS and sex education. The conflicts over AIDS education in the New York City schools has been described as "trench warfare," with leaders of the opposing factions calling each other "killers."[32] But New York City is just one theater in a cultural war. The Sexuality Information and Education Center notes that parents in at least 250 other cities and towns have been embroiled in similar disputes over how to balance abstinence and condoms in sex education, and over how much sexual detail should be included in the elementary school curriculum.[33]

A lack of civility has become a glaring problem in the nation's schools, where getting by often means getting hostile. In the hallways, it's shove or be shoved. "If you're standing in the hallway and someone's coming, you better move," explains one high school student, "because if you don't, they're just going to take you down and keep on going."[34]

Conflict within the public school system is also reflected in the increasing numbers of lawsuits between parents and schools. "It used to be if a student was accused of doing something wrong, the parent said: 'If the teacher said you did something wrong, they're right,'" according to August Steinhilber, general counsel for the National School Boards Association. "Now they say, 'We'll sue.'"[35] A New York mother sued a junior high school when her son wasn't chosen for the National Honor Society. Several Pennsylvania students sued their school, arguing that the school's requirement of unpaid community service amounted to "involuntary servitude." A Baltimore student's parents sued their public high school over its refusal to allow the student to wear an antiabortion T-shirt, which depicted a bloodied, dismembered fetus, to school. Many high school students have sued their school district for refusing to authorize a Bible club. A New Jersey middle school student sued her school when it adopted a ban on backpacks in classrooms. Although teachers sought to justify the ban by citing such problems as tripping over backpacks left in aisles, getting whacked in the face by careless students turning abruptly, and the use of them as weapons of intimidation, the plaintiff, with the support of her father, took the school and its ban to court, arguing that her rights had been infringed.

These cases illustrate an educational environment that has become more adversarial and combative. Objective intellectual pursuit has been replaced by ideological conflict. Not surprisingly, this shift in attitudes has been accompanied by more litigation against schools and teachers. Although it once may have been the practice for parents to side with the teachers, it is now becoming common to sue if the teacher or school does something disagreeable to students or parents.

Workplace Warfare

Like education, the workplace is becoming increasingly combative. Unity in pursuit of a common endeavor has greatly eroded. A 1993 survey conducted by the National Study of the Changing Workplace by the Families and Work Institute found a labor force that has little loyalty to employers and is deeply divided.[36] Increasing points of division are emerging not only between workers and management, but also between workers themselves. One such division that is growing in intensity is that between workers who are parents and those who are not.

Working parents resent the lack of flexible working hours and employer-sponsored day care, whereas childless workers are tired of seeing their colleagues with children get additional time off when the kids are sick and of having to work late to make up for the parents who rush out the door at 5 o'clock to pick their children up from day care. Childless workers also claim they don't get equal treatment, that working parents receive special benefits. For instance, whereas maternity leave has become a standard benefit in many workplaces, general personal leave time for serious matters unrelated to having children is much harder to come by. Angered by this disparity, a single, childless flight attendant sued her airlines for discrimination in their benefits. Although the airline offers unlimited free flights to employees' spouses and children, it refused to let her fly her grandmother out for a visit. Another case involved an assistant college professor who claimed unfair treatment when a colleague who had just become a father was awarded an extra year to complete his tenure requirements.

Besides the working-parent–childless-worker conflicts, numerous other divisions have erupted in the workplace. Gays clash with straights over benefits for companions. Tensions arise between the advocates of a dress code and those who wish to dress according to their ethnic heritage. (In one case, a woman who was prevented from flying on an employee pass because she was wearing traditional Muslim garb with open-toe sandals and no hosiery sued the airlines for discrimination. Company policy required passengers using such passes to conform to a dress code, which banned sandals and required hosiery.) Smokers and non-smokers, especially in regard to 10-minute smoking breaks, have become hardened adversaries. Then there are the loyalists versus the job-jumpers, the civil libertarians versus the drug-test supporters, and the flextimers versus the nine-to-fivers.

Religious conflicts have produced particularly sharpened divisions in the employment arena.[37] A growing number of cases have involved discrimination claims by religious employees who have been prevented from discussing religion on the job. In one case, an employee who didn't want to hear about his employer's beliefs filed a harassment claim. In another, an employee sued to retain the right to wear a "Stop Abortion" button at work. In yet another, a federal court characterized an employee's hanging of certain pictures of the Ayatollah Khomeini in her own cubicle as harassment of an Iranian employee who saw the pictures. Elsewhere, a state court concluded it was religious harassment for a Christian-owned company to put Bible verses on paychecks and religious articles in the company newsletters.

Reflecting the escalating adversity in the workplace, employment litigation has exploded. In general, employees seem to be even more litigious than the country as a whole. It has been called a "legal war" in the workplace. For instance, the number of discrimination lawsuits has risen by more than 2200 percent over the past two decades and now account for an estimated one-fifth of all civil suits filed in U.S. courts. Stressful firings have increasingly invited lawsuits from terminated employees who felt humiliated or emotionally distressed. In one case, a Connecticut jury awarded $105,000 to a woman who sued her employer for the way she was fired. After 7 years of service, the woman was forced to leave her personal belongings in a plastic bag and was escorted out the door by security guards in full view of gaping co-workers. A supervisor told her that she would be arrested for trespassing if she returned, even though there had been no allegations of criminal wrong-doing or any indications of disloyalty. The incident caused "utter humiliation" to the woman and led her to file the lawsuit. In another case, the family of a Massachusetts metal shop employee who was killed in a workplace accident sued the employer for working the man to death. According to the complaint, the employer knew that the worker was driven by mental illness to put in long hours, and that the stress of those long hours caused the accident.

A growing number of employee/plaintiffs have claimed that duress on the job can touch off the same kind of emotional symptoms as battle fatigue. Claims for posttraumatic stress disorder, the psychological disorder best known for the combat flashbacks experienced by many Vietnam veterans, have begun to appear in many employment-related lawsuits.[38]

Sexual harassment in the workplace is similarly a growing subject of litigation. According to one observer, the "American workplace has resembled an embattled frat house where boys struggle to discern the boundary between sexual civility and salacious misconduct."[39] Even aside from actual conduct, however, employers have been charged with discrimination for using "sexist" job titles such as "draftsman" instead of "draftsperson," and for the use of "Men Working" signs. In 1989, the Equal Employment Opportunity Commission and local Fair Employment Practices agencies received 5623 charges of sexual harassment, whereas in 1994, the number of charges amounted to almost 14,000.[40] In one notorious case, the nation's largest law firm, Baker and McKenzie, was ordered to pay $7.1 million in a sexual harassment case brought by a secretary. In another, the directors of W. R. Grace and Company, in March of 1995, ousted the firm's president and CEO because of sexual harassment charges—the incident being the first time that a corporation has fired a CEO for sexual harassment.

In addition to sex, age is yet another focus of litigation warfare in the workplace. Disputes over age discrimination have become far more frequent and have gained new urgency because of the restructuring of corporate America. "People are calling lawyers sooner, even before they are fired," according to one age-discrimination lawyer.[41] Between 1990 and 1993, the number of age-discrimination cases rose fourfold. These complaints, however, often cause a backlash among younger workers, who say they can't get a job, even though they are less expensive, because all the older workers are protected by law and can't be laid off or reassigned.

Not only is the workplace becoming more adversarial, it is also becoming more violent. Almost 40 percent of Americans consider workplace violence to be a growing problem.[42] According to a Justice Department report, one in six violent crimes occurs at work.[43] A 1993 survey by Northwestern National Life Insurance suggests that more than 2 million employees suffer physical attacks on the job each year and more than 6 million are threatened in some way. Homicide is now the leading cause of death in the workplace in New York City and the second-leading cause across the nation.[44] The number of bosses killed at work has doubled over the past 10 years.

Whereas in the past, the labor disputes were between management and labor, the disputes have now arisen within labor as well as between labor and management. The types of disputes have also expanded: Workplace tensions that once involved primarily economic issues now entail social, cultural, and behavioral matters. Even efforts to lessen this adversity have themselves often erupted in further conflict. For instance, in 1993, the Department of Transportation suspended diversity training programs for its employees after repeated occurrences of men being groped, women sobbing for hours, and the encouragement of racial epithets.

Just as the workplace has become more adversarial, the relations between the genders have turned increasingly antagonistic.

The Sex and Gender Wars

In the war between the sexes, rage takes many forms. Feminism is linked with communism, whereas traditional men are labeled Neanderthal. Books are written about "toxic men." Hillary Clinton is depicted as an evil tyrant. At the publishing house HarperCollins, a woman editor even designed a "Stamp out HarperCollins men" button that was later worn by many of the female staffers.

Relations between the sexes have probably never been worse. Even in the field of romance, the mood between men and women is growing more litigious and less libidinous. Sexual harassment complaints have more than doubled in the past 2 years. But sexual litigation is not just waged by women. Increasingly, men are also claiming to be harassed by their female bosses. Eight male former employees sued the Jenny Craig weight-loss organization in 1994, alleging that their female colleagues had created a sexually hostile working environment.

Even more divisive than the wars between the genders are the wars between straights and gays. Dozens of states and localities have grappled with ballot initiatives that would omit sexual orientation from a list of other protected categories such as race, creed, gender, and age. Other controversial legislative programs deal with extending government health benefits to "domestic partners" of government employees. These battles are turning into the most divisive and ugly of any seen in recent decades. They have gone beyond a political conflict to a cultural and religious war. "I've polled for 20 years," said pollster Tim Hibbitts, "and this is the ugliest, most divisive issue I've ever seen."[45]

Many middle-of-the-road Americans are being forced to pick sides—by gay-rights advocates insisting that homosexuality be declared a normal practice, and by religious conservatives attempting to portray homosexuality as a moral wrong. Although there once may have been a middle ground, staked out on the old-fashioned American notion of tolerance—a notion that held that neither society nor the government had business punishing the private sexual practices of consenting adults—such a ground now seems nonexistent in an increasingly polarized culture. Among many gay-rights advocates, this version of tolerance is not tolerance at all. Instead, they are looking for sexual parity—a demand that homosexual identity be viewed as normal as heterosexual identity. According to Suzanne Pharr, founder of the Little Rock, Arkansas, Women's Project, "The elimination of homophobia requires that homosexual identity be viewed as viable and legitimate and as normal as heterosexual identity."[46]

Relations between the genders have become more like those between litigants. Combative, divergent interests engaged in a win–lose struggle characterize these relations. And an increasingly adversarial media has intensified these struggles.

An Adversarial Media

The news media have increasingly taken an adversarial stance toward the subjects they cover. Critics argue that the attack mode of American journalism has made the press more interested in scandal and in negative journalism, and that reporters have acted like junkyard dogs eager to tear their victims to shreds. Newsweek reporter Steven Waldman admits that "cynicism is the dominant ideology of the press."[47] According to White House correspondent Kenneth Walsh, the "traditional adversary relationship between the media and the presidency has deteriorated into a mutual cynicism."[48]

As Larry Sabato notes in Feeding Frenzy, journalists seem much more interested in scandal than in issues of policy.[49] Such journalism further drills into an apathetic public all the ills of society and government. Thomas E. Patterson, a professor of political science at Syracuse University, argues that "the press nearly always magnifies the bad and underplays the good" in its coverage of the White House.[50] "News that incessantly and unjustifiably labels political leaders as insincere and inept fosters mistrust on the part of the public, and makes it harder for those in authority to provide the leadership that is required if government is to work effectively," Patterson declares.[51]

The American press in the past 20 years "has undergone a transformation from an access culture to an aggression culture."[52] To a post-Vietnam, post-Watergate generation distrustful of authority, no reporter wishes to appear insufficiently prosecutorial. The measure of good journalism today seems to relate directly to the severity of the attack on the subject of the story or investigation. Consequently, the press is often seen as too intent on stirring up conflict and too adversarial in its approach to politics. This adversarial culture pushes journalists to curry favor with anyone who has a grievance or a score to settle with a politician. In such a culture, the media appear more anxious to launch attacks on the government from the outside than to reveal facts about it from the inside. Individual journalists are rewarded for being aggressive, not in order to accomplish something but simply in order to be seen as aggressive. This elevation of aggression to a virtue has characterized the "Sam Donaldson era in the American media."[53] Such aggression sells because its audience is living in an increasingly adversarial society shaped by the combative values of litigation.

Not only do the media take a cynical and adversarial stance, but they often reduce issues to a simple win–lose contest. *Time's* weekly scorecard of "Winners and Losers" is just one example. Politicians are cast either as good guys or bad guys, as media emphasis remains on the drama of personalized conflict. But on a broader scale, virtually all public activity is treated as a fight in an alley. Even stories on budget debates and welfare reform are handled as personal combat. One study by Kathleen Hall Jamieson, dean of the Annenberg School for Communication at the University of Pennsylvania, found that the country's most influential news organizations dedicated 54 percent of their healthcare coverage in 1994 to the strategic aspects of the debate, such as which politician was "winning" and which was "losing." Only 35 percent of news accounts were primarily issue oriented or factual.[54]

The adversarial mode of modern journalism has been called

"gotcha journalism," and it reflects what President Clinton and others have called the "gotcha" mentality of those journalists who cover politics.[55] Far removed from traditional investigative reporting, this "gotcha journalism" may be defined as the effort to catch public officials in personally embarrassing positions. Journalists who practice it focus on catching *faux pas* instead of reporting on what a person actually does in carrying out his or her official job.

"Gotcha" journalism was evident at the 1993 meeting of the National Conference of State Legislatures in San Diego. A Minneapolis television station sent an undercover reporter to the conference. To avoid detection, he fraudulently obtained press credentials and even lied to a South Dakota lawmaker who asked him where he was from. The reporter obtained footage of the Minnesota Speaker of the House playing golf on Sunday—the day of the conference with the lightest meeting schedule. Although the Speaker paid her expenses on the days she did not attend working sessions, it was implied she would not have done so had the reporter not followed her around. In addition, the reporter also uncovered a second Minnesota lawmaker who brought his family with him at his own expense, although his wife and children did stay in his hotel room without paying anything extra. Elsewhere at the conference, a Seattle station sent a film crew to photograph people sitting around the hotel pool. And a Utah television crew set up near the spot where the pleasure boats departed from the marina, trying to spot Utah legislators getting on those boats. The crew, however, never even registered to cover the conference.

"Gotcha" journalism has put many legislators in a state of paranoia.[56] They are afraid of the press in a way that is unhealthy. They fear they are going to be followed by a reporter who will distort everything they do. For their part, journalists say that is what their editors want—conflict and corruption. Government and politicians, however, are not the only targets of the increasingly adversarial media. Over the past two decades, the media have claimed what amounts to prosecutorial powers to peer into private lives. A January 1990 Harris poll reported that 79 percent of Americans felt their personal privacy was threatened by the press.[57] In one of the most blatant media invasions of privacy,

Arthur Ashe was forced to admit in 1992 that he had AIDS because *USA Today* had threatened to expose the story.

The adversariness of the traditional news media has been fueled by increasingly conflict-oriented opinion talk shows such as "Crossfire" and "The McLaughlin Group." And then there are the more sensational, scandal-prone shows such as "Geraldo" and "Hard Copy" that reflexively assume an adversarial stance toward anything they cover. Even more respected television news programs such as "60 Minutes" and "Dateline" often employ a litigation-type format, presenting their programs not in an objective, detached documentary manner, but in an aggressively prosecutorial way. Even when the media are not prosecuting, they are fueling an adversarial culture. Extremists such as Louis Farrakhan and David Duke are granted huge television audiences, provided their messages are sufficiently shocking and confrontational.

No segment of the media, however, is as confrontational as the growing numbers of television talk shows, including "Jenny Jones," "The Ricki Lake Show," "Jerry Springer," "Sally Jessy Raphael," "The Montel Williams Show," "The Maury Povich Show," and "Rolanda." The combative approach of these shows was highlighted when a guest on a March 1995 segment of "The Jenny Jones Show," after being confronted and humiliated by a surprise coguest, allegedly killed the person 3 days later. But "Jenny Jones" is no different from its competitors. They all focus on emotional confrontations and employ a format designed to include an on-camera surprise calculated to embarrass a guest, and then to encourage guest conflict. Strung across the stage in their chairs, the guests snarl at one another, hurling insults that bring gasps from the studio audience and repeated beeps from the censor. For its part, the audience screams like Romans at gladiatorial combat. On some days, there might even be physical assault. Another of Ms. Jones's shows offered confrontations between women who got, as the screen caption put it, "Dumped after Sex," and the cads who dumped them. Some of the high-decibel confrontational episodes on "The Ricki Lake Show" have included "Pack Your Bags or You'll Wish You Were Dead" and "You're the Rudest Thing Alive ... and I'm Sick of Your Attitude."

Not surprisingly, in response to this practice of encouraging guest warfare, a growing number of disgruntled guests have been humiliated enough to bring lawsuits. One California woman won a $614,000 settlement from the producers of "The Montel Williams Show," who she claimed lured her on the program under false pretenses.

The present-day media are drawn overwhelmingly to conflict. This attraction to conflict is yet another example of the media following the lead of the combative litigation process.

An Increasingly Contentious Politics

Like most every other aspect of society, politics too has become more adversarial. Some have described the current political climate as the "age of defiance."[56] According to a former Democratic Congressman, Thomas Downey of Long Island, "This is very much the age of 'in your face.' It wasn't that way in [former] times. [Then there] was a far more civil and polite era."[59] In a political system that seems hopelessly polarized, *compromise* has become a dirty word. Synonymous with capitulation, compromise is no longer an acceptable part of the political process. The gridlock discussed so often during the 1992 presidential campaign is but one sign of the increasing divisiveness in the political arena. The growing ideological battles are yet another.

Bipartisanship has been an endangered species in politics in the 1990s. The ideological gulf between the parties has widened. There are fewer liberal Republicans in Congress than there were in the 1970s and fewer conservative Democrats. But even within the Democratic Party, which controlled all branches of government in 1992, consensus was elusive. Liberals fought moderates; Northerners clashed with Southerners.

This ideological division at the party level has rippled down into the voting public. Whereas constituents once tended to vote for the person, not the party, surveys conducted after the 1994 election show that voting has become as sharply polarized on partisan and philosophical lines as Congress itself has become. With conservative voters becoming much more Republican and liberals much more Democratic, a permanent and sharp ideological divide is developing among the American electorate.

The contentious and adversarial practice of modern politics contrasts sharply with that of the postwar period earlier in this century, when a more nonideological style helped avoid much conflict. The genius of the American system, as revealed during that period, has been its ability to compromise. The most effective politicians—such as Sam Rayburn, Everett Dirksen and Lyndon Johnson—employed a basic courtesy in dealing with their opponents. They knew politics was about power, but they did not think it necessary to destroy their opponents. But most of all, they respected what they had in common, particularly the presidency. That era, however, is long gone.

Another sign of the intensifying warfare in politics is the bitter confirmation fights. Robert Bork, Clarence Thomas, and Lani Guinier were among the most notorious victims of this increasingly nasty process. According to Bobby Inman, a Clinton appointee for Secretary of Defense, men and women named to high government office are often savagely abused. After his CIA-director nominee Michael Carns had to withdraw amid accusations of immigration-law violations, President Clinton once again condemned the poisonous and harsh atmosphere that the confirmation process had become.[60]

Yet another symptom of increasingly adversarial politics appears in the constant barrage of ethics inquiries being aimed at political opponents. Such inquiries have led to the resignations of Speaker Jim Wright and Senator David Durenburger. Within weeks of the 1994 election, which gave Republicans a majority in the House of Representatives, Democrats called for an outside counsel to investigate ethics charges against incoming Speaker Newt Gingrich, relating to his teaching of a college course. Several months later, in February of 1995, House Democrats formally filed a new ethics complaint against Gingrich, charging that a cable television station's airing of Gingrich's college course constituted an illegal gift. This new complaint followed a previous one that alleged Gingrich used improper, tax-deductible donations to fund his course. Yet a third complaint was filed, charging that Gingrich promoted a toll-free telephone number on the House floor to sell tape recordings of the college course. Finally, in December of 1994, Democrats attacked Gingrich for entering into a book contract with HarperCollins. In response to this barrage against their leader, House Republicans filed ethics charges against Richard Gephardt.

The adversarial conduct of politics goes much deeper than the national level. Experts in both politics and politesse say bad public manners "are spreading to the once-decorous suburbs, replacing Beaver Cleaver-like courtesy with what some call—in 90's-speak—democratic dysfunction."[61] Local elected bodies across the country are experiencing more personally directed conflict. Elected officials in Oak Forest, Illinois, passed a "civility resolution" to force themselves to mind their manners in public. A similar ordinance was passed in Pasadena, California. Other local bodies have hired conflict-resolution specialists to help them conduct their business in a peaceful manner. Although several decades ago decorum was as firm as the parliamentary procedures laid out in *Robert's Rules of Order*, the present is very much the age of "in your face."

The aggressive adversarial mode of politics was especially evident in the 1994 elections—an election season called "mean and ugly" by the *New York Times*. Across the nation, the level of political discourse was among the nastiest and most combative ever. The blitz of attack ads never let up. The way to win was first to squash opponents as persons, reducing them to agents of Lucifer, then to think about the issues. In the Minnesota Senate race, the candidates accused one another of being late paying their property taxes. In the vicious California gubernatorial race, the candidates attacked each other for hiring illegal immigrants. The Pennsylvania race was called a "muddy slugfest." The Virginia race saw the use of the cover of *Playboy* to remind voters that one of the candidates had had an affair with the woman on the cover. Of course, accusations of lying and infidelity were common in campaigns across the nation. But even political positions such as opposition to affirmative action and welfare programs were accusingly translated into reflections of "a politics of hate" or a "politics of anger."

After the 1994 elections concluded, the politics of combat continued. The tone of open hostility that would mark House proceedings in the first 100 days of the 104th Congress was hinted at on the first of those days, when Representative Maxine Waters made an obvious show of declining to applaud or stand during Gingrich's maiden speech as Speaker. Waters's display proved to be a trendsetter. This harsh combativeness continued throughout the session. The Democrats, now in the minority, pledged to fight the Republican agenda and to stall it at every turn, calling Newt Gingrich and his allies "trickle-down terrorists" and "budgetary terrorists." As political observers noted, the "parties were girding for war." Headlines proclaimed the beginning of a "2-year war" in Congress. Very quickly, events occurred to harden the attitudes on both sides. Democrats accused Republicans of trying to silence them with "totalitarian" behavior.[62] Representative John Dingell, a Michigan Democrat, compared the Republican majority to "the *Reichstag*." Representative John Lewis compared Republican lawmakers to the Nazis and conjured up images of GOP storm troopers jackbooting across the land. Republican Dick Armey referred to the openly gay Democrat Barney Frank as "Barney Fag," while David Bonier kept up a relentless attack on Gingrich over ethical questions. And during a particularly savage welfare debate, Representative Sam Gibbons responded to Republican heckling by shouting at his colleagues, "You-all sit down, sit down and shut up!" According to political scientist Christopher Deering, "this high-voltage partisanship is virtually unheard of in American history."[63]

The culture of confrontation so pervasive in modern politics has made many departing politicians glad not to be coming back. "Haiti is a better place to be," said Representative Fred Grandy, Republican of Iowa, who relinquished his seat to make what ended up being a losing primary bid for Governor. "People don't like one another," he said. "There's an overall sense of fatigue and frustration—I'm glad to be getting out."[64] Senator Paul Simon, who announced his retirement after the elections, cited the cynicism and negativism in politics. "I am worried about a rancorous atmosphere in this nation," he said.[65] Another retiring senator, David Boren of Oklahoma, talked about the complete breakdown of a sense of bipartisanship in Congress. Parties have become more extreme, and Congress has become more partisan, he claimed. Even the personal and social relationships in Congress have broken down, Boren noted. "Too often now, senators only get to know the members of their own party."[66] When Howell Heflin, the 73-year-old Senator from Alabama, announced his decision to retire, he denounced what he said was a tendency for politicians and the news media to "pit one group of Americans against another."[67] In making his decision not to seek reelection, Senator Bill Bradley castigated both parties, accusing them of being more interested in feuding than in addressing the needs of the nation. And in being honored for his 14,000th vote, Senator Robert Byrd despaired of the incivility to which the Senate had succumbed.

The suspicion, the paranoia, the rising dislike of the opponent have become as much a part of politics as the door knocking and literature drops. The enmity between two candidates becomes personal and deep, and is revealed in the charges, countercharges, and, not uncommonly, legal complaints alleging violations of state fair-campaign-practices laws. One reason is that, just as in sports and in litigation, winning becomes everything. "The mentality becomes almost of war or a Vince Lombardi football game," said one former legislator. "You have to hate your opponent. That's the only way you can be successful."[68]

In the highly adversarial atmosphere of contemporary politics, images of terror are conjured up far more often than images of inspiration. Hitler, rather than George Washington or Abraham Lincoln, seems to be the historical figure most frequently cited. Opponents have taken to firing accusations of Hitler-like tactics at each other. Opposing political strategies are likened to Nazism. Dissenters are labeled terrorists. The horrors of the Holocaust are used to oppose a budget bill.

The growing contentiousness of politics is yet another sign

that American society and culture is increasingly following the adversarial example of litigation. Such an adversarial approach is especially damaging to a democratic political system, relying as it does on such values as compromise and consensus. As the litigation explosion has promoted an increasing adversariness in American society, politics has suffered a steady erosion, for the adversarial orientation of a litigious society undermines the nation's political foundations, turning its politics into a battle of litigants.

CHAPTER 5

A Litigation Democracy

As envisioned by the Constitutional framers, of the three branches of government—executive, legislative, and judicial—the first two were supposed to be the ones in which the public most actively participated. Indeed, throughout most of American history, the political branches have commanded more of the public's attention and energies than has the judicial. But with the litigation explosion erupting in the late decades of the 20th century, the courts have increasingly drained public attention and involvement from the political process. In effect, the litigation process has subverted the political process. It is as though, through the litigation explosion, the courts have become the arena for the political involvement of society, with the act of suing superseding the act of legislating.

With the United States becoming an adversarial society in the litigation age, the social practices and cultural values supporting its democratic politics have eroded. Whereas politics looks to the majority, litigation focuses on the minority. Whereas politics rewards compromise, litigation is an act of conflict in which one side wins and the other loses. Instead of existing in the kind of balance envisioned by the Constitutional framers, the values and activities of the judicial branch have, through the litigation explosion, undermined those of the political branches.

Many indicators reflect such an erosion in America's political foundations. Among democratic nations, the United States has the fewest citizens voting and has experienced a 20-year decline in voter turnout.[1] In the 1994 New York primaries, for instance, only 7.8 percent of the voting-age population bothered to vote. According to the Higher Education Research Institute at UCLA, college first-year students in 1994 cared less about the political process than they did ever before.[2] Not only is there voter disinterest, but there is also mistrust—the kind of mistrust found among combative litigants. In 1964, when University of Michigan scholars asked people how much of the time they trusted the government to do what's right, 76 percent said most or all of the time.[3] When the question was asked again in 1992, only 29 percent agreed. By 1994, the figure had fallen to 19 percent. A *New York Times*/CBS News poll conducted on the eve of the 1994 elections found that three-fourths of the public disapproved of the job Congress as a whole was doing.[4] By a margin of two to one, they could not name one public official they admired. In the political ads, the dome of the Capitol was often used as a symbol of government corruption. As Senator John McCain admitted on the eve of the 1994 elections, "Most Americans want us to get out of town.... They think we have done enough harm."[5]

This hostility to politicians reflects not only an increasingly ineffective political system that, during the litigation age, has followed all too closely the adversarial orientation of the courtroom, but it also reflects the public's opposition to the growing drift of politics toward the litigation model. Seventy-nine percent of the public thinks lawyers have too much influence in government, and this suspicion is heightened by the fact that there are 224 lawyers among the 535 elected members of the House and Senate.[6] In one political cartoon, meant to illustrate the negative tone of the 1994 campaign, a candidate's billboard proclaiming of his opponent "Did I mention he's a lawyer?" was portrayed along with a passing motorist commenting, "These last-minute campaign ads are getting dirty."

Reflecting the escalating combativeness in politics is the growing ideological polarization of the two parties, especially in the House of Representatives. E. J. Dionne Jr. argues, in *Why*

Americans Hate Politics, that American politics has become domi-nated by divisive debates about cultural and social issues.[7] Al-though Americans still believe that the purpose of politics is to solve problems and resolve disputes, that is exactly what politics is not doing. That is why, according to Dionne, so many have come to hate politics. As Dionne notes, candidates seek to win elections by reopening the same divisive issues, such as abortion and capi-tal punishment, over and over again. Old resentments and angers are stirred up to get voters to cast yet one more ballot of angry protest.

According to Dionne, both conservatives and liberals have turned politics into a form of moral warfare in which much of the debate is over which set of sins should preoccupy government. Instead of practical discussions on how to reduce crime, political dialogue centers around the moralistic symbolism of the death penalty. Instead of debating policies that directly impact the fam-ily, discourse occurs on the vague yet divisive notions of tradi-tional family values. Instead of addressing the specific problems most women face in the workplace and on the streets, focus is continually redirected to the polarizing subject of abortion rights. Instead of crafting policies that would help minorities fully partic-ipate in society, energy is used to debate the merits of multi-culturalism and political correctness. These are all evidence of a politics that has become too much like the litigation process: a process focused on uncompromised conflict between polar ex-tremes, out of which one party wins and the other loses.

Another sign that the political process has become divisive and uncompromising is the gridlock that has come to characterize the lawmaking branches of the federal government. One of the major issues of the 1992 presidential campaign was "gridlock." According to the Democrats, this gridlock was caused by a Repub-lican president opposed to the general will of the people as ex-pressed through the Democratic Congress. Consequently, with Democrats controlling both houses of Congress, the Clinton presi-dency was supposed to bring an end to the legislative bind that undermined the presidency of George Bush. But this did not happen, perhaps because gridlock was caused by something more

fundamental than a divided government—something as fundamental as a political system that now reflects the adversarial society that America has become in the litigation age.

The first 2 years of the Clinton presidency, despite the promises of 1992, saw the continuation of gridlock, even though the
Democrats held comfortable majorities in both houses of Congress. Among the legislative measures that succumbed to gridlock
were bills to overhaul the financing of Congressional election
campaigns, tighten controls on lobbyists, update the nation's tele-
communications laws, and revamp the Superfund law providing
for the cleanup of toxic waste dumps. Filibusters also killed bills
addressing replacement of striking workers and product liability.
In addition, the fear of filibusters kept many other measures,
including national health insurance legislation, from coming to
any kind of vote. As The New Republic editorialized, "The bicker-
ing in Congress surely reflects the nastiness of political debate in
the country at large."[8]

Although the framers of the Constitution envisioned political
conflict, they did not foresee the guerrilla warfare between political parties that often crippled Congress in 1994. Almost twice as
many filibusters occurred in the 1993–1994 term as occurred in the
entire 19th century. As typical headlines put it, "Awash in Filibusters, Senate Limps Toward Adjournment,"[9] or, "Rancor Leaves Its
Mark on 103rd Congress."[10]

Despite the public's reaction against political gridlock—
voting out the Democratic majority in Congress and installing the
first Republican one in 40 years—Democrats just days after the
1994 election vowed to persist in it. Democratic leaders in the
House declared that they would use every device they could—
procedural and oratorical—to stall the Republican agenda. They
declared a "2-year war" on the Republican majority, and condemned their Republican colleagues as "supply-side terrorists."

Besides making politics more gridlocked and adversarial, the
growing prevalence of litigation-like behavior has also undermined the legislation that actually gets passed. Increasingly, any
controversial legislative enactments get challenged in court by
dissatisfied groups. Litigation is becoming a routine step in the

lawmaking process, and lawsuits are becoming an automatic political strategy. After months of political wrangling to reach a compromise plan for removing New York City's antiquated system of street-corner fire-alarm boxes (a system city officials said was expensive, inefficient, and the source of many false reports), Mayor Giuliani and his plan were taken to court in October of 1995 by a deaf group who claimed the plan violated their civil rights, even though they had never raised the issue during public hearings on the plan.

Increasingly, opponents to a legislative program announce even before the program is enacted that they will tie it up for years in court. Shortly after Clinton announced his gays-in-the-military policy in 1993, for instance, gay activists initiated a class-action suit against the Department of Defense to overturn it. In another case, disgruntled senators from Pennsylvania, who did not like the closure of the Philadelphia Naval Shipyard, went to court in 1994 in a last ditch effort to reverse the law. They petitioned the Supreme Court to nullify the government's selection of which military bases to close, even though the law had been created to remove the partisan obstacles that had made it practically impossible previously to close any bases. A lawsuit challenging the use of certain 1990 census data has been brought against the federal government by several cities and states seeking to realign, outside the legislative process, the distribution of federal money. Observers have noted that the case will require "years of litigation over what is required in terms of redistribution of federal money."[11] And within hours of the closing of the polls in November 1994, lawsuits were filed to block enforcement of Proposition 187—the California ballot initiative that sought to render undocumented aliens ineligible for most governmental social services. Legal experts predicted that there would be years of litigation over the meaning and scope of Proposition 187—litigation that would precede even any attempt at enacting or implementing in any way the provisions of Proposition 187.

The legal battles over term limits further reflect the attempt to control the political branch through the judicial. To a public growing increasingly frustrated with politics, term limits have become quite popular, having already been democratically adopted in nearly half the states. But entrenched politicians are fighting the public on this issue, and this fight is being waged through litigation. Former Speaker of the House Tom Foley outraged many of his constituents when he filed a lawsuit to overturn his own state's term-limit initiative. In addition, the Clinton Administration has opposed in court a term-limits amendment adopted in the President's home state of Arkansas.

Litigation is even being used to dictate the outcomes of political elections. Redistricting suits, for instance, have been brought to determine how far the Voting Rights Act goes in mandating electoral outcomes for minorities, or in guaranteeing them a specific number of elected offices. In other types of litigation challenges to election results, defeated candidates sue their victorious opponents, alleging violations of fair-campaign-practices laws. Nearly 2 months after her defeat in the 1994 Maryland gubernatorial race, and only weeks before the scheduled inauguration of her opponent, Ellen Sauerbrey filed a lawsuit asking the court to declare her the winner of the election. In her suit, she alleged that voter fraud and technical improprieties were responsible for her loss. In a more novel variation of candidates turning to litigation, some have sued their opponent for sexual harassment, claiming that the opponent's aggressive politicking constituted sexual harassment. A Massachusetts woman, who lost the election for presidency of her union, sued her opponent for sexual harassment and won a $35,000 verdict. The case revolved around an opponents' campaign poster that depicted the plaintiff in an uncomplimentary sexual light—although she admitted that the poster did not cause her to lose the election.

Yet another example of litigation directly inhibiting or squelching the political process is the growing use of SLAPPs—Strategic Lawsuits against Public Participation in government.[12] These lawsuits have been used by political opponents to discourage citizens from engaging in such activities as circulating a petition, testifying at a public hearing, or lobbying for legislation. People have been sued, in lawsuits seeking millions of dollars in damages, for writing a letter to the President of the United States to oppose a political appointment, reporting violations of environmental laws to federal agencies, and complaining to school boards about teacher performance. A Long Island, New York, woman who opposed the cutting of oak and beech shade trees by a subdivision developer was hit with a $6 million harassment suit. And in Contra Costa County, California, citizens opposing a waste-to-energy plant were sued by the sanitary district in a $42 million lawsuit.

Even in matters affecting such everyday issues as property taxes, litigation has increasingly encroached upon legislative and executive decisions. An entire business of property-tax reduction specialists has sprung up to help property owners challenge in court their tax assessments. In 1989, for instance, there were only 4042 cases of such tax appeals. By 1993, however, the number had grown to 36,234.[13]

As it intrudes ever more into the legislative process, litigation is at times becoming an alternative to the political process, offering political activists a secondary venue in which to pursue their political agenda. As a Massachusetts Superior Court judge has observed, Americans "tend to regard litigation as the panacea that will cure all society's ills—quickly, painlessly and cheaply."[14] From school desegregation to redressing gender inequities, to ensuring fair voting districts, political problems are increasingly getting taken to court. The antismoking campaign, for instance, has moved from the legislatures to the courts. Unable to pass anti–tobacco company legislation in Congress, advocates have turned to lawsuits against those companies. In one class-action suit filed in federal court in New Orleans, a group of plaintiffs' attorneys have asked for $50,000 in damages for each of the 100 million Americans who have ever smoked—a number representing almost half of the U.S. population. And just as lobbyists fund their political lobbying campaigns, plaintiffs' attorneys were expected to contribute $100,000 a year to a litigation fund supporting the lawsuit.[15]

Litigation has also been used as a substitute for political action in the gun-control area. As advocates have had difficulty passing their strict gun-control measures through Congress, they have taken to suing the gun manufacturers. In May 1994, on behalf of the families of eight people who were shot and killed when a man burst into an office and sprayed it with bullets, the Center to Prevent Handgun Violence sued the manufacturers of the guns used in the shooting. The lawsuits maintained that the gun manufacturers negligently sold products that could be used by violent criminals to kill innocent people. Although the gun makers attempted to have the suit dismissed, the San Francisco Superior Court, in April 1995, ruled that the suit could proceed, marking the first time that an assault-weapon maker could be held accountable for misuse of its product. In related litigation, promoters of a gun show have been held liable for injuries suffered by a man who was shot by a gun stolen from the show.

Like gun control, abortion has been another area in which litigation has been used in lieu of legislation. The most recent strategy of the antiabortion lobby, for instance, has been the filing of malpractice suits against doctors who perform abortions. Increasingly, lawyers associated with antiabortion groups are seeking to file claims against doctors who do abortions. Life Dynamics, Inc., an antiabortion group in Denton, Texas, claims it is involved in 80 such cases—the goal of this litigation, of course, being to discourage doctors from performing abortions by subjecting them to lawsuits and causing their malpractice insurance rates to rise. As one doctor who has been sued said about plaintiffs such as Life Dynamics, "The problem is, even if they lose, they win—whatever happens in court, they've had the press conference and I've been damaged."[16]

Through the imposition of punitive damages in civil lawsuits, the courts have been assuming functions traditionally left to the political branch. What was once a very limited legal tool used in cases of intentional torts, such as assault and battery, has become a powerful means for juries to send their regulatory "messages" to corporate America. Unlike compensatory damages, punitive damages are meant to punish conduct deemed outrageous and egregious. They are intended to perform a function that lies largely with criminal justice, namely, punishment, but because they are awarded in civil courts, they are much easier to obtain that a criminal conviction. Take, for instance, the case of the Alabama doctor who in 1990 bought a new BMW, only to discover later that the paint on one section had been damaged and then refinished. He sued and got $4,000 in compensatory damages, along with $4 million in punitive damages. Yet, if the company was guilty of the type of gross and wanton fraud that would justify such punitive damages, that conduct should have been prohibited by criminal laws passed by legislative bodies. In a study of the Cook County courts, the RAND Corporation found that between the early 1960s and the early 1980s, the number of punitive damage verdicts rose 25-fold, and the average award soared from $7,000 to $729,000.

Several other high-profile punitive damage awards illustrate the growing tendency of juries to take on a legislative role. Although G. D. Searle Corporation won most of the lawsuits against its Copper-7 intrauterine devices (IUDs), one jury ordered $7 million in punitive damages for a contraceptive that had been approved by the federal government and that had not been found defective by juries in several previous cases. The California jury that awarded the $2.7 million in punitive damages against McDonald's (later reduced by the judge to $480,000) to a woman who suffered burns when the take-out coffee cup she was balancing in her lap spilled, decided to send a message that, as one juror put it, "the coffee's too hot out there." This decision, however, was essentially legislative in its effect. It strove to regulate the temperature of beverages served in restaurants across the country. Yet in so deciding, the jury was subject to no political accountability, conducted no research, and held no public deliberations. If a legislature were considering whether to prohibit restaurants from selling coffee hotter than 160 degrees, all concerned parties—coffee-machine vendors, coffee distributors, restaurant operators, and the coffee-drinking public—could provide input. Legislatures also issue relatively precise edicts, for example, "Coffee hotter than 160 degrees may not be sold." Jury verdicts, however, are quite the opposite. The verdict may be that 180 degrees is too hot, but it does not say that 160 or even 170 degrees might be acceptable. Moreover, even if one jury finds that 170 degrees is fine, the next jury in the next case may find it too hot.

As punitive damage awards have come to be used in a regulatory function, litigation has also served as an alternative funding mechanism for many political endeavors. In a creative attempt to use litigation as a source of funding, various types of public interest groups now receive a significant share of their financing from funds left over in large class-action lawsuits.[17] When plaintiffs' attorneys won a class-action lawsuit against Wells Fargo Bank, for example, the judge distributed $3 million of unclaimed funds to, among other interests, advocates for battered women, the disabled, and immigrant and single-parent families. In San Francisco, the Consumers Union now gets about 20 percent of its annual budget from such sources. A federal judge in Chicago has upheld distributions to such groups as the American Civil Liberties Union and the Chicago Lawyers' Committee for Civil Rights under Law in a case that involved price-fixing charges against a bottle manufacturer. In another antitrust case, excess funds helped pay the salaries of public interest lawyers representing AIDS patients. Elsewhere, a federal judge awarded a museum several thousand dollars with funds left over from yet another antitrust case. Although this source of funding obviously pleases the recipients, who may have trouble obtaining legislatively appropriated funding, its critics view the awards as a way for plaintiffs' attorneys and consumer groups to perpetuate litigation and to pursue their political agenda outside of the political process.

One problem posed by the increasing intrusion of litigation into the political process occurs when legislative bodies get sued. The increase in the number of such lawsuits and the cost of resolving them—from sidewalk trip-and-fall claims to police brutality cases—has become a significant and often unpredictable aspect of municipal budgets. From 1993 to 1994, as a result of lawsuits against it, New York City spent a record $300 million on judgments and settlements.

Litigation also poses a difficult policy dilemma for elected officials. Trying to settle or defend lawsuits presents a much different task than trying to enact legislation. The former requires secrecy, the latter openness. Yet, facing increasing litigation, elected officials find themselves more frequently behind closed doors in deciding the fate of millions of dollars in public funds. Even these closed-door sessions of strategizing, however, have themselves become the subject of litigation from groups who claim that the sessions violate open-meeting laws. But public meetings can put elected officials at greater risk in a lawsuit; and the dangers of telegraphing legal strategies to opposing lawyers can hamper public debate, since elected officials don't know what they should or should not say that might help or hurt their legal case. Dealing with increasing litigation, one Minneapolis council member noted, "Open government is on the run. We've had a lot of these [closed] meetings because we've had a lot of litigation," she explained, "and we're going to have more and more."[18]

As litigation has intruded more and more into the political process, politics in America has come to mirror the adversarial litigation model. Interest-group politics—the phrase commonly used to describe the state of contemporary politics—reflects the type of "victim mentality" that pervades the litigation process. Political interest groups have found that, just as in litigation, power lies in defining themselves as victims. Yet the maintenance of that power requires that the victim-groups continue celebrating their victimization, which in turn leads other groups to compete for power by defining themselves as victims. This chain reaction of victimization creates political divisiveness and undermines democratic community, as the contest for victimhood serves to isolate groups rather than to assimilate them into the broader society.

Interest-group politics, modeled as it is after the adversarial nature of the litigation process, has contributed to the erosion of the Jeffersonian concept of public virtue—the duty of each citizen to consider the public good apart from his or her private interest. President John Kennedy's famous phrase—"Ask not what your country can do for you"—is a modern expression of the classical civic-virtue ethic. Interest-group politics, however, does not encourage a consideration of the common good, or of anything but self-interest. Like the litigation model, interest-group politics simply envisions combat between self-serving parties to produce public policy. It is assumed that this combat will produce good policy, just as it is assumed that the conflict of litigants in court will produce the truth. And just as parties battle in a lawsuit with no consideration of their mutual concerns or of what might be best for both sides, interest-group politics ignores the existence of a public interest apart from the sum of private, individual interests.

As a constituent-oriented political creed, interest-group politics looks only to the agendas of client groups. Writing in 1950, Arthur Schlesinger warned of those who would use politics, similar to the way litigation is used, as an outlet for private grievances and frustrations. Under the litigation model, however, interest-group politics today is used for just such purposes.

Whereas litigation looks at individuals as litigants, interest-group politics regards citizens as members of interest groups. The groups, in turn, are awarded specific benefits *as a group*, just as parties to a lawsuit are awarded damages as litigants. And politicians are identified with the interest groups they represent, just as lawyers are seen in the courtroom as advocates for their clients.

In another similarity with litigation, interest-group politics has created a politics of rights and entitlements. Yet rights are the language of litigation, not democracy. Compromise is what democratic politics is about, but rights frustrate compromise. And the current interest-group politics of rights has suffocated the political life of the nation. In pursuing such politics, interest groups seek not to participate in the democratic process on an equal basis with other individuals and groups, but to actually bypass the democratic process by establishing a system of rights and entitlements that will guarantee fulfillment of their interests, regardless of popular opinion. The same strategy is used in litigation.

This focus on rights has led interest groups to favor the courts over the legislatures as their political forums. Under the guise of public-law litigation, they have increasingly tried to pass their public agenda through the courts—as litigation is often perceived as a faster and less expensive process than the passage of legislation. This politically oriented litigation, though still more widely practiced by liberal groups, is used by conservatives as well. For instance, the Washington Legal Foundation, a conservative public interest firm, litigates on behalf of businesses, property owners, and other "victims of liberal orthodoxy." Whereas liberal public interest law firms have fought for an expansion of civil liberties, conservative groups have opposed affirmative action and property regulations. Consequently, under interest-group politics, courts have become more legislative in their functions. This has given rise to the judicial activism of recent decades. Yet each time judicially created rights overrule legislative acts, the principle of majority rule and self-government is weakened.

Faith in the democratic process has atrophied as interest groups have increasingly relied on the judiciary rather than the democratic legislatures for their political goals. These groups have become so focused on the courts that their democratic impulse has turned to the judiciary and has advocated greater citizen participation in the judicial process through more relaxed procedural requirements. A concern for access to the courts has virtually overshadowed that for access to the voting booth or the political caucus. The great democratic value of equality has taken on a new interpretation in the litigation age. Now the emphasis on equality focuses on the right to sue, on opening up the courts to give everyone a greater ability to litigate grievances. Thus, rather than widening and improving the democratic political process, interest groups have tried to "democratize" an inherently undemocratic institution—the courts. Democratic equality has consequently come to mean an equality to litigate in the courts, rather than an equality to participate in the political process. Under this new sense of equality, the United States is becoming a democracy of litigants.

Interest-group politics, with its view of society as a fragmentation of various conflicting special interests, reflects the adversarial society and culture that America has become in the litigation age. The nation's culture wars—with its battles involving capital punishment, affirmative action, abortion, religious freedom, and gay rights—are increasingly fought in the courts, as the opposing sides have virtually lost any hope in reaching a consensus. Although the aim of democratic politics is to unify people and to create consensus, a political process increasingly modeled after the adversarial nature of the courtroom cannot do that. Instead, such politics accent and magnify the divisions in society.

Experts have offered many explanations for the decline of politics in modern America. But the most fundamental, and often unnoticed, explanation is that politics has declined because it has recently followed the model offered by the litigation process. The litigation model has undermined the political health of America, because courts are essentially undemocratic, operating with a set of concerns and assumptions quite different from those with which a political process must function. As recent history has shown, a litigation-oriented democracy is a self-eroding democracy.

CHAPTER 6

Litigation and the Rise of a New American Role Model

THE APPEAL OF THE VICTIM

The victim has become the modern American archetype. From the Jeffersonian yeoman farmer to the Horatio Alger self-made industrialist to the Kennedy Cold War warrior, descriptions of American cultural evolution have centered on particular individual traits that most characterize the time. As the 20th century comes to an end, the individual-as-victim has come to reflect American culture. More and more, Americans are choosing victimhood as the image by which they see themselves. The victim-label is becoming more popular than the hero-label; victimhood is the social status to which increasing numbers of Americans are striving.

America is awash in victimization. The self-reliant citizen has given way to the grieving victim. "Blame the person who made you a victim" has become the cultural creed. From talk shows such as "Oprah" and "Sally Jessy Raphael" to the accelerating numbers of various 12-step programs, victims are unabashedly venting their grievances. From criminals who claim they are the real victims of a violent society to adults who claim to be victims of their own toxic parents, the urge to claim victimhood has overcome society. From "lookism" to "ageism," proclamations of suffering and resentment have been glorified by the vanity of victimhood. Even the supposedly most privileged social group—white males—has pursued the moral prestige and political spoils of victimhood. Men's advocates often rail against the victim mentality, but they are hardly immune to its temptations: high school football is "male child abuse"; circumcision is socially sanctioned violence against infant boys; and women who walk around looking sexy yet remaining unavailable are abusers of men. Men's higher mortality rates are even cited as unassailable proof of male victimhood.

The contemporary appeal of the victim is inspiring more and more people to discover their victimhood. There is even a desire to see public figures or "heroes" confess that they too are victims. Social role models are not those who have escaped victimhood, but those who have lived it. Throughout his presidential campaign, Bill Clinton talked about growing up in an alcoholic family, while 30 years earlier his political hero, John F. Kennedy, dared not even talk about the physical ailments he had to endure. There is even a desire to see the heroes of the past turned into victims. Athletes such as Mickey Mantle become known as much for their drinking as for their athletic accomplishments; presidents are remembered for their extramarital affairs; writers are analyzed for their dysfunctional family histories.

Victimhood is becoming so popular that even the rich and famous crave its status. In her autobiography, Roseanne Arnold divulges at length the ways in which parental abuse wrecked her life, forcing her into prostitution, drug use, and theft. "Every day I teeter on a razor blade," she writes.[1] Contrast the contemporary rush of celebrities to publicize their victimhood with the attitudes of an earlier era, as exemplified by actress Helen Hayes. Though she lived into her 90s and wrote three sets of memoirs, only in the third, written just a few years before her death, was she able to admit in print that her husband, Charles MacArthur, had been an alcoholic.

VICTIMIZATION AND THE LITIGATION PROCESS

Although victimization exists at every level of American society and in every aspect of American culture, the one unifying thread is the litigation process. Nearly every story of victimhood either begins or ends at the courthouse. It is no coincidence that the litigation explosion is occurring hand in hand with America's victimization epidemic.

The victim strategy has become a profitable one in court. A woman who sued McDonald's because the coffee she bought at a drive-up spilled and burned her was awarded $2.9 million by a jury. It didn't matter that the woman spilled the coffee when trying to remove the cup's lid while driving in her car with the cup wedged between her legs. She was a victim of fast-food-chain hot coffee, her lawyer argued. In another case, a man was awarded $7 million because he was paralyzed in an accident that occurred while he was riding a bike at night without a light, and after he had been drinking. His lawyer said it was the bicycle manufacturer's fault—his client shouldn't be expected to know that riding without a light was dangerous. After a Massachusetts man died while driving a stolen car, his family sued the parking-lot owner for failing to take steps to prevent such thefts. The widow of a man electrocuted when he urinated on electrified rail tracks of the Chicago Transit Authority sued and won $1.5 million, even though, to get to where he was killed, her husband had crossed wooden barriers that read "Danger," "Electric Current," and "Keep Out." In New York City, a couple sued the Transit Authority for $10 million because they were run over by a subway train while having sex on the tracks. They were, their lawyer claimed, innocent victims of a transit system's indifference to safety.

Litigation has contributed to transforming employees into victims, because as victims, individuals' potential monetary rewards far outweigh the rewards as employees. In *Hunio v. Tishman Construction Company*, a California jury awarded $5.1 million to the former vice president of a construction firm who claimed to have been victimized by his company after he had walked out of a major project because he found a customer abrasive and abusive.

In response to the company's mistreatment, which included giving him "minor projects" and leaving him sitting in his "glass-walled office working only 20% to 25% of the time," the plaintiff, a $104,000 per year construction manager at the time, checked himself into a psychiatric hospital, quit his job, and filed a lawsuit.[2] His jury award included $2 million for emotional distress and $1 million in punitive damages. As a litigant, the plaintiff was more richly compensated than he was as a corporate vice president. But to qualify for this kind of compensation, he had to prove victimhood—a victimhood that proved richly rewarding.

The litigation explosion breeds victimization, for it is in the litigation arena that the victim becomes champion and is accorded the most tangible rewards. In sports, the hero is the winner. In business, the hero is the profit maker. But in litigation, the hero is the victim. The courtroom is where America officially recognizes and rewards the victim. In the civil suit, it is the victim who wins; in a criminal action, defendants who prove that they too are victims are excused and acquitted. Consequently, the more litigation, the more the victim is exalted—and the more litigation fuels and reinforces America's victimization culture.

The litigation arena also institutionalizes victimhood. The courts are the only social/political institution specifically geared toward the victim. All across the nation, petty disputes between "victims," involving the mundane activities of daily life, are besieging the courts. In Rochester, New Hampshire, the parents of a 9-year-old boy filed suit against an 88-year-old woman who refused to return the boy's kickball after it went into her yard. She claimed that she was tired of being "victimized" by the neighborhood children, whereas the child's parents argued that their son was a victim of theft. Elsewhere, a student sued his college because his roommate partied too much. Another sued because of a bad haircut. A Georgia bank receptionist sued a colleague for maliciously directing pipe smoke at her. In another case, a radio talk-show guest sued an employee of the radio station for blowing cigar smoke in the guest's face. According to the lawsuit, the whiff of smoke caused "physical discomfort, humiliation and distress."

As usual, both compensatory and punitive damages were sought for this injury.

The language of victimization is becoming the language of social interaction in America—and litigation often provides the vocabulary of that language. Often the first place where individuals and groups achieve victimhood is in the courts. The courtroom lawyers articulate the elements of victimization, providing the arguments for new ways of being victimized. Litigation teaches the public how to see themselves as victims. A lawsuit filed in 1993 by the Welsh-American Legal Defense Fund against several prominent newspapers and television stations exemplified this trend of finding new claims of victimization. Upset that the media's use of the verb *to welsh* constituted, in their view, a slur on the Welsh people, the plaintiffs in their suit contended that the media defendants "degraded the Welsh and Welsh-Americans in a manner in which the same media modernly do not, and dare not, defame any other ethnic group or nationality."[3]

The American bias toward finding victimization was apparent in the repressed-memory sex-abuse lawsuit filed in 1993 against Cardinal Joseph Bernardin, the head of the Chicago archdiocese. Even though the charges against Bernardin stemmed from decades-old events that had no corroborating evidence to support them, and even though Bernardin himself had long enjoyed a public image of virtue, his reputation was immediately damaged by the charges. Members of the "victim community" automatically assumed the Cardinal was guilty, simply because the accusations had been made. Little media attention was given to the possibility that the charges might be false, which, in the end, they turned out to be.

Victimization has become a powerful weapon. It can exempt a person from complying with the rules of society, as in the case of a San Francisco couple who sued Northwest Airlines for kicking them off a flight because of their verbal harassment of other passengers—the result, the couple claimed, of a disorder that causes them to scream obscenities involuntarily. They charged the airline with illegally discriminating against them because of their disability, and they demanded damages for the public humiliation they say they suffered when they were ejected from the airplane. Claims of victimization can be used by the victimizer to deflect blame. When in August of 1994 the NAACP dismissed its leader, the Reverend Benjamin Chavis, Jr., after learning that he had secretly used hundreds of thousands of dollars of the organization's money to ward off a sex discrimination lawsuit against himself, Chavis claimed he was being "crucified" and threatened to sue. The victim status also enables an individual to seek benefits not otherwise available. A woman, calling herself a victim of callous insurance companies, sued her health insurance company that, after paying for two unsuccessful attempts at *in vitro* fertilization, refused to reimburse her for further infertility treatments. "They're depriving me of my right to become a mother," the irate plaintiff argued.

THE CREATION OF NEW VICTIMS

Litigation feeds victimization through the creation of rights. Victims and rights go hand in hand: more rights leads to more victims whose rights have been violated. And with rights as the key to victory in the courtroom, new types of victims demand new types of rights. A relentless cycle develops in which more rights must be generated to keep up with newly recognized victims. Such is the case with "lookism," as the practice of preferring the pretty over the plain is called in rights jurisprudence. Adam Cohen of the ACLU argues that ugly people need to be protected against the discrimination of lookism. According to Cohen, "People don't realize how pervasive the preference for the beautiful is in our society, starting with teachers who give attractive children better grades."[4] He argues that "there is nothing wrong with giving people who have a hard life a legal remedy—we can always set enforcement priorities later."[5] However, as the litigation explosion has shown, these priorities are rarely set.

In providing the arena for and the language of victimization, the litigation process has prompted the spread of victimhood into unusual areas. A 360-pound woman, for instance, sued to force movie theaters to provide seats large enough for obese patrons. Her 1994 suit asked for $15 million in damages for the emotional suffering she endured when the manager of the theater victimized her by refusing to let her bring a portable chair into the auditorium. In another case, a 280-pound man sued his former employer, arguing that he was fired because of his weight. Claiming that his weight qualified as a disability, and that he was protected by the Americans with Disabilities Act, the man alleged that he had been singled out at his job for "a calculated campaign of harassment and discrimination," including making hostile references to his size and holding an "intervention" at which family members and co-workers asked him to get treatment.[6] The employer, a pest-control firm, claimed that the man's weight prevented him from doing basic job duties such as climbing ladders and getting under sinks and counters. Yet another California woman sued a health food store, claiming it did not hire her because she weighed 305 pounds.

The inclusion of overweight people in the pantheon of victims is a new departure in American civil rights. Previously, protection has been confined to groups (i.e., racial minorities, women, the elderly) whose conditions were entirely due to factors outside their control. But now plaintiffs argue that obesity should be considered a disability even if it is caused by gluttony. "This is litigiousness run wild," according to Fred Siegal, a political science professor at Cooper Union.[7]

Similarly, "addictions" are also being claimed as disabilities that confer victim status. A worker fired for absenteeism, for instance, sued on the grounds that his pinball addiction led him astray, and his employers were therefore obliged to accommodate his disability. Yet another new status of victimization was created by a 47-year-old bankruptcy clerk who sued her employer, Citicorp Credit Services, Inc., for discriminating against her because of her body odor. Her suit sought $1.2 million and demanded that the company accommodate her body odor, just as it would any other handicap, instead of treating her rudely and insensitively. Cases such as these illustrate the degree to which lawyers create new victims through the litigation process. They preach the message that anyone can be a victim—even lawyers themselves. Claiming they have been victimized, lawyers have sued their clients and their firms. One New York lawyer brought suit against his client—a black musician—for firing him. The lawyer, who is white, claimed he was a victim of discrimination. In another New York lawsuit, the family of a lawyer who committed suicide sued his former law firm, arguing that the stress from long workdays and "inappropriate workloads with unrealistic deadlines" pushed the young man over the edge. According to the family's lawyer, the workload expected of the lawyer was "inhumane"; even though the job was high-paying, it made a victim of him.[8]

The litigation culture is becoming such a powerful force in breeding victimization that even law students are seeing themselves as victims. Many female law students are now complaining about the methods of legal education, claiming that "the large classes and the confrontational atmosphere [are] intimidating."[9] "I'm uncomfortable when a professor takes my ideas and subjects me to some sort of public humiliation," one student claims. "A man who's more used to competition maybe can take that kind of intense scrutiny."[10] Consequently, a group of women are pushing for smaller classes, more discussion, different ways of grading students, and more emphasis on political and social issues. "We're not whining because we're not doing well," one of the women explains. "We're whining because we're not happy."[11]

VICTIMIZATION AS A POTENT POLITICAL TOOL

The use of victimization as a weapon has extended beyond the litigation arena. It has, for instance, become a valuable political strategy. In a culture of victims, the politics of joy—as Hubert Humphrey once termed it—has been replaced by the politics of sorrow. Although Theodore Roosevelt never spoke of the death of his first wife, and Franklin Roosevelt did everything possible to camouflage his disability, candidates now openly boast of their sufferings, for in the 1990s, politicians run as victims.

The 1994 election season certainly had its share of victim–candidates. Michael Huffington (the Republican Senate candidate in California) spoke of the miscarriage that marred his supposed storybook life. In Georgia, Guy Millner, the Republican nominee for governor, devoted a television ad to his daughter's account of discovering an intruder in her bedroom. California gubernatorial candidate Kathleen Brown announced that her daughter was a victim of date rape. In Virginia, Democrat James Moran told reporters about his 3-year-old daughter's terminal cancer. And in seeking the Washington, D.C., mayoral office after his drug conviction, Marion Barry claimed to be a victim of a racist law enforcement system.

Presidential politics has likewise taken a victimist turn. In the 1992 election, candidate Bill Clinton proclaimed that as a childhood victim of an alcoholic stepfather, he was able to "feel the pain" of the American voter. During the first term of his presidency, he was often called the nation's "First Mourner" for his easily adopted, politically profitable mournful demeanor in the wake of disasters and tragedies. But perhaps nothing reveals how much the victim mind-set has come to dominate American politics than the display at the 1996 Democratic Convention. Delivering one of the convention's most highlighted, prime-time speeches was actor Christopher Reeves, the paralyzed victim of a horseback-riding accident. Though Mr. Reeves held no political role or office, his appearance was aimed at portraying the Democrats as in step with the nation's victim-oriented attitudes. Indeed, the entire convention appeared to be one huge sympathy-fest, as if the politicians felt that sympathy, even more than tax cuts, would draw voters. Jeff Greenfield, the ABC political commentator, suggested that Ricki Lake, the syndicated television talk-show host, "should have been the chair of [the Democrat's] convention."[12] Throughout the convention, tales of personal suffering were abundant: Senator Barbara Boxer played a videotape of the father of a boy who died from eating a tainted hamburger at Jack-in-the-Box; the President shared the story of how his brother had fought cocaine addiction; the First Lady revealed the trauma of Chelsea's night at the hospital after a tonsillectomy; Keynote speaker Evan Bayh talked about the loss he felt from his mother's death; and the Vice President shared his grief over his sister's death of lung cancer. All in all, it was a convention of victim-politics—a convention devoted more to eliciting sympathy than to debating public policy.

In contemporary politics, just as in litigation, individuals in their quest for victory actively try to portray themselves as victims. Such portrayals are becoming an increasingly popular campaign ploy. For instance, in the 1994 New Orleans mayoral campaign, one candidate—a Jewish lawyer—mailed thousands of scurrilous fliers containing anti-Semitic attacks in a fund-raising letter he sent to Jewish voters throughout the nation. In that letter, he claimed that the fliers had been created by his opponent. The opponent, on the other hand, argued that the fliers had been fabricated by the Jewish candidate to portray himself as a "candidate under siege,"[13] because by acquiring the victim-image, the candidate had greatly increased his fund-raising ability. Regardless of who actually did create the fliers, however, the lesson revealed is that politicians rush to cast themselves as victims and then use that victimhood as a powerful offensive tool.

Political groups have also adopted victimization as their driving force. Feminism in particular has been prone to victim rhetoric, labeling boys who flip girls' skirts in elementary schools as "gender terrorists." Catharine MacKinnon has asserted that "some 47 percent of women are victims of rape or attempted rape."[14] MacKinnon argues that when comparing victims' reports of rape with women's reports of sex, the two look a lot alike. Romance, according to Andrea Dworkin, is "rape embellished with meaningful looks."[15] And as Naomi Wolf claims, boys rape and girls get raped as a normal course of events.

According to some dissident feminists, the victimization mentality has come to dominate American feminism. In a hotly debated book, *Who Stole Feminism?*, Christina Hoff Sommers argues that feminism has been derailed by a self-indulgent leadership with a direct personal interest in grossly overstating the woes of womanhood. Sommers writes that the number of stories about women's oppression is greatly exaggerated.[16] (She claims, for example, that around 100 women die each year from anorexia, not the 150,000 often cited.) In women's studies classes, according to Sommers, young women are indoctrinated to believe they are downtrodden victims of discrimination. Likewise, in *The Morning After*, Katie Roiphe disagrees with how feminists have portrayed women as helpless victims in the date-rape crisis. Rophie claims that the statistics on campus date rapes are vastly overblown so as to portray women as victims.[17]

As the feminist movement shows, victimization has become a potent political weapon. Victimization has also become a trump card that any individual can use against most forms of social authority. In the employment context, for instance, individual's victimization releases them from their duties or obligations as employees. A man, claiming that he suffered from a chemical imbalance, sued his employer, who had tried to fire him because he brought a gun to work. In another case, a man sued his company after he was fired for having arrived late to work nearly every day for weeks. Although his employer had repeatedly warned him that his behavior was grounds for dismissal, he argued to the court that he suffered from an ailment called "chronic lateness" and that he deserved reinstatement to his job. He won.

A CULTURE OF COMPETING VICTIMS

As it proliferates through society, victimization can also be competitive and envious. In 1993, when New Jersey Governor Christine Todd Whitman proposed the showing of *Schindler's List* in the state's high schools, for instance, minority groups attacked the decision, saying that the emphasis on the Holocaust elevated Jewish suffering while ignoring the injustices suffered by other racial groups.

Battles between victims have occurred on college campuses that have adopted disciplinary systems for dealing with charges of sexual assault among students. In the age of litigation, however, helping one group often leads to lawsuits by another. Claiming that they have been unfairly treated by these disciplinary processes, men who have been punished have in turn sued the colleges over such procedures. Lawsuits have been filed against schools such as Yale University, Old Dominion University, the University of New Hampshire, and Valparaiso University by men arguing that they are "victims" of sexual hysteria. One Valparaiso student, who had been found to have violated the college's sexual-assault guidelines, sued the college for $12 million. As colleges have discovered, claims of victimization occur on both sides.

Because of this counterattack, colleges are now backing away from disciplining offenders. Among other things, the threat of litigation against disciplinary panel members discourages faculty members from participating. But then, doing nothing can also result in lawsuits. In 1991, for instance, four female students who had been sexually assaulted sued Carleton College. They claimed that the school knew that their attackers had a history of sexual abuse and yet did nothing to prevent further attacks.

Conflicts between victims have produced an endless cycle of litigation. The case of Holt Euliss illustrates this cycle. Euliss, a 12-year employee of AT&T, was charged with sexual harassment by a woman he had known since his school days and whose son he coached. The harassment charged revolved around a single joke told by Euliss one day at work. Though he protested his innocence every step of the way, he was suspended without pay from the company, ejected from the premises, fined, transferred, and ordered to undergo counseling. Two weeks after the complaint against him was made, he committed suicide. His note read, "I have lived all my [life] trying to help and please others, and the one thing in life that I had was pride. But in the last two and a half weeks, I have heard so many lies about me that the pride I once had has deteriorated almost to nothing."[18] After his suicide, his family commenced a wrongful-death suit against AT&T for its treatment of the sexual harassment complaint against Euliss, alleging that its mishandling of the matter caused Euliss's suicide.

A VICTIM-ORIENTED EDUCATION

Although the litigation explosion has fostered a victim-mentality throughout every area of American society, the field of education has been particularly affected. Speech codes reflect this pervasive victimhood. Having been enacted at hundreds of colleges, these codes aim to protect the victims of speech—those who may be insulted by the insensitive speech of others. The codes reflect a recognition of a victim's right not to be offended.

This "politically correct" victimization—used by those who perceive themselves as victims of long-term abuse by "the system"—also shows up in the curriculum. The *National Standards for United States History*, a federally funded curriculum guide that outlines what students in grades 5 through 12 should know about American history, illustrates this victimization.[19] These standards, released in 1994 and backed by the American Federation of Teachers and the National Education Association, place a disproportionate emphasis on the plight of "victims" in American history. Harriet Tubman, the African American who helped organize the pre-Civil War underground railroad, was cited six times in the *Standards*, whereas Lincoln's "Gettysburg Address" was mentioned only once in passing. Although the 1848 Seneca Falls convention on women's rights was heavily emphasized, the inventions of Thomas Edison and Alexander Graham Bell were not even mentioned. Although the American Historical Association vehemently opposed any emphasis on Western civilization in the *Standards*, the "achievements and grandeur" of Mansa Musa's court in West Africa were praised. Students were also encouraged to study Aztec architecture and labor systems, but not its practice of human sacrifice. The traditional aspects of American history that were mentioned were often presented in a critical light. Senator Joseph McCarthy and the Ku Klux Klan receive frequent mention, whereas John D. Rockefeller is put on trial for his "unethical and amoral business practices." Although Daniel Webster and his eloquent oratory was not mentioned at all, the *Standards* did cite Pat Buchanan's speech at the 1992 Republican convention for its bigotry.

The message conferred by the *National Standards* is that America victimizes, and the only heroes in American history are the people who today are considered victims. It replaces the "great leader" view of history with a "victim" view. By dismissing the "great-leader and great civilization theory" of history, however, the Standards go one step further and turn any previously recognized "great leaders" or "great civilizations" into racist and oppressive villains. At a time when people from all over the world are immigrating to America, the *Standards* proclaim that American civilization is not worth studying, and that America has little, if any, redeeming value to offer the world. In a culture of victimhood, history is interpreted as primarily a history of oppression.

As America's culture of victimhood has flourished, its former culture of victory, with its sense of triumph, has declined.[20] Reflecting this transformation and the view of America as more a victimizer than a victor, one of the most popular American history textbooks (Todd and Curti's *Triumph of the American Nation*) was given a new title in 1995, with the word *Triumph* conspicuously absent (Todd and Curti's *The American Nation*).

The "victim historians" have replaced the idyllic view of America as representing the highest aspirations of humanity with a conviction that the United States was, and to a considerable degree still is, an oppressor nation with a history of injustice and deceit. To them, the vital history lesson is not the myth of opportunity embodied in the Statue of Liberty, but immigration laws that have restricted the numbers of Hispanics and Asians coming to the United States. Instead of the remarkable engineering feat of the transcontinental railroad, they see the abuse of its laborers. They consider the culture that shaped America not as a desirable legacy to be embraced, but as a corrupting and alien force that needs to be eradicated. For them, history is a story of victims who were once oppressed and now must be exalted. They regard the Vietnam War, for instance, not as a policy mistake, but as a moral disgrace, proving that America is inherently imperialistic, militaristic, racist, and even evil.

This obsession with victimhood has a distorting influence on historical truth. If traditional historical study tended to ignore people who suffered injustice, the new victim-view of history has moved to the opposite extreme by unconditionally canonizing them as noble heroes. In a 1994 three-part TBS series titled "The Native Americans," for instance, the producers single-mindedly and uncritically exalted the victimized Native American cultures. It repeatedly lectured about how perfect North America was before white people arrived, and it created the impression that there was never a dreary day until the arrival of Europeans. Almost totally ignored were the bloody intertribal wars of the past. For a series meant to illustrate the rich Native American culture, it instead focused on the white world and all the ways it has victimized the Indian. It ended up as a series not about Native American culture and history, but about Native American victimization.

The distortions of the new victim-view history became quite apparent in the highly publicized and controversial proposed exhibit by the Smithsonian Institution to commemorate the 50th anniversary of the bombing of Hiroshima. The exhibit, whose theme was American vengefulness and Japanese suffering in World War II, had outraged veterans' groups. What rankled these groups most was the exhibit's anti-American description of the Pacific War as American racist pillagers intent on destroying Japanese culture. According to the original text, "For most Americans … it was a war of vengeance, [whereas] [f]or most Japanese, it was a war to defend their unique culture against Western imperialism."[21] Incredulous veterans wondered how the Smithsonian could have forgotten the Japanese invasion of China in 1931 and the long years of ruthless fighting and atrocities that cost China 3,211,419 casualties, or the sneak attack on Pearl Harbor, or the fall of Guam, the Philippines, Hong Kong, Singapore, and Rangoon.

The one-sided contradictory messages of the contemporary victim-view of culture and history have led school districts to remove from their libraries books on Christianity, while books on Native American religious traditions were allowed to remain. Harvard professor Bernard Bailyn, a winner of two Pulitzer Prizes, was attacked for reading in class from a diary of a Southern planter without giving equal time to the recollections of a slave. Such equal time was impossible, argued Bailyn, because no journals or diaries written by slaves had ever been found. At the University of Michigan, a young man who expressed the opinion that homosexuality was immoral was sent to a harassment officer and ordered to complete 6 weeks of sensitivity training; later he was directed to write an essay of self-recrimination under the title "I Was Wrong."[22] When a University of Pennsylvania student member of a committee for diversity education expressed in a memo her "deep regard for the individual," a university administrator circled the passage and commented that "this is a red flag phrase today, which is considered by many to be racist. Arguments that champion the individual over the group ultimately privilege the individuals belonging to the largest or dominant group."[23]

In forming educational goals and judging the quality of education, the victim rather than the achiever has become the focal point. Primary and secondary public schools now seem to operate on the assumption that no child is smarter than another. When one boy asked for harder work, he was told he couldn't get too far ahead of the rest of the class—it would run counter to the school's group-oriented philosophy. Bright kids are required to perform at the level set by the most "intellectually challenged" of students. Although the gifted student is said to have a positive influence on the slower students, any emphasis on the needs and abilities of the former is condemned as elitism, for in a victimized culture, it is better to be a victim than an elitist. But a focus on the victim has resulted in a decline in the amount and quality of work expected in class.

Further reflecting the powerful victimization forces in culture and society is the emergence of a new genre of art. In the 1994 year-end issue of *The New Yorker*, one of America's most admired art critics, Arlene Croce, decried the emerging "victim art."[24] Croce, in her controversial article, deplored what she considers the politicization of grants given by the National Endowment for the Arts and the effects of political correctness on the arts in general. To Croce, a work of art should be judged by its realization of truth and beauty, not its adaptability to an agenda.

Although current trends in art and education reveal the tight hold of the victim mentality on the social mind-set, the litigation explosion has shown that just about anything can create a victim, including classic art. A 29-year-old California computer operator, for instance, charged in a 1993 complaint that drawings of partially nude women constituted sexual harassment, because they disrupted her work environment.[25] The drawings were part of an exhibition in Menlo Park City Hall of woodcuts by Brazilian artist Zoravia Bettiol. Goya's *Naked Maja* was the target of a sexual harassment complaint in 1991 by a Pennsylvania college professor, who claimed that the painting of a recumbent courtesan inspired sexual fantasies among her male students and thereby rendered her classroom a hostile working environment. But the outbreak of visual sexual harassment is by no means gender specific: A male janitor working in the Oglesby, Illinois, post office in 1993 complained that depictions of naked Native Americans in a mural commissioned by the Works Progress Administration (WPA) in 1941 and displayed in the lobby violated his civil rights.

BLURRING THE LINE BETWEEN VICTIM AND CRIMINAL

Victimization is not only being fueled by the civil litigation explosion, but it is also being reinforced in the criminal justice system. Both the civil and criminal courts are teaching the lesson that victimhood carries a reward: in the former, it pays money; in the latter, it offers acquittal from criminal conviction.

In the modern criminal court, the concept of "victim" has been greatly expanded. It no longer relates only to the person who was innocently injured by someone else's criminal conduct; it also refers to the helpless criminal who caused such injury. As in the civil litigation process, the criminal justice system has helped teach society the mechanics of claiming victimization and of blaming others. Polls may show that Americans think the value of responsibility needs a resurgence, but in litigation, responsibility translates into liability.

The criminal courts have recognized new types of victims that in turn have provided new excuses for deviant behavior. Traditionally, only a few defenses provided a legal justification for behavior that might otherwise be considered criminal. Self-defense was one; mental incompetence, or insanity, was another.

These defenses, however, were only rarely available. Self-defense required a real and imminent threat to one's personal safety, and the insanity defense required not only psychiatric proof, but also an indefinite stay in a psychiatric hospital if insanity was proved. To most people, confinement in a psychiatric ward was not much better than imprisonment behind bars. But the rise of victimization has supplied a host of new criminal defenses, without the adverse aftereffects of a mental hospital. All accused defendants need do is argue that they were not responsible for their actions because they had been previously victimized in one way or another. Consequently, defendants are escaping responsibility for their otherwise criminal actions by painting themselves as victims who were uncontrollably forced into such actions.

One of the first of the new victim defenses was used by the man who shot San Francisco Mayor George Moscone and Supervisor Harvey Milk. He was not found guilty of first-degree murder because, among other mitigators, the refined sugar in his junk-food diet had made him depressed. The "Twinkie defense" painted him as a victim of a junk-food society.

The first trial of the Menendez brothers for the murder of their parents presents perhaps the most notorious recent use of the victim defense. Traditionally, their dead parents might be thought of as the victims in the case, but because of the wave of victimization defenses now available, the brothers portrayed themselves as victims of their parents' abuse. Invoking the "child abuse" defense, the brothers claimed they were driven to the killings by years of abuse and trauma inflicted by the parents. Their case ended in a hung jury, when they were able to garner enough sympathy by claiming to be among the millions of alleged abuse victims in the United States. This victimology approach was so powerful with the jury that it could not convict a couple of adult men who pleaded an abused-child defense that is typically used in cases involving minors, and who chose the maid's night off to pump 16 rounds of ammunition into their parents as they ate ice cream and strawberries in the family room in front of the television.

As the Menendez case revealed, child abuse has become the victimization of choice. In a case involving the attempted firing of a St. Paul, Minnesota, policeman who had been convicted of sexual misconduct involving a 14-year-old, the police officer claimed that because he himself had been a victim of sexual abuse as a child, he was not only not responsible for his own misconduct, but also he should be given special treatment and therapy as a victim of past abuse. The judge must have agreed, because she ruled against the firing of the policeman.

Perhaps almost as notorious as the Menendez case was the 1994 trial of Lorena Bobbitt for maliciously wounding her husband. Having severed her husband's penis while he slept, Ms. Bobbitt invoked the "battered wife syndrome"—a defense previously used by a Massachusetts woman in 1989 to justify the beating death of her husband who, she claimed, had been beating her for years—to show that she was not responsible for her actions that night. Years of being victimized by her husband had left her susceptible to an "irresistible impulse" to strike back. Like the Menendez brothers, Ms. Bobbitt was found to be the pathetic victim of physical abuse, humiliation, and sexual torment. And such victimhood was seen by the jury to justify violent assault.

The Los Angeles riots in the aftermath of the first trial of the police officers accused of beating Rodney King produced another new victim defense. During that rioting, several men were videotaped beating and hurling bricks at the head of truck driver Reginald Denny, causing more than 90 skull fractures. In their subsequent trial, these men successfully used the "riot defense" to excuse their actions. A central argument of the defense was that people caught up in a riot are less answerable for their misdeeds because they are in the grip of a mob psychology. After acquitting them, one juror, speaking about the defendants, explained that "they just got caught up in the riot. I guess maybe they were in the wrong place at the wrong time."[26] The defendants, their lawyers had argued, were just victims of fate, just as was poor Mr. Denny, who obviously was in the wrong place at the wrong time—although it was Mr. Denny's skull that had been beaten. As the "riot defense" reveals, in an age of the victim, just about anyone can claim victimhood. While rioting used to be a crime, it can now be a defense.

As with the Denny trial, some of the most frightening social crimes are producing some of the most bizarre claims of victimization. One such claim was made by Colin Ferguson, the man who went on a shooting rampage during rush hour on the Long Island Railroad in December 1993, killing 6 people and wounding 19 others. For his defense, Ferguson blamed his shooting on "black rage"—the sheer anger over racism in America. Perhaps most surprising, however, was that this "black rage defense" was found to be at least somewhat compelling by almost half of the people polled in a comprehensive telephone survey of public attitudes toward crime.[27] So once again, in the aftermath of a shocking crime, there were only victims: the dead and wounded, and the shooter who was a victim of racial prejudice and its resulting "black rage."

Another somewhat-related defense is the "explosive rage disorder." This defense was asserted in the 1994 trial of Eric Smith, who was charged with brutally murdering 4-year-old Derrick Robie. Derrick was on his way to a town recreation program when Smith lured him into a field and bludgeoned him with a 26-pound rock. During Smith's trial, the jury was subjected to the usual testimony of psychiatrists and disorder experts that has become all too commonplace in today's courtrooms. Their testimony, of course, was that Smith's actions were not his fault—he was a victim of his "explosive rage disorder."

The proliferation of victim defenses has resulted in a corresponding multitude of "syndromes." These syndromes arise from a legal profession that is increasingly arguing that individuals are helpless over their circumstances and do not have power over their destiny. In a Los Angeles murder trial for the beating of his wife with a wrench, Moosa Hanoukai successfully asserted the "meek-mate syndrome." He argued that his wife had destroyed his self-esteem by psychologically emasculating him—forcing him to sleep on the floor, calling him names, and so on.

Daimion Osby, a black 18-year-old who shot two unarmed black men in a Fort Worth parking lot, managed to get a deadlocked jury after his lawyer argued that he suffered from "urban survival syndrome"—the fear that inner-city blacks have of other blacks.

Joel Rifkin, in his trial for the killing of two women, asserted the "adopted child syndrome." This syndrome apparently developed because Mr. Rifkin was rejected by his biological mother, whom he believed to be a prostitute. Consequently, he sought refuge among prostitutes and then strangled them to ease his suffering.

Other recently used syndromes include the premenstrual stress syndrome, which was the grounds for the acquittal of a woman doctor charged with drunken driving in Virginia; the Super Bowl Sunday syndrome, which asserts that there is a direct link between men watching professional football and violence against women; and the "failure to file syndrome," which has been used to avoid punishment for failing to file income taxes. According to this latter syndrome, the failure to file results because of an "overall inability to act in one's own interest," according to a description of the syndrome by a New York University psychiatry professor.[28] This syndrome had been used to defend a surgeon who had not filed tax returns in 10 years because of an aversion to filling out forms. But the failure-to-file syndrome is not recognized in any psychological diagnostic manual, says Douglas Fizel, spokesman for the American Psychological Association. "It sounds more like this is coming out of the legal arena than the psychological," he adds.[29]

VICTIMIZATION AND THE SOCIAL MIND-SET

The psychological arena has been a vital contributor to the victimization defenses in the criminal courts. Even more generally, however, the collaboration between lawyers and therapists has had a particularly stimulating effect on the litigation explosion as a whole, since most claims of victimization, even in the civil courts, require some type of psychological testimony. And there is every indication that the success of victim defenses will only grow over time, especially since the baby-boom generation has flocked to the social work, psychology, psychiatry, and human services professions. In reacting to the perceived harsh judgmentalism of the past, these professions have tried so earnestly to avoid "blaming the victim" that they excuse anyone who possibly could be a victim. Yet, the more that society looks on people as controlled by their environment, or by genetic and psychological factors, the less they will be seen as individuals who have free will and hence are responsible for their actions.

As Americans burrow more deeply into the victim mentality, they will intensify the litigation explosion. Victimology has turned out to be a winning tactic in the legal arena. Once a victim is identified, the litigation system almost reflexively turns to compensate that victim. The cycle goes on and on. But the courts tend to treat all victims the same. It tends to make all suffering equal so that all remedies will be equal. It is a trend that would make the college student who is insulted by a racial joke comparable to James Meredith barred at the door of Ole' Miss, and a sexually explicit joke as detrimental to job security as a supervisor who takes away the duties of a clerk who has rebuffed his advances.

The nation's courts during the litigation age have fostered a cultural belief that any injury or disappointment confers victimhood, and that this status warrants retribution. In a litigation culture, people become convinced that they are entitled not just to the pursuit of happiness, but also to happiness itself. A litigation culture celebrating victimhood refuses to acknowledge the limitations inherent in the human condition. Whenever disappointments occur, the language of victimization stands ready to translate them into lawsuits.

The litigation explosion and the rise of victimization, however, cannot be understood without examining yet another aspect of contemporary American culture—the therapy movement. It is this movement that is most tangibly helping to move potential victims from their self-pity to their courtroom seat, for without their partnership with therapists, lawyers could not bring many of their victim cases to the litigation arena. Consequently, the litigation explosion is closely intertwined with the therapy explosion.

CHAPTER 7

An Explosive Partnership: Therapists and Lawyers

AMERICA'S THERAPEUTIC CULTURE

The litigation explosion, and particularly the rise of victimization, is fueled by the growth of America's therapeutic culture. Psychologists have teamed up with lawyers to bring new and more victims to the courtroom. As the therapy movement discovers more and more psychological and emotional injuries, the litigation explosion gets more lawsuits. As more Americans explore their victimhood in therapists' offices, the more they litigate that victimhood in the courtroom. And as America becomes more a therapeutic culture, juries and judges become more sympathetic to new lawsuits seeking damages for new kinds of psychic injuries.

The symptoms of America's therapeutic culture exist everywhere. As Barbara Ehrenreich writes, "We are all ... in recovery."[1] Pop psychology books are perennial bestsellers. In a culture obsessed with psychic healing, psychology has become the academic darling of the 1990s and the most popular course of study among college students. Therapy and analysis are becoming as commonplace as flu shots. The most indulged child in America is the "inner child." Support groups aimed at boosting self-esteem have become phenomenally popular, with an estimated 40 percent of all Americans belonging to such groups.[2] As Ellen Herman states in *The Romance of American Psychology*, "Psychological insight is the creed of our time."[3] Even the President reaches out to voters with his therapeutic mantra: "I feel your pain."

As the therapeutic culture has taken root, the language of politics has come to bear striking similarity to that of pop psychology. Like states-rights in the mid-19th century and economic security in the 1930s, psychology has become the commodity of politics in the 1990s. Social programs are aimed at improving the self-esteem of their beneficiaries. Affirmative action programs are needed not only to provide jobs but also to raise the self-image of minority groups. Even the campaigns take on the language of a therapist's office. With the end of every political campaign, it is time "for the healing to begin."

America's therapeutic culture has intensified the victim mentality in society. The proliferation of 12-step programs and books such as *I'm Not My Fault* and *Toxic Parents* all contribute to the national conversion to victimhood. People are now assumed to be emotional victims, offsprings of dysfunctional families. As John Bradshaw, Melody Beattie, and other gurus of the 12-step program are quick to point out, 96 percent of American families are dysfunctional.[4] Ubiquitous recovery-movement phrases such as "We're all victims" and "We're all codependent" strive to leave no one out of the victim circle. Women in some 12-step programs even claim to having been "metaphorically raped."[5]

Perhaps the most blatant sign of America's therapy culture appears on the plethora of television talk shows—Oprah, Phil, Sally Jessy Raphael, Geraldo Rivera, Montel Williams, Ricki Lake, Jerry Springer, and so on. Millions of viewers ingest daily servings of pop therapy from these talk shows, where both the guests and the audience compete for who has suffered the most psychological injuries. Dr. Lillian Glass, a Los Angeles therapist, has herself appeared on "a couple of hundred shows" to dole out some quick psychological cliches during the final minutes of the program.[6] Serving as public confessionals and therapy sessions in which nothing is left unsaid, the shows have been instrumental in promoting the language of a therapeutic culture, with words and phrases such as inner child, emotional reality, dysfunction, self-actualization, and, most of all, self-esteem dominating the discourse. And on these shows, psychological trauma and dysfunction are the presumed norm. On one show, Sally Jessy Raphael announced that there were 40–60 million survivors of incest in the United States.

THERAPY CULTURE AND VICTIMIZATION

Self-esteem has provided a whole new foundation for victimhood in America. It has become the "sacred cow of American culture."[7] It is the answer to every ill in society, from crime to broken families to educational reform. No longer is victimhood confined to those who suffer some objectively defined ailment or injustice, such as physical handicap or criminal violence. Therapy has injected a powerful egalitarianism into American culture. A victim can now be anyone whose self-esteem has been injured. And the only judge of that self-esteem injury is the person who has incurred that injury.

The quest to combat psychic pain and achieve self-esteem is the crusade of the 1990s, much as was the quest to employ the unemployed in the 1930s and the crusade against communism in the 1950s. Whereas the generation of the 1930s fought an economic depression, and the war generation fought Nazi tyranny, the generation of the 1990s fights emotional depression and personal unfulfillment. Emotional "healing" has become the national obsession. In a culture of self-absorption in feelings, "healing" is a never-ending process. And in a litigation age, lawsuits have become yet another stage of the healing process, with lawyers joining the rapidly growing array of counselors, sensitivity facilitators, and analysts dedicated to healing the increasing numbers of emotional victims.

Psychic disorders and dysfunctions become the norm in a therapeutic culture, and the acceptance of such disorders and dysfunctions further promotes the spread of victimization. With each new edition of the *Diagnostic and Statistical Manual of Mental Disorders* (DSM)—the one book sure to be found on the shelf of every psychiatrist—the number of disorders multiply. The latest edition includes over 300 mental disorders, more than three times the number in the first edition. Mental disorders now include such maladies as the "disorder of written expression" (which afflicts people who can't write well) and age-associated memory deficit. According to some doctors and psychologists, the growth of the DSM reflects the way in which people are being defined— according to their disorders. As one critic noted, "The crazy is now the normal." Consequently, there are more and more accepted victims who are justified in suing on behalf of their victimhood.

In a therapeutic culture, psychic pain is a trump card against any other kind of pain or tragedy. Even convicted criminals' psychic restoration rivals the permanent physical injuries of the people they bombed—if their self esteem has been restored, they should be leniently treated. A man convicted of killing a 14-year-old girl during a sexual assault similarly argued for his parole with the words: "I feel good about myself, I have good self-esteem."[8]

EDUCATION AS THERAPY

Perhaps no area of society reflects the dominance of the therapeutic culture more than the field of education. Intellectual development no longer seems the primary focus of elementary education— it is the nurturing of self-esteem. Unless students feel better about themselves and unless they acquire greater self-esteem, the argument goes, they cannot learn. This focus on self-esteem occurs so widely in educational and popular writings that it has led to the creation of a self-esteem movement—the practice of supplying positive feedback regardless of the quality of performance. Every student in class gets at least a "satisfactory" grade; every member of a fifth-grade baseball team that failed to win a game all season gets a trophy at season's end. Classrooms in which students are urged to recite from a list of nice things to say to each other—"You brighten my day" or "I'm lucky to know you" or "You're a special friend"—resemble more a Hallmark store than a place of learning. In a number of states, most notably New York, the basic subjects required for academic advancement are being replaced by a "Rainbow" curriculum more preoccupied with inspiring self-esteem than with teaching reading or writing. As many critics of this approach argue, the time is approaching when 8-year-olds will have more knowledge about Native American totem rituals than about the multiplication table, and will be better instructed in a positive image of gay lifestyles than in how to apply the rules of grammar. The point was made in a newspaper cartoon depicting two little girls walking down the street. One of them says, "My friend has two mommies," and the other replies, "How much is two?"

The therapeutic worldview has become a dominant one in higher education as well. Women's studies programs around the country, for instance, are heavily "therapized." Reporting on her tour of such classes at various colleges, Karen Lehrman wrote: "Sometimes they consist of consciousness-raising psychobabble, with the students' feelings and experiences valued as much as anything the professor or texts have to offer."[9] Not all programs are as bad as this, but Lehrman saw plenty to object to: "touchy-feely classes," an emphasis on self-revelation, and the celebration feelings over facts. Women's studies programs, according to Daphne Patai and Noretta Koertge in *Professing Feminism: Cautionary Tales from Inside the Strange World of Women's Studies*, often depict women as victims in need of self-esteem. Likewise, Christine Hoff Sommers has reported that conventions of the National Women's Studies Association Conference are marked by therapeutic uplift and healing rituals, such as holding hands to form "a healing circle" and assuming the posture of trees to gain a feeling of rootedness and tranquility.[10]

Elsewhere at the university level, the influence of group self-esteem has been significant. Students are demanding courses that reflect and affirm their own identities and are devoted to psychic uplift and the raising of group self-esteem—thus the proliferation

of departments such as gay studies. In the field of history, for
instance, the notion of education as therapy has had a particularly
distorting effect, for it is in that field that the need to create positive
self-images is surpassing the quest for truth. Finding that certain
minorities have been oppressed throughout history, some historians now want to write history in a way that gives a sense of pride
and heightened self-image to those minorities. Yet in pursuing
self-esteem, truth is often left behind, because truth can be highly
subjective when victimization and low self-esteem are its determi-
nants. Afrocentric history may improve black students' self-
esteem by legitimately highlighting the accomplishments of African civilization, but in striving to elevate African culture, it often
presents European culture as nothing more than a bastardized
version of itself. Afrocentrists, for instance, argue that Africans
were in the New World even before Columbus's journey, that
ancient Greece stole their culture from Africa, and that all Western
culture derives from Africa.

Even in the workplace, the currency of feelings is rising in
value. Corporations are going through "sensitivity training"
courses arranged by personnel officers—the resident psychologists of the workplace. For when employees feel slighted, they
sue—as they have increasingly done if they are rudely treated or
insensitively terminated. Some litigators and psychologists are
even trying to develop the legal theory that employees who yell at
their bosses cannot be disciplined if they can establish that their
outbursts result from an emotional condition.[11]

THE LITIGATION EXPLOSION IN A THERAPY CULTURE

In a therapeutic culture, emotional tranquility and self-esteem
are easily damaged; and in an age of litigation, such injuries end
up as lawsuits. A high school senior, alleging injury to her psyche,
sued a university for its clerical error in sending her information
suggesting that she had been accepted for enrollment when in fact
she had not. Her lawyer publicly stated that the girl's feelings had
been so wounded that she would continue to press her lawsuit

even if the university now accepted her. In another case, a man who was offended by the ability of a CD-ROM encyclopedia to find instances of a racial slur in its own text sued the encyclopedia's publisher for $40 million. The plaintiff claimed he suffered emotional distress after finding the word *nigger* in such references as a book by comedian Dick Gregory titled *Up From Nigger* and a passage from the biography of Dr. Martin Luther King Jr., in which he recalled incidents in which he was called "nigger." A former sales representative won an $8 million punitive damages award for the psychological distress he suffered from the insensitive way in which he was fired. Alleging severe emotional trauma, a lesbian couple sued a doctor who declined to artificially inseminate one of them. And a 360-pound woman sued a movie theater chain for $15 million in damages for the emotional suffering incurred when the manager of a theater refused to let her set up a portable chair in the theater's aisle.

Therapy has injected a powerful egalitarianism into American culture. It proclaims that everyone is, or can be, a victim. Anyone who has ever had parents can be a victim. Anyone who has ever felt offended or hurt can be a victim. Take the case, for instance, of the 20-year-old woman who sued her former softball coach and high school counselor for failing to prevent, and then handle with sufficient sensitivity, a team initiation rite carried out by her teammates. Or consider the complaint filed against Northwest Airlines by a woman who was offended when she was not allowed to use her husband's reduced-rate travel pass because her attire did not conform to the dress code required by such passes.

As more cases involving psychological claims get litigated, more potential litigants seek therapy. Living in a litigious society, individuals quickly learn that a visit to a therapist may yield a substantial return at the courthouse. In this way, the litigation explosion fuels and reinforces the therapeutic culture. The possibility of a large settlement sends more people to the therapist. In turn, the more therapy that occurs, the more victims are created, and the more litigation that ensues.

The psychology profession has not only created new causes of action for which plaintiffs can sue, but it has also created a whole new set of damages that can accompany many existing types of lawsuits. Now, as part of nearly every employment or personal injury case, plaintiffs claim damages for "severe emotional and psychological distress" that allegedly occurred in connection with the employment termination or automobile injury. Consequently, psychologists have become increasingly frequent witnesses in civil trials. Psychologists are even providing psychological autopsies in cases involving a deceased person. In one such case, for instance, an Iowa court called in three psychiatrists to conduct a psychological autopsy for the purpose of determining why a man killed himself and, hence, whether his widow was entitled to certain workers' compensation benefits.

A therapeutic culture has another stimulating effect on the litigation explosion. It makes everyone feel especially sympathetic to psychic pain. It's like the Great Depression, which made everyone feel economically insecure, even those with jobs. Juries, attuned to the healing needs of psychological victims, are more likely to reward litigants who claim emotional and psychic injuries. Because of the pervasive influence of the therapeutic culture (i.e., through the television talk shows), juries have become more familiar with the language of therapy and more susceptible to novel theories about how a plaintiff has been injured psychologically.

In a therapeutic culture, the courts have increasingly become a forum for "healing." Testifying psychologists are telling jurors that lawsuits are a necessary part of a person's healing process, and consequently, jurors are increasingly being asked to participate in that process. When Lorena Bobbitt was acquitted for the admitted sexual mutilation of her husband, her lawyer came before the microphones and called the verdict "a giant step forward for Lorena in the healing process," suggesting that a jury's job is not to find the truth, but to aid in the healing. Similarly, shortly after Michael Jackson reached a multimillion dollar settlement for alleged child molestation, his lawyer explained that Mr. Jackson just wanted to get on with his life and let the healing process begin. When the Justice Department agreed to pay $3.1 million to settle a suit brought by the family of Randy Weaver, the white separatist whose wife and son were killed in a 1992 gun battle with federal agents, it said that the settlement was made with the hope of "taking a substantial step toward healing the wounds the incident inflicted."[12]

America's therapy culture has affected the two types of courts differently. In the civil courts, it is psychology that identifies all the hurts and abuses that form the subject of million-dollar lawsuits. And in the criminal courts, psychologists testify to the plethora of victim syndromes that have been used to convince juries to excuse the actions of defendants. In 1992, for instance, the "urban psychosis" defense was first used in the case of a teenager charged with shooting a girl and then stealing her coat. A psychologist testified that the teenager had grown up in the inner city and had been frequently exposed to violent behavior. This exposure, the psychologist argued, induced an urban psychosis that in turn made the teenager not responsible for his actions. In commenting on this type of defense, constitutional scholar Bruce Fein observed that "we have a whole raft of lawyers today arguing that individuals are just helpless over their circumstances, [and] that's nonsense."[13]

REPRESSED MEMORY:
AN EXAMPLE OF THERAPY LITIGATION

Perhaps the most controversial psychological theory currently used to support a lawsuit is the repressed memory theory. Under this theory, adults come to believe that their parents or other relatives abused them when they were young and that they blocked out all memory of this abuse until undergoing recovered-memory therapy later in life. With encouragement from therapists, they then cut off their relatives and sue them. In one case, a 91-year-old Minnesota man was sued by his 60-year-old daughter for incest, the memory of which she says she repressed for 57 years before a therapist helped her recover it. And, of course, there was the much-publicized case involving Joseph Cardinal Bernardin, the Chicago Cardinal sued by a man who claimed that more than two decades earlier Bernardin had had sex with him, which was subsequently dropped after the plaintiff admitted that his recovered memories were false.

Critics claim that recovered memories of abuse are the product of a therapeutic theory gone out of control. The number of people who say they've been falsely accused, lost their children and grandchildren, and suffered financial ruin due to lawyers' fees has soared. By 1994, nearly 9000 people had sought help from the False Memory Syndrome Foundation in Philadelphia, a parents' advocacy group started by an accused couple. A year earlier, the number had been about 3000. Proponents of recovered-memory therapy, however, have dismissed the critics and their public crusade against the therapy as a typical defense mounted by "perpetrators in denial." Some therapists actually believe that a lack of memory of being a victim of sexual abuse proves one of two things: that the abuse whose memory is being "repressed" was truly traumatic, or that the person's definition of sexual abuse is grossly inadequate. As one therapist who supported a client in a $20 million suit against her parents for sexual abuse explained: "I don't care if [the specific allegations] are true—what's important to me is that I hear the child's truth, the patient's truth." According to the therapist, "We all live in a delusion."

Although great controversy surrounds recovered-memory therapy, the psychology profession has offered little solution. Psychologists and psychiatrists are bitterly divided over the idea that the memory of repeated abuse can be completely wiped out and then recovered, virtually intact. The American Psychological Association appointed a task force in 1993 to develop a consensus on the issue, but the group quickly stalemated. Despite this scientific confusion, however, the courts have continued to march ahead, litigating a matter that has befuddled the experts. Lawsuits keep piling up, and judges and juries are left to answer the key question: Which of these memories are true? As is usually the case, uncertainty and ambiguity breeds more litigation. Millions of dollars in damages have been awarded to thousands of victims who have allegedly recovered repressed memories of abuse, and many states are encouraging such lawsuits by extending the applicable statutes of limitations.

Increasingly, repressed-memory theory is coming under criticism, even within the psychology profession.[14] Coinciding with this criticism, therapists are facing a new wave of lawsuits by former patients who have renounced their "memories," by those who say they have been falsely accused of abuse, and even by patients recovering memories of abuse committed by the therapists themselves. For instance, a California man, whose family broke up after his daughter accused him of abusing her 25 years earlier, was awarded $500,000 in his malpractice suit against two therapists charged with implanting false memories in his daughter. Experts call such recovered-memory lawsuits the "next big wave" of malpractice litigation to hit the psychology profession. And insurers are bracing for the onslaught. The American Professional Agency, the nation's largest insurer of therapists, is predicting that the recovered-memory field will incur litigation costs of $300 million by the year 2000.

THE THERAPEUTIC CULTURE
AND THE TRANSFORMATION OF LAW

The injection of psychology into the courtroom has become so prominent that the traditional notions of individual responsibility and free will have undergone a profound transformation. According to many attorneys, "Using the psychological effects of the past to explain the actions of the present has become so common in the courtroom that now it is assumed that your past is to blame for everything."[15] Free will and rational choice are becoming less relevant. Adult problems are simply seen as the inevitable result of having been raised poorly. To psychologists, people are in the grip of emotions that are beyond their control—that is, until they undergo therapy. In their search for a cause of all deviant behavior, psychologists turn to a person's past, to everything outside of that person's control. Everything, that is, except the traditional concept of free will.

In a therapeutic culture, the independent individual with a free will has been replaced by the injured individual imprisoned by the past and vulnerable to outside influences. Fragile individualism has overtaken the older frontier tradition of self-reliant individualism. The Enlightenment view of free will and the rational person is being supplanted by neomedieval notions of people as helpless victims whose dysfunctional pasts control them like evil spirits. Under this notion, a criminal defendant's sense of inner worth can lessen the degree of responsibility for his or her actions. In 1992, for instance, a federal appeals court in San Francisco ruled that a bank robber's sentence could be reduced because she had been abused as a child and, as a result, had experienced profound feelings of inadequacy, isolation, confusion, low self-esteem, and guilt.

This concept of individuals, as helpless puppets of their past, has increasingly taken hold in a litigious therapeutic culture. It has forced the courts to delve into complex examinations of the psychological past of the litigants. But since psychologists rarely meet a person who is normal or healthy, or capable of independent judgment, any definition of objective behavior or intent becomes impossible. Consequently, law becomes reduced to a psychological analysis of each person. No objective guidelines exist. Such a condition is emerging in the area of harassment law. Employees, for instance, can sue if they encounter at work a "hostile environment"—an ambiguous description that can include a wide array of speech or actions, including tuning an office radio to right-wing talk shows, deemed upsetting or humiliating. "Our basic rule of thumb is what we call a 'gut-check,'" says William Petrocelli, coauthor of *Sexual Harassment on the Job*. "If you feel you've been sexually harassed, then you have been."[16]

Traditionally, the law assumed an objective standard for judging human behavior—in other words, that there is a capable, normal mind. But in a nation in therapy, it is becoming less appropriate to make such an assumption. In a nation in which people are victims of various psychological syndromes, it cannot be assumed that a rational individual sits in court. The courtroom must then become, in effect, a therapists' couch for each litigant. But without objective, predictable standards for people's actions, even the existence of a rule of law becomes questionable. And, of course, without such objective standards, there will be nothing to control or curtail the litigation explosion.

In a therapeutic courtroom, the rule of precedent also withers. When each person must be judged according to his or her particular psychological makeup, the precedents set in previous cases become irrelevant. Since each person is different, no two cases will automatically have the same result. Instead, each person must be judged according to his or her past and individual psychological identity. No general rules can therefore apply, because every person's psychological makeup is different. This decline of precedent further fuels the litigation explosion, for even though others have failed in a particular type of case, the next plaintiff just might succeed. Consequently, litigation becomes like a slot machine—if there are enough attempts, there will eventually be a winner. Instead of inhibiting uncontrolled and abusive behavior, this legal approach—of allowing any behavior if motivated by emotional disability—will only encourage more lawsuits and criminal cases. Furthermore, justice will be impossible when the victimizer is nothing more than another victim.

The workplace has been one site of such escalating litigation. The 1992 Americans with Disabilities Act (ADA), which protects workers with physical disabilities, also covers those who suffer from mental disorders ranging from severe depression to paranoia. But it is the mental disorders that have proved to be the real litigation minefield, producing such horror stories as workers claiming "chronic lateness syndrome." Psychiatric disabilities already constitute the third-highest category of complaints filed under the ADA. Under the ADA, any employee can claim depression as a disability, even a Harvard-educated lawyer. When fired because of poor work performance, the lawyer sued his employer, alleging that his periodic depression was the cause of his job problems and that the company should instead have cut his hours and made other accommodations for his disability. The court agreed and awarded him $1.1 million.

CONCLUSION

Caught at the vortex of a litigious society and a therapeutic culture, the nation's courts are being increasingly influenced by the therapy movement. Psychologists are telling jurors that lawsuits are part of a person's healing process, and jurors are becoming partners with therapists, being asked not to dispense justice but to participate in the healing process. Likewise, lawyers have increasingly emulated the therapist/talk-show host, leading juries through a 12-step courtroom program in which they can experience the recovery needed for the litigants to begin their healing process. In a culture of self-esteem, the lawsuit becomes another form of therapy.

As members of a therapeutic culture, juries have become quite familiar with the language of therapy and recovery, with the new psychological syndromes, with the fragility of the psyche and the ways in which people can be overcome by the psychological traumas of the past. Consequently, they have become increasingly receptive to claims of emotional victimization. Because of this receptivity, a jury was quite comfortable with a psychiatrist's description of Lorena Bobbitt's behavior at the time of her violent attack as "brief reactive psychosis."

With courtrooms increasingly addressing psychological claims, the growth of the therapeutic culture will further fuel the litigation explosion. Similarly, more lawsuits involving psychological injuries will in turn feed the therapy movement. The two will be locked in a symbiotic relationship.

CHAPTER 8

An Inadequate Social Regulator

THE EMERGENCE OF LAW
AS THE PRIMARY SOCIAL REGULATOR

In the litigation age, law has become the primary regulator of social behavior. With every kind of dispute involving even the most traditionally private of matters ending up in court, law has superseded any other set of social customs or cultural values as society's governing standard. Being continually refined through litigation, law has been charged with governing all the intricate possibilities and complexities of modern life. The litigation explosion has conveyed the delusion that the legal process can serve as an all-wise Solomon for American society—dictating answers to every question, anticipating all future occurrences, remedying every ill, and eliminating every uncertainty. As experience has revealed, however, the expectation that the litigation process can be such an all-encompassing social regulator is indeed a misplaced expectation.

In the litigation age, the question of "Is it legal?" has eclipsed that of "Is it wrong?" Discovering legal rights has replaced the investigation of what is right. Avoiding illegality has risen above complying with what is decent and ethical. Schools increasingly focus on students' rights, not students' curiosities. Employees concentrate on their rights as much as their jobs. Even members of sports teams have taken on the language of rights over the demands of teamwork.

Lawsuits relating to participation on sports teams provide one of the clearest examples of how litigation concepts have come to govern social relations and behavior. Membership on a sports team is, or should be, governed by the individual's athletic abilities and contributions to the team. But in the litigation age, a third consideration has been added—that of due process. Cries for *due process*—a term meaning the legal procedures to which an individual is entitled in a judicial action—have been the common response when an athlete is ejected from a team or punished for inappropriate behavior. Take, for example, the case of Tonya Harding and her attempt to remain on the 1994 U.S. Olympic Team after she had been implicated in the attack on fellow teammate Nancy Kerrigan. Even though she admitted lying about her knowledge of that incident, her supporters argued that she should not be ejected from the team until she had been given due process. Harding even filed a $20 million lawsuit against the U.S. Olympic Committee, seeking to prevent it from interfering with her participation in the games. Arguing that everyone is entitled to due process, her supporters claimed that until Harding was convicted on some criminal charge, she should be considered innocent until proven guilty. To them, the only thing that mattered was due process.

Yet, due process is not the only consideration, nor perhaps even an appropriate one, when determining whether one is to be given the privilege of representing her country in the Olympic games. There are other concerns, such as sportsmanlike conduct and team morale and national image. Due process is important only in legal cases, in determining whether someone is criminally guilty or legally liable. The standard for determining whether someone should be sent to prison is not the same as one for deciding who should be a member of a team representing the United States on the world stage. But in a litigious society, due process has become the overriding social standard. It intrudes into private organizations and activities that were never meant to be governed by the same standards that prevail in a court of law. When a California high school student was ejected in 1993 from the cheerleading squad for failing chemistry, she turned not to a tutor, but a lawyer, and sued the school over its academic policies. Likewise, an Indiana high schooler sued when he was found ineligible for his school's golf team. Thirty years ago, however, high school students were as unlikely to consider filing such a lawsuit as they were to find a judge who would have taken it seriously. "We've almost reached the point where, as we go through life, we have to have a lawyer at our side to do anything," observes Henry Manne, dean of the George Mason University Law School.[1]

As with sports in general, coaching, in particular, has become an activity increasingly conducted in the minefield of liability. In May 1995, two former members of the University of Minnesota women's tennis team sued the university because of their coach's alleged pattern of abusive behavior, including verbal abuse and forcing players to run laps when they felt ill. Among other allegations, one of the players said the coach grabbed her as a form of punishment on three occasions, belittled her, and gave her teammates the impression that she was not pulling her weight. In his response, the coach admitted to being a demanding coach but denied abusing any authority.

THE WORKPLACE AS A LEGAL QUAGMIRE

With the breakdown of sexual etiquette and basic courtesy, the law has flooded into the workplace to regulate personal interactions between employees. Now, employers must do much more than provide jobs and pay wages—they must also maintain a "nonhostile" work environment, free from any offensive language or sexual innuendo. In October 1994, a Connecticut jury awarded $105,000 to a woman who was "utterly humiliated" in the way her employer fired her. Escorted out the door by security guards in

full view of gaping co-workers, the woman claimed that she suffered great "emotional distress" by the ordeal of her termination.
Not *why* she was fired, but *how* she was fired became the subject of
her lawsuit. In another case, a former sales representative for
Schering-Plough Corporation won an $8 million punitive dam-
ages award for the insensitive way in which he was fired—in a
diner by two company executives, who then followed him home
and took his drug supplies and company car. As these cases
reveal, litigation has become the dictator not only of what employers must do, but also of how they do it.

With the increasing intrusion of litigation, the workplace is
being governed more by the commands of lawyers than by the
necessities of the common economic endeavor in which all employees are engaged. Despite the thousands of workplace safety
regulations, for instance, actual safety conditions have not im-
proved much. This is because, according to Philip Howard, author
of *The Death of Common Sense*, the great majority of accidents are
due to human error, not to equipment malfunctions.[2] Consequently, the real effect of all those safety regulations is simply to
breed more litigation. According to Howard, 96 percent of OSHA's
health standards are appealed in court.

Even the most ordinary incidents of workplace life, such as a
conversation over job performance, are now being driven by legal
considerations. The "rights revolution" in the workplace has not
made it a more harmonious and productive place, but one suffocated and sometimes torn apart by diverse employees asserting
their various legal rights. As "rights" in the workplace have prolif-
erated, more than 70 percent of American employees now fall into
a protected category and can sue if they feel their rights have been
violated.

Employers have even been held liable for the domestic abuse
suffered by their employees. After Patrick Thomas was convicted
in 1993 for shooting his former girlfriend at her Houston office, the
family of the former girlfriend sued her employer for failing to
protect her—even though a restraining order had been already
issued against Mr. Thomas. The case was settled for more than
$350,000. Not only is liability for domestic abuse a relatively un-

explored area for corporations, but also experts predict that such lawsuits against employers will increase under the federal Violence against Women Act, which makes battering a civil rights' violation and stiffens compensatory damages.[3]

The increasing legal regulation of the workplace has put some employers into a no-win situation, leaving them with a legal catch-22. This quandary was demonstrated when the U.S. Postal Service, seeking to prevent further workplace violence, fired Thomas Lussier after another former postal worker went on a shooting spree in Royal Oak, Michigan, in 1991. Lussier's supervisor had described him as "mentally unbalanced and capable of a Royal Oak–type incident."[4] Lussier, a Vietnam vet, had been diagnosed with posttraumatic stress disorder. But a federal judge ruled that Mr. Lussier's discharge was illegal, because he had a mental disability that was protected by an antidiscrimination law. Consequently, the employer was left with an unsolvable dilemma. On the one hand, courts are increasingly holding companies liable for the violent outbreaks of their employees. On the other hand, the Americans with Disabilities Act (ADA) and other antibias laws are making it difficult for employers to fire mentally unstable and violence-prone workers.

Although an employer's duties regarding the handling of an employee's mental disabilities under the 1992 ADA are still unclear, many employers are reluctant to seek advice from state or federal agencies for fear of getting sued. An unfortunate consequence of the ADA, mental health experts say, has been to discourage employers from quietly working things out with troubled employees.[5] Privacy laws also restrain companies from exhaustively screening job applicants for hints of violence. For instance, in a controversial 1991 decision, a California appeals court ordered Dayton Hudson Corporation to stop administering a personality test called "Psychscreen" at its Target discount store chain. The court said that some questions on the test, which was used to gauge applicants' emotional stability, violated privacy rights.

Of course, the quagmire of confusion wrought by the litigation explosion is not confined to the workplace. Consider, for instance, a lawsuit filed by the National Federation of the Blind against an amusement park in Minnesota. The suit alleged discrimination in the park's refusal to allow blind persons to go unescorted on three rides—Go Carts, Antique Cars, and Bumper Cars. In rationalizing its policy, the park explained that all three of the rides required the rider to steer the vehicle and that a blind person could not safely steer. A spokesperson for the Federation answered that the blind "are part of society [and] are all entitled to inclusion in that society." In a litigation age, the park was doomed either way. If it refused to allow blind persons to go on the rides without restrictions, it would have to fight a discrimination lawsuit. If it relented and permitted ridership, it subjected itself to the inevitable lawsuit from someone injured by a blind person driving a motorized vehicle.

LITIGATION AS THE CURRENCY OF SOCIAL EXCHANGE

The litigious atmosphere of the workplace similarly exists in the marketplace. Routine business relations, once governed by handshakes and promises, are increasingly conducted through litigation. Debts are not paid until a lawsuit is filed, defective products are not repaired until a judge so orders. Disgruntled customers had to sue more than a dozen retailers and restaurant chains, including Kmart and Montgomery Ward, because those businesses would not honor their gift certificates. Even business dealings involving matters of trust are degenerating into litigation. Lawyers sue their clients for disputed bills, and patients sue their doctors when treatments don't work. Insurance policyholders, relying on the company to offer financial protection, increasingly have had to sue to obtain coverage. "If we knew a way other than patients suing insurance companies, we'd be happy to follow that course," remarked a director of a program at the University of Colorado offering fetal tissue implants for patients with Parkinson's disease, "but it seems that the established procedure is pressure and lawsuits."[6]

Litigation, however, is not confined to claims involving large sums of money. It has become the way people deal with any type of dispute. A New Jersey lawyer sued a restaurant for allegedly serving him a double espresso instead of decaffeinated coffee. A student at Tennessee State University, in 1994, sued his fraternity—an organization supposedly based upon fraternal bonds—because of the hazing he said he had to endure to become a member. An Arizona high school sophomore sued her no-show prom date. A Boston mother, reacting against a 3-year-old boy who kicked her daughter while the two children were playing in a playground, filed a lawsuit in March of 1996, asking that the boy ar̶d̶ ̶h̶i̶s̶ ̶m̶o̶t̶h̶e̶r̶ not be allowed in the playground while she and h̶e̶r̶ ̶d̶a̶u̶g̶h̶t̶e̶r̶ were there. The boy's lawyer remarked that "maybe̶ ̶i̶t̶'̶s̶ ̶a̶ ̶s̶i̶g̶n̶ ̶o̶f̶ how people are starting to rely too much on the c̶o̶u̶r̶t̶s̶ ̶t̶o̶ ̶s̶o̶l̶v̶e̶ problems that just don't belong there."[7]

This "constant escalation of personal grievances in̶t̶o̶ ̶l̶a̶w̶s̶u̶i̶t̶s̶ is a very dangerous societal thing," according to Richard Epstein, professor at the University of Chicago Law School.[8] Grievances are litigated in court just as casually as one would order a sweater from a catalog. Take the case of the young couple who celebrated their honeymoon at The Rainbow Room in New York City. Seated near the smoking section, they were occasionally subjected to drifting smoke during the evening. They finished their meal and left without incident. A few weeks later, they sued the restaurant for $1 million, maintaining that they were so upset by the smoke at dinner that it "upset their expected right to conjugal happiness."[9] Elsewhere, more than 100 neighbors of a San Francisco woman they term a "vexatious litigant" have gone to court to ask that she be barred from commencing any more lawsuits.[10] The woman has filed over 50 lawsuits covering all types of claims, from suing a neighbor over a backyard basketball hoop, to suing a tenant for failing to leave a gate open for garbage collectors.

The litany of legalese recited in connection with every advertised contest or promotion or special offer reveals how ridiculously legalistic American society has become. The recitation of the indecipherable list of legal restrictions is made so rapidly that no one could understand, even if they wanted to. The only good it does is to provide a legal defense in a future lawsuit. The satirical manner in which the copyright notice is read at the end of each broadcast of "Monday Night Football" is done not to educate anyone, but it is just part of the legal requirements of a litigious society.

THE INEFFECTIVENESS OF LAW
AS A SEXUAL REGULATOR

Perhaps the area of American life undergoing the most rapid pace of legalistic regulation is sex. The collapse of traditional social codes and the corresponding rise of sexual litigation have led to the increasing regulation of sexual conduct. Some legal pioneers on the sexual litigation frontier are pushing judges to adopt a new legal action for "sexual fraud." Such fraud suits could be brought by women whose sexual partner lied about being unmarried, or by men who have slept with women who deceived them about using birth control. In another attempt to regulate romance, a group of state lawmakers in Washington introduced a bill in February 1995, that would require marriage licenses to come with warnings about spousal abuse.

Even college campuses, once the site of love-ins and free sex, have gone to regulating such matters. Having once thrown off all social and cultural rules regarding sex, colleges are now adopting a new set of legal rules governing sex. On some campuses, hand-holding and kissing require explicit verbal, if not written, consent. At others, administrators have been sued for not preventing unwelcome sexual advances from one student to another. And at still other colleges, professor–student romances have become increasingly restricted. In 1995, for instance, the faculty at the University of Pennsylvania called for an outright ban on professors dating their students. This proposed ban came in response to a lawsuit against the school by Lisa Topol, who claimed that a professor with whom she was sleeping during her senior year sexually harassed her after she tried to break off the affair. Not only did Topol sue her professor and the University of Pennsylvania, but she also sued Bates College in Maine—the professor's previous employer—for failing to warn Penn about the man's proclivity to sexually harass.

It is not just professor–student relationships, however, that are being increasingly regulated at college campuses. Even the sexual conduct between students is becoming subject to rules. The code of sexual conduct adopted by Antioch College in Ohio, for instance, spells out in great detail the boundaries of acceptable behavior among students and faculty. A portion of the code reads as follows:

> All sexual contact and conduct between any two people must be consensual; consent must be obtained verbally before there is any sexual contact or conduct; if the level of sexual intimacy increases during an interaction (i.e., if two people move from kissing while fully clothed—which is one level— to undressing for direct physical contact, which is another level), the people involved need to express their clear verbal consent before moving to that new level; if one person wants to initiate moving to a higher level of sexual intimacy in an interaction, that person is responsible for getting the verbal consent of the other person(s) involved before moving to that level; if you have had a particular level of sexual intimacy before with someone, you must still ask each and every time.... Asking "Do you want to have sex with me?" is not enough. The request for consent must be specific to each act.[11]

These legalistic rules of sex reflect a society caught up in a vicious cycle of litigation thinking. Despite the hours of lawyerly work expended in drafting the Antioch rules, it seems very unlikely that any young students will carefully consult them prior to commencing their romantic adventures. Yet, the regulations proliferate, as if coming from a naive belief that the mere existence of rules will eliminate all sexual improprieties. As one defender of the Antioch rules noted, "All rules are artificial, but, in the absence of generally agreed-upon social conventions, any new prescription must feel artificial."[12] And that is the basic truth underlying a litigious society—that law provides the only, and sometimes even artificial, social conventions.

The attempts by colleges and universities to regulate sex have themselves set off a litigation aftershock. As many schools are discovering, it is easier to create new rules than to enforce them, especially in the litigation age. Men who have been disciplined under college-sponsored disciplinary procedures designed to handle sexual-misconduct complaints have in turn sued their colleges. A Yale University basketball player, expelled in 1993 for an alleged rape, counterattacked with a lawsuit against the university. Similar lawsuits have confronted Old Dominion University and the University of New Hampshire. A Valparaiso University student, suspended in 1993 for violating the school's sexual assault guidelines, sued the university in federal court for $12 million. Although colleges are being sued for instituting disciplinary procedures, they are also being sued when they do not do so. In 1991, for instance, four female students sued Carlton College in Northfield, Minnesota, for not preventing students who had a history of sexual abuse from assaulting them.

In an attempt to supply standards of behavior in the area of sexual conduct, courts have been the site of intense activity. Having morally deregulated sex in the 1960s, college campuses in particular, and America in general, are now reversing course and legally regulating it. According to the Equal Employment Opportunity Commission, sexual-harassment complaints more than doubled from 1991 to 1993.[13] In a case brought by a woman against an unwanted suitor, a Minnesota court was called to decide if flowers and an anonymous love note constituted "stalking" under an antistalking law. And some lawyers are trying to make street remarks, such as "Hey baby," legally punishable as assaultive behavior. Even grade-schoolers' sexual teasing is becoming the subject of sexual harassment lawsuits. Schools have been sued for the sexual remarks and gestures made by students on the school bus and the playground. Before young children even know the meaning of their words, they are being taken to court. In such a litigious society, sex education in the future may well take place more in the courtroom than at home or school.

Just as sexual harassment complaints have multiplied, more accused men have responded by filing lawsuits of their own. In the area of sexual harassment, litigation has bred more litigation.

In 1993, a federal jury in Texas awarded $3 million in a defamation suit brought by a man falsely accused of sexual harassment. But men are not just suing their accusers, they are also suing their employers. A Continental Airlines pilot, after being investigated by his employer in connection with sexual harassment charges, sued the company for $1 million for defamation.

Another litigation backlash has come from men who have filed sexual harassment suits against women. Perhaps the most notorious of such suits was filed by the "Jenny Craig Eight." In Massachusetts Superior Court, eight men who were formerly employed as counselors at Jenny Craig weight-loss centers charged the company with firing them or giving them unfavorable assignments just because they were males in a female-dominated corporate culture. Some of the men said they were asked to perform demeaning tasks, such as shoveling snow, emptying the trash, or fixing the boss's car. Several of them said they were taunted about their "tight buns" and excluded from office chitchat about pregnancy and menstrual periods. The men also claimed that they were very uncomfortable wearing the smocks and neck scarves that are the company-issue uniform. This lawsuit by the Jenny Craig Eight subsequently provoked a flood of inquiries from men with similar stories, according to the Massachusetts Commission Against Discrimination. One official at the Commission compared the flurry of calls to those prompted by Anita Hill's testimony against Clarence Thomas.[14] Yet, even in a workplace inundated with sexual harassment concerns, one female manager displayed on her wall a sign that read, "If you want a job done right, get a woman to do it."[15]

The legal regulation of sex has both followed from and fed into the litigation explosion. It is perhaps the natural result of a litigious society whose primary social regulator is the law. But as such a regulator, the law has not proved to be very effective, particularly in the field of sex. Not only has the incidence of sexual harassment and abuse continued to skyrocket, with reverse harassment claims by men now making up more than 10 percent of the total number of sexual harassment complaints to the Federal Equal Employment Opportunity Commission, but also the public seems even more confused about what behavior is acceptable and what is not. One reason for this is that litigation produces no clear standards. In fact, litigation often produces no guidelines whatsoever. Since most cases are settled, and most settlements carry confidentiality provisions, the public never knows the outcome or resolution of the dispute. Such was the result of a highly publicized sexual harassment suit against Stroh Brewery.

Heralded as a pioneering event in the crusade for changing the social roles of women, the 1991 lawsuit alleged that Stroh's television ads featuring the "Swedish Bikini Team" set the tone for the way women were treated at the company. But instead of sparking major social change in the way sexual stereotypes are used, the case was quietly settled in 1993 with a confidentiality agreement. No public debate or discussions were held about how the case was resolved or what it meant for gender relations. This was in great contrast to how the lawsuit began, with a public relations campaign waged by the plaintiffs' attorney that reverberated on the television talk shows. The campaign centered on the bold assertion that there was a connection between the ads and the way the brewery treated its female employees. Although the attorney promised that the case would tackle the important issue of how sexual stereotypes were used in marketing, the secret settlement provided neither answers nor discussion concerning that issue.

A similar lawsuit was filed by six employees of Hooters restaurant. The suit alleged, in part, that the revealing uniforms the employees were required to wear amounted to, or was evidence of, sexual harassment. But again, the case was settled, and the settlement was confidential.

Litigation has also failed to provide clear guidelines for social behavior, because it frequently produces conflicting and even contradictory messages. For instance, at the same time that the University of Pennsylvania was being sued by a female student for not preventing sexual harassment by a professor whom she had been dating, the school was being charged by a male professor for sexually harassing him by asking him about his relationship with a former student and then denying him a promotion. This dilemma has likewise handcuffed corporations, which have found it increasingly difficult to set policies shielding them from liability without invading employees' privacy. Attempting to lessen the occurrence of sexual-harassment lawsuits occurring because of broken or soured office romances, many companies prohibit dating between supervisors and subordinates. Yet plaintiffs, armed with lifestyle-discrimination statutes, have sought to penalize companies for enforcing such no-dating policies. Now enacted in more than 20 states, such laws are aimed at preventing discrimination based on off-duty behavior. In 1994, IBM lost a suit filed by a manager who said he was forced out of the company because he had dated a subordinate. The man won a $375,000 jury verdict after arguing that IBM's no-dating rules constituted an invasion of privacy.

LAW'S INABILITY TO REGULATE EVEN THE LAWYERS

Another indication that law is not providing very effective social regulation is that even the high priests of the litigation age are sinning. For instance, although lawyers should perhaps be the best-behaved lovers in an age of litigious love, they clearly are not. Lawyers seem as prone to violating the sexual rules as anyone else in society. According to experts, the percentage of lawyers getting sued for sexual harassment is no less than in other professions.[16] In a 1994 survey, 43 percent of female lawyers reported that they had experienced unwelcome sexual advances in their office during the previous year.[17] A 1995 study of 57 major law firms by the Harvard Women's Law Association issued a harsh indictment of the profession's double standards for men and women.[18] And in response to growing concerns about divorce lawyers taking sexual advantage of their vulnerable clients, four states—New York, Minnesota, Oregon, and California—have adopted explicit restrictions on a lawyer's sexual relations with his or her client.

Lawyers, in fact, seem as incapable as anyone else of having their sexual behavior modified by the law. In the largest award ever in a sexual harassment lawsuit, a California jury in 1994 awarded $7.1 million to a former law secretary in her suit against Baker and McKenzie, the world's largest law firm. As revealed during the trial—a trial carried daily to a national cable audience by Court TV—the offending lawyer had a history of harassing behavior, some of it long known to his partners. In the wake of this stunning jury award, consultants reported a surge of calls from law firms eager for advice on how to head off similar complaints.[19]

Lawyers' legal transgressions, however, are not confined to the area of sex. A 1994 racial discrimination lawsuit by a black former associate against the New York law firm of White and Case resulted in a settlement of more than $500,000 to the plaintiff. In a San Francisco case, an aging attorney alleged that his former firm violated federal age-discrimination laws by taking him off a project because the client wanted someone younger. Although clients and law firms often choose and assign lawyers based on potentially discriminatory factors, the courts have never ruled on this kind of discrimination in the legal profession, but they have nearly always stricken down "customer preferences" when companies use them as an excuse to make discriminatory employment decisions. In 1981, for example, a federal court ruled that an oil company could not refuse to promote a woman simply because it feared its Latin American clients would react negatively.

The failure of law to provide adequate guidance even for the most knowledgeable lawyers was especially evident in a lawsuit between two companies engaged in the business of offering review courses for law-school graduates taking state bar exams around the country. When two former executives of the Bar/Bri unit of Harcourt General, Inc., the market leader, resigned and went to work for West Publishing, a competitor of Harcourt, they were sued by their former employer for fraud and breach of loyalty. In response to its suit, Harcourt was sued by West, who claimed that Harcourt's lawsuit was designed to disrupt West's entry into the bar-review market. Commenting on the tangled web of lawsuits, the lawyer for one of the former Harcourt executives called the Harcourt lawsuit "absolutely baseless," whereas West's lawyer called the suit "sham litigation," and Harcourt's attorney described West's lawsuit as "ridiculous."[20] Even though

Harcourt's Bar/Bri division prepares about 70 percent of the nation's law students for their bar exams, it has not been able to avoid its own litigation problems. In 1994, a Los Angeles jury ordered it to pay $4 million for attempting to monopolize the bar-review business. And in 1992, it paid $150,000 to settle a lawsuit accusing it of anticompetitive behavior.

Not even the American Bar Association (ABA) has been able to avoid legal transgressions. In response to a Justice Department investigation and a lawsuit charging antitrust violations in June of 1995, the ABA agreed to change the way it accredited the nation's law schools. It was the first time that accreditation standards set by a professional organization had been investigated as a possible subterfuge for anticompetitive practices.

As another example of the inadequacy of law as the exclusive behavioral standard, the steadily rising numbers of ethics complaints against lawyers certainly proves that legal training and knowledge do not translate into more ethical behavior.[21] In 1992, for instance, the State Bar of California received 100,000 complaints from clients against their lawyers. The number of lawyers disciplined in Texas rose 90 percent from 1993 to 1995. And in Illinois, 25 percent of the lawyers sanctioned were from large, established law firms. In fact, the increasing ethical problems of lawyers forced the ABA's Committee on Ethics and Professional Responsibility to issue a report explaining in detail the various rules of ethics. This report illustrated the sometimes infantile status of ethical knowledge within the legal profession. For instance, the document declares, as if it needed to be declared to any grade-schooler, that a lawyer is never justified in charging a client for hours not actually expended. Moving on to more complex ethical situations, the report states that if a law firm pays an economist $200 an hour for his or her services as an expert witness, it may not bill the client more than $200 an hour for those services.

Another common ethical transgression of lawyers relates to the rules prohibiting them from soliciting clients in person or by phone. In response to widespread abuses of this rule, the Texas State Senate passed a bill in 1993 that would make soliciting clients a felony, punishable by 10 years in prison and a $10,000 fine. The problem of lawyer solicitation was highlighted in 1989, when a school bus carrying 81 students in southern Texas slid into a water-filled pit after being hit by a truck. Twenty-one students were killed, attracting a swarm of plaintiffs' attorneys, drawn by the deep pockets of the bottling company that owned the truck. One lawyer allegedly paid $10,000 to a go-between to refer him to the parents of a child who had died. Another allegedly forgave a $700 debt owed by a local woman and offered $500 for each client she helped solicit. In other cases, plaintiffs' lawyers in Texas have posed as Red Cross workers and priests to get at injury victims or grieving families.

Within days of the May 11, 1996, crash of the ValuJet airplane in Florida, dozens of personal-injury lawyers tried to solicit families of the crash victims. This occurred despite the state's ban on solicitation of disaster victims and their families. Some lawyers mailed out color brochures promoting their air-disaster expertise. Others sent flowers or offered the chauffeur services of sympathetic young women carrying business cards. Still others, according to written complaints by victims' families, lurked behind the potted palms in the lobby of the hotel where the families stayed. One of the firms soliciting those families included the firm in which Greta Van Susteren, cohost of CNN's "Burden of Proof," was listed as "of counsel."[22]

In addition to ethical violations, criminal prosecutions are increasingly being directed at lawyers for illegal acts committed in the course of their practice. In one case involving insurance fraud in New York City, 21 lawyers were indicted in what the grand jury called "a pervasive pattern of criminal conduct."[23] It is not just the shady or marginal lawyers who are facing criminal prosecutions, it is the lawyers from the most respected firms in the country. In 1992, Harvey Myerson, founder of the now-defunct New York firm Myerson & Kuhn, was found guilty of defrauding four former clients with bogus billings. A former managing partner of one of Chicago's largest firms, Winston & Strawn, pleaded guilty in 1994 to bilking his firm and former clients of more than $784,000. Not only was the lawyer one of the most prominent members of Chicago's legal community, but he was a former federal prosecutor. Another large corporate law firm in Chicago, Chapman & Cutler, was also investigated by federal authorities in 1994 for overbilling its clients more than $1.3 million.

THE LEGAL TROUBLES
OF A LAWYER-FILLED WHITE HOUSE

In addition to the legal and ethical transgressions of lawyers, perhaps the most telling sign of the ineffectiveness of law as the primary social regulator is found in the legal troubles of the Clinton Administration. An "atmosphere of lawyerly evasion," according to *Time*, "suffused an Administration so plump with law degrees."[24] Headlines in the established media proclaimed the administration as a "Culture of Deception" and the First Lady as "Slippery Hillary."[25] Not since the late days of the Nixon White House have there been so many presidential aides and cabinet members under investigation. A record number of independent counsels were set up during Clinton's first term alone to probe various alleged misdeeds, and these were in addition to a series of Congressional probes, some of the most important of which began when the Democrats still controlled the Congress.

Throughout Clinton's presidency, including his campaign, a clear pattern of "lawyering the truth" emerged, observed *Newsweek* senior editor Joe Klein. In explaining his use of marijuana as a student, Clinton nonetheless claimed that he "never broke a state law." This lawyerly evasiveness reappeared when Clinton repeatedly revised his story regarding his draft controversy. It returned when Hillary Rodham Clinton hedged the explanations of her commodities trading. Then there were the string of evasive, and then contradictory, White House responses regarding the First Lady's alleged role in illegally terminating seven employees of the White House travel staff. Next came the stonewalling and reversals concerning documents taken from Vince Foster's office after his suicide. Though the White House steadfastly claimed that no documents had been removed from Foster's office, months later it finally admitted that some had indeed been taken. Likewise,

though the administration evaded the Whitewater special prosecutor's subpoena of Rose law firm billing records for two and
one-half years, it expressed shock and disbelief when the records
were "discovered" in the private quarters of the White House by a
secretary.

It was in the course of investigating the Clinton finances that
government regulators found that the First Lady's Little Rock law
firm, from which an entourage of Clinton administration aides
had been recruited, had violated several conflict-of-interest rules,
had falsified transactions relating to its representation of a savings
and loan association, and overbilled clients. But the most disturb-
ing incidents of lawyerly evasions in the Clinton White House
occurred in connection with the Whitewater investigations.

In testifying about the subject of a White House cover-up,
aides paraded failed memories, studied evasions, and half-truths
before the grand jury. On the issue of whether the White House
attempted to influence or interfere in the investigation, for instance, disjointed testimonies suggested a persistent pattern of
deception practiced among White House staff members. When
the diary of Joshua Steiner, Treasury Chief of Staff, showed that
the White House exerted "intense pressure" on Deputy Treasury
Secretary Roger Altman to oversee the investigation, Steiner later
claimed that his diary was no longer a reliable source of information. As the involvement of Altman became a significant issue,
Altman neglected to tell Senate investigators about all his contacts
with the White House regarding the Whitewater investigation.
Altman also denied the testimony of Treasury general counsel
Jean Hanson that she had conveyed to him confidential information on the Whitewater investigation and that Altman had told her
to pass this information along to the White House. For his part,
Treasury Secretary Lloyd Bentson contradicted the testimony of
both Altman and Hanson, claiming that he knew of no contacts
between the Treasury and the White House regarding the Whitewater investigation. And with Bentson citing errors of judgment
by Altman, Clinton nonetheless refused to fire him, explaining
that although Altman "had not given all the information in a
timely fashion,... there was no violation of the law."[26] Yet in the

end, this display of contradictions and falsities in their testimonies led to the resignation of the entire top leadership of the Treasury Department, as well as that of White House counsel Bernard Nussbaum.

In an administration that prides itself on intelligence, it is surprising how many "I don't recalls" were given in response to questions on Whitewater. Senior policy advisor George Stephanopoulos, whose memory is legendary among his colleagues, used the expression "I don't remember" 31 times in his Senate deposition. Hillary Clinton's chief of staff, Maggie Williams, did not recall saying what Mr. Altman's diary claims she said, and everyone disagreed with the diary of Joshua Steiner. The First Lady's closest advisor, Susan Thomases, gave "couldn't recall" responses some 180 times during her Senate testimony. Even Hillary Clinton was generous in her "I don't know" responses.

All the evasive responses in the Whitewater investigation may not have qualified as a lie in Washington, but they certainly were not the truth. What is most surprising is that many of the lawyers in the Clinton Administration, including both the First Lady and White House counsel Bernard Nussbaum, participated in the investigations of the Watergate cover-up that brought down the Nixon presidency. Yet there seems to be no lessons learned from that monumental legal precedent. They have completely failed to learn the main lesson of Watergate—that the cover-up is just as illegal, and more dangerous, than the original misdeed. Nor has the Clinton administration even learned a much more recent lesson, one from which they had benefitted during the 1992 campaign and which involved the attempt by aides from the Bush campaign to examine Bill Clinton's passport files for damaging information. The Clinton campaign was justifiably outraged when it learned of the Bush campaign's scrounging through Clinton's files in the State Department, yet just 1 year later, a couple of Clinton appointees rifled through the State Department's confidential personnel files of hundreds of Bush-appointed department employees. Furthermore, at about the same time, the White House began illegally obtaining more than 600 FBI files on a host of private citizens who had left government service. When this scandal was discovered, the White House once again could give no straight answers. In fact, it took weeks for it to come up with an answer to the simple question of who had hired one of the aides who had obtained the files. But in true "Nixonesque" language, the White House attributed the whole episode to an innocent "bureaucratic snafu."

The First Lady's "I-am-litigator" evasiveness has been a consistent strain throughout the scandals that have plagued the Clinton White House. The First Lady explained her suspicious commodities trades by claiming that she turned $1000 into $100,000 just by reading the *Wall Street Journal*. On several occasions she has changed her story regarding the travel office firings, and on several others she has been contradicted by other witnesses. She expressed complete dismay as to how the long-subpoenaed billing records of the Rose law firm finally turned up in her private quarters. And with each new stage of the Whitewater investigation, the Clintons amend yet again their tax returns. This evasive example of "lawyers as First Family" does not support the theory that more laws will make for a better-behaved society.

The Clinton's legal troubles, however, were not confined to Whitewater. Paula Jones filed a sexual harassment suit against the President. Associate Attorney General Webster Hubbell was forced to resign when he was charged with overbilling clients and padding his expense accounts while he was a lawyer at the Rose firm in Little Rock. Later, in December of 1994, Hubbell pled guilty to two felonies for fraud and tax evasion, and admitted to stealing $394,000 from the Rose firm and its clients. Agriculture Secretary Mike Espy resigned amid ethics charges, although once again the lawyerly evasive Clinton argued that "although Secretary Espay has said he has done nothing wrong, I am troubled by the appearance of some of these incidents."[27] Transportation Secretary Federico Pena came under investigation by the Justice Department. An independent counsel was appointed in 1995 to investigate matters relating to Housing Secretary Henry Cisneros's misleading statements to Federal investigators regarding payments he made to a former lover. The Justice Department opened an inquiry in 1995 into Secretary of Commerce Ron Brown's business dealings to determine if he violated tax or financial-disclosure laws and whether he was paid money by people seeking to influence the Commerce Department. After finding that Mr. Brown failed to properly report large payments from a former business partner, the Justice Department asked for the appointment of an independent counsel to investigate the matter. It was the fourth time that the Attorney General had sought an independent counsel to investigate questions of possible wrongdoing among top officials of the Clinton Administration. White House operations chief David Watkins was forced to resign in 1994 after it was disclosed that he took a $2,380-per-hour Marine helicopter ride to play a round of golf. Watkins had also been involved in the firing of the White House travel office staff for financial improprieties, and was the subject of a sexual harassment lawsuit brought by a female Clinton campaign worker. In acknowledging a settlement of the lawsuit, a lawyer for the campaign said that there was "no finding of wrongdoing or violation," but declined to discuss the settlement further, saying that "there was a confidentiality agreement between both parties."[28] Another litigation setback occurred when a federal judge, in a lawsuit against the Clinton healthcare task force, imposed sanctions against Administration officials for their "misconduct" pertaining to the disclosure of documents from that task force.[29] Finally, top White House advisor Bruce Lindsey was named as an unindicted coconspirator regarding charges of illegal campaign finance practices.

The shortcomings of law as the primary social regulator are further illustrated by the legal problems of lawmakers. During each decade from the 1900s to the 1970s, less than four congressional representatives on average faced criminal charges. In the 1980s, however, 22 faced such charges; and in the first three and one-half years of the 1990s, 15 had criminal charges served against them, the most notorious being House Ways and Means Chairman Dan Rostenkowski. In the 1995 campaign for the Chicago City Council alone, five convicted felons were candidates.

The competency and behavior of federal judges has also come under criticism. In 1994, the Chicago Council of Lawyers released a groundbreaking evaluation of the judges from the U.S. Court of

Appeals for the Seventh Circuit.[30] Believed to be the first evaluation of its kind, the report was, at times, harshly critical. It questioned whether several judges possessed the legal skills to be on the bench. Several years later, the Illinois system of disciplining state court judges came under fire. As critics charged, "Illinois's system for disciplining judges has been something of an inside joke."[31] Shockingly, judges had not been disciplined for such behavior as refusing three defendants their right to a jury trial and then directing courtroom workers to lie about what happened, suggesting that Danish women are floozies and then citing that belief in acquitting a man of invading a Danish woman's home, and describing jailhouse rape to juveniles in graphic language.

There is no indication that ethical or law-abiding behavior will increase as law becomes the primary social regulator in a litigious society. In fact, indications are just the opposite. For instance, in a survey of college students conducted by a University of Nebraska professor over an 8-year period (1984–1991), the respondents viewed themselves as law-abiding citizens, yet their behavior suggested otherwise. Although 87 percent of the students said they were law-abiding, 81 percent admitted to cheating on a test, 75 percent said they had driven while drunk, and 58 percent admitted to stealing. As this example once again demonstrates, law does not seem to automatically produce the kind of social behavior required of a stable society. But as the litigation explosion continues, Americans increasingly turn to law as their only social regulator.

CHAPTER 9

A Casualty of the Litigation Explosion

As the 20th century draws to a close, courtroom trials in America have become like the great gladiatorial contests of ancient Rome. They are followed as sporting events are followed, always with speculation as to who is winning and who is losing, and who has the better lawyer. Yet, in the midst of all the dramatic courtroom battles, the first casualty has been one of the original justifications for conducting such trials—the truth. In the litigious society that America has become, the notion that truth emerges from the court-room has been largely discredited.

Trials have become contests rather than discoverers of truth. After a famous trial ends, the litigants write their books telling what really happened. Even the public senses that trials do not necessarily reveal the truth. Reflecting this mood, contemporary courtroom novels and movies often withhold the truth from reve-lation at trial. In the movies *Guilty as Sin*, *Jagged Edge*, *Defenseless*, *Presumed Innocent*, and *An Innocent Man*, the truth is discovered only after the trial has ended, and only after the trial produced the wrong result. These movies suggest what is becoming apparent: The judicial system is not necessarily the reliable producer of truth that Perry Mason led us to believe it was. On the long-running television show, "L.A. Law," for instance, the viewer rarely saw the truth behind the trial, just the outcome of it and the agonizing of the lawyers.

A comparison of "L.A. Law" with the 1950s television series "Perry Mason" reveals how the public image of trials and truth has changed. In "Perry Mason," the trial always produced the truth behind the mysteries presented at the beginning of the show. On the other hand, "L.A. Law" set out not to unravel a mystery in the courts but to deal with "the ambiguities of the system," according to creator Steven Bocchco.[1] In doing so, it did not portray the great matters of justice that "Perry Mason" did, but often depicted such trivial legal spats as a case involving the barroom sport of dwarf tossing.

As the litigation explosion demonstrates, Americans are quite willing to go to court. But in spite of this litigiousness, there is an eroding confidence that court decisions will be based on the truth. Without a trusted ability to produce the truth, however, trials are no more than just another form of sporting contest. And in such a sporting atmosphere, lawyers have come to be less officers of the court and more bitter adversaries bent on winning at any cost while inflicting maximum damage to the other side.

In the American litigation process, determining the truth is not a direct focus. It is an indirect goal that the courts hope to fulfill through the workings of the adversary system. Out of the combat of the litigants, it is hoped that truth will somehow prevail, that it will emerge as a by-product of an adversarial combat between litigants. Rather than truth, the judicial process focuses primarily on the rights of the litigants. The parties are responsible only for what they can prove in their favor, not for revealing the truth. And the winner is not necessarily the one with truth on his or her side, but the one who had the best legal strategy. As constitutional lawyer Floyd Abrams notes, "It is time to ask whether it really leads to justice to have a system in which many lawyers spend far more time avoiding truth than finding it."[2]

Because the courts' main focus is on following procedural rules rather than on independently discovering the truth, the role of truth becomes relative and ambiguous. The jury, which must make the final determination of fact, sees only the evidence the parties choose to present and to which there are no successful objections. As passive spectators during the trial, the jurors cannot actively question the witnesses, the evidence, or the lawyers.

Objecting to the backseat role that truth has come to play in modern trials obsessed with process and procedure, a new movement has arisen within the legal profession. The "truth school," adhered to by increasing numbers of judges and legal scholars, stresses that a trial is, after all, a search for the truth. According to this school, the judicial system spends too much time and energy on combat between the opposing lawyers and too little on the ultimate question of what actually happened.[3] Not only does the truth school seek to minimize the jockeying between opposing lawyers and the importance it plays in the trial, but it generally believes that the jurors should hear all the information and draw their own conclusions. "Trials shouldn't be a sport or a game where judges just try to even the odds between the two sides," argues Akhil Amar, a professor at Yale Law School.[4] Members of the truth school favor the elimination of many of the technicalities that are used by lawyers to conceal evidence. But at the moment, of course, the truth school remains just a minority view within the legal profession.

The litigation explosion has changed neither the way trials are conducted nor the rules pertaining to the jury's final determination of truth. It has, however, greatly changed the public's perception of the probability and capability of a trial to produce the truth.

In many ways, for instance, the magic of the jury box has been eroded. The public no longer believes that behind closed doors the jurors can sift through the evidence and their own biases to discover the truth. Perhaps it is because, in this litigious age, lawyers have learned to exploit and intensify, through the use of "litigation consultants," any existing juror bias.

The growth of the litigation consulting industry testifies to the success that lawyers have had in manipulating juries. From 1983 to 1994, the number of jury consultants increased sevenfold.[5] This industry now generates over $200 million a year in revenues.

Made up of psychologists and sociologists, the litigation consulting industry boasts that it can assemble and then mold a jury to reach a desired verdict. One successful southern California consultant promises a 96 percent chance of a favorable verdict if he's allowed to convene jury focus groups and advise on strategy.[6]

A traditional assumption of the litigation process is that the jury can competently evaluate evidence and see through most efforts by the advocates to distort the truth. But this assumption is obviously undermined when consultants enable lawyers to exploit juror biases in ways that are so subtle that even the jurors may not fully be aware of how and why they are being persuaded.

The first task of a jury consultant is to discover the subtle prejudices and hidden biases of potential jurors. This information helps lawyers pick a favorably biased jury and then exploit those biases. Consultants strive to enable a lawyer to exploit jury bias in ways so subtle that the jurors, judge, and opposing lawyers may not know what is happening. According to jury consultants, trials can be predetermined by assembling a jury with a particular racial, ethnic, and gender makeup.

After assisting in the selection of a favorably biased jury, the consultant then suggests what evidence to offer and how to package that evidence to take advantage of the jury's particular biases. In the unguarded words of one consultant, "All in all, we help lawyers position their cases to juries in much the same way you would sell a bar of soap."[7] But jury selection and packaging of the evidence is only part of a litigation consultant's job. Every aspect of the trial, from the clothing and demeanor of the lawyer to the manipulation of the media, is influenced by the consultant.

When the litigation explosion meets the media age, trials involve image as much as they do facts. Lawyers must master the art of media image even before they perfect the legal strategies of their cases. It is not unusual to see a lawyer change his or her image or demeanor as a case unfolds, particularly if the consultants have suggested such a change. Frequently, the wars of lawyerly media manipulation overshadow the legal issues of the trial.

The growth of the litigation consulting industry has even eroded the credibility of scientific and technical facts in the courtroom. Because of its objective nature, scientific knowledge is not perceived by nonscientists as a matter of debate or dispute. In the modern courtroom, however, scientists and technicians argue and disagree as much as the lawyers who retain them. Courts have come to regard scientific and medical experts as mere advocates. Since each side has its own experts to support its version of the case, those experts become no more than dueling advocates with their own biases that can only be brought out by crossexamination. Juries in personal injury cases, for instance, hear completely different explanations of the plaintiff's injuries from the medical experts testifying on behalf of the two parties. In cases involving an alleged construction defect, two teams of engineers and architects offer radically different theories of the defect, depending on which side has hired them. Science and technology has become, in a litigation age, as relative and ambiguous as the law, because, as juries have come to realize, trial lawyers can get an expert to testify on anything.

With trials becoming carefully waged contests between two sides armed with their own set of consultants, the public has begun to lose hope that truth will actually emerge in the courtroom. As portrayed in the 1950s classic movie *Twelve Angry Men*, a jury that would earnestly and peacefully wrestle with the facts and their prejudices to reach the truth seems in the 1990s to be just a fictional fantasy. In highly publicized trials, the public has witnessed jury verdicts that are an astounding contradiction to the facts. The jury in the first Rodney King case let the police officers walk, despite the videotaped portrayal of their beating. As much as the country was shocked by that result, however, a similar outrage occurred in the trial of the men accused of beating truck driver Reginald Denny during the riots occurring in the wake of the first Rodney King verdict. Again there was a videotape and, again, the jury let the defendants off.

In addition to spawning an industry of consultants geared toward manipulating juries, the litigation explosion has hindered truth in a more general and socially pervasive way. Too often people are afraid to tell the truth because of a fear of getting sued. Liability has replaced truth as the governing standard for the content of speech. Employers are reluctant to provide candid references about former employees, and landlords are hesitant to give an open assessment of tenants they have known out of fear of being sued. Because of the constant barrage of libel lawsuits, even news organizations hesitate to print or broadcast controversial facts. In the litigation age, a culture of subterfuge has emerged. One of the truths that has been supplanted by the litigation explosion is perhaps the essential truth of the human condition— the truth of limitations and tragedy. Life has its inevitable disappointments, and not all the risks faced in the process of living turn out as desired. In the litigation age, however, lawsuits have become an insurance against risk. They have served as an antidote to tragedy, a remedy for disappointment. Whenever anything bad happens, a lawsuit can reverse it or, at least, compensate for it. When beset by tragedy, people sue. As the litigation explosion teaches, there's always someone to blame and to sue. Any disappointment can be eased at the courthouse.

It used to be that some tragedies, such as natural disasters, were not litigated. Called "acts of God," they were seen as things beyond the control of any human and, hence, unavoidable. They were the price of living. Since humans had no control over the workings of God or nature, no one was to blame for their occurrences and consequences. This attitude, however, has changed during the litigation age. Natural disasters are increasingly spawning lawsuits. A flood of suits, for instance, resulted from the damage caused by Hurricane Andrew in Florida in 1992, and even more followed the 1994 Los Angeles earthquake. Although in the past earthquakes rarely resulted in lawsuits, changes in liability law and public litigiousness have made such suits more common. After the 1994 Los Angeles earthquake, a *Los Angeles Times* headline read "Legal Aftershocks Will Keep Lots of Lawyers Busy."[8] Within a week of the earthquake, several law firms ran advertisements soliciting clients with earthquake damage. Insurance experts said the volume of damage claims was nearly five times higher than in any other recent and similarly severe quake.

One reason for this increased litigation is the evolution in California case law that now holds that an "act of God" is not an automatic defense to litigation. In the words of a former chairman of the American Bar Association's litigation section, "Acts of God can be anticipated."[9] But if they can be anticipated by humans, how can they be acts of God?

In a litigious society, disasters attract lawyers. Although an airplane crash is much different from an "act of God," such as an earthquake, it follows the same grim ritual that is conducted after most mass disasters—the mad dash by lawyers to sign up clients. Shortly after the USAir crash in September of 1994, before funeral services for the dead had even been held, surviving relatives had to fend off lawyers seeking to represent them in a lawsuit against the airline. It got so bad that the Pennsylvania state bar had to warn USAir crash victims' families to be wary of lawyers trying to solicit them. Then, of course, there were the legal feeding frenzies that followed the 1989 Texas school bus accident and the 1996 ValuJet crash discussed in Chapter 8.

The impulse to litigate is becoming the first reaction to tragedies. Litigation is turning these events into economic opportunities. When a bus crashes in Chicago, pedestrians rush to climb aboard, hoping that they will be counted among the victims. In wrongful death actions, the surviving family members reconstruct the life of the dead person in an attempt to boost the damage amount. Affections are inflated, memories are cleansed, and dreams are magnified. The person created in the lawsuit no longer resembles the individual who once lived.

Litigation has attempted to cover up an awful truth about life in America. Despite the sense of entitlement and expectation Americans developed in the period of prosperity since World War II, Americans cannot be shielded from anxiety, uncertainty, and disappointment. Yet the age of entitlement has bred the age of litigation. In turn, the litigation explosion has maintained a false sense of entitlement—it has provided the means by which Americans can maintain their heightened and unrealistic sense of expectation. Litigation has been the American response to times when expectations fell short, or when failure occurred rather than success. A lawsuit becomes the antidote to disappointment. Losing a job, buying the wrong house, or making a bad investment has been met with filing a lawsuit. In the litigation age, there has developed the attitude that what life doesn't provide, the courts will. When prosperity is threatened, the courts will come to the rescue. It is as though litigation has become the flip side of the American dream—for those that do not find health and prosperity and happiness, litigation is always available.

The litigation explosion has helped prop up the illusion that in the United States there should be no such thing as failure, tragedy, and disappointment. In a litigious society, it is presumed that all should go well and there should be no losers—and if someone does lose, he or she has a right to sue. Consequently, the litigation explosion has shielded Americans from a full realization of the basic truths of human life. Rather than questioning whether its unfulfilled expectations are realistic, the country has turned its sights to the courthouse. Instead of recognizing that life is full of accidents, mistakes and cruel deeds—and that all too often those miscues and misdeeds lead to tragedy—litigious Americans look for people to blame. And the search for that blame often leads to lawsuits. "Americans feel if anything goes wrong in their lives, it's because someone violated their rights," says Stephen Presser, a professor of legal history at Northwestern University School of Law.

In a sense, litigation is the price of living in an age of entitlement, for litigation offers a second chance to reverse or amend reality, a way of denying the harsh realities of life. One woman, refusing to accept her physical inability to bear children, sued her insurance company to force it to continue paying for her fertility treatments, which had previously proved unsuccessful. Rather than recognize her inability to conceive as a tragedy and disappointment, the woman litigated, for in a litigious society, there is no tragedy, just violations of rights.

Americans have become so loathe to any interruption of their expectations of happiness and prosperity that even their psychological fears have spawned litigation. For instance, passengers on a plane have sued and recovered damages from the airline just for the fear they suffered during their flight. In other cases, plaintiffs have gone to court to recover damages for their fears that they might contract a disease. One plaintiff, after learning that her physician was HIV-positive, sued him for the brief time during which she feared that she might have contracted the disease from him. It is as if fear is an unjust abnormality that no one should have to suffer. But if fear can be grounds for a lawsuit, then litigation has created a false reality.

Rather than being the agents of truth, the courts in the litigation age have undermined the value of truth. Litigation has been a way for people to create their own truth and to deny unwelcome realities. The lesson taught is not that truth controls life, it is that truth is irrelevant—what matters is only what a jury can be convinced to do. With truth so irrelevant in the litigation age, however, courts can offer little direction to society. And unfortunately, people are less and less often looking for the truth—they are only waiting for the outcome.

CHAPTER 10

False Prophets

PUBLIC ANIMOSITY TOWARD LAWYERS

An ominous sign of America's litigation culture is the state of its leaders—the lawyers. If the psychological condition of lawyers is any indication, a litigation culture will not prove to be an enriching one.

Increasingly, disgruntled lawyers are either fleeing their profession or dreaming of fleeing. A 1992 poll conducted by *California Lawyer* magazine found that 72 percent of lawyers enjoyed practicing law less than when they began.[1] An American Bar Association (ABA) poll revealed that one-third of the lawyers were actually dissatisfied with their work.[2] Nearly 40,000 lawyers drop out of the profession each year; despite average big-firm starting salaries of $70,000 a year, the turnover rate at many large law firms has doubled in recent years.[3] In addition to job dissatisfaction, lawyers are also increasingly suffering from mental and psychological illness. A 1990 Johns Hopkins University study found that severe depression is more likely to occur among lawyers than among 103 other occupations; and researchers at Campbell University in North Carolina discovered that 11 percent of attorneys in the state thought about committing suicide at least once a month.[4]

The gloom within the legal profession mirrors social attitudes outside of it. On the scale of social respect, attorneys are bottom-dwellers. Public cynicism about the legal profession is rampant and getting worse. A 1993 Gallup Poll placed lawyers among the lowest ranked in popularity, along with television talk-show hosts and car salesmen.[5] In another survey, almost 40 percent of the public said that their image of lawyers had "gotten worse," and one-third said that lawyers were less honest than most people.[6] More than half could not name a lawyer they admired, and among those who could, the top two were fictitious lawyers—Perry Mason and Ben Matlock. In general, the people most likely to deal with lawyers had the lowest opinion of them. Only one-third of the survey respondents called lawyers a constructive part of the community. According to a 1993 *National Law Journal* poll, just 5 percent of American parents wanted their children to become lawyers.[7]

The public's animosity toward lawyers also appears in a growing mistrust of them. In an ABA poll, for instance, only 22 percent of the respondents believed that the phrase "honest and ethical" was descriptive of lawyers.[8] Consequently, a whole new industry has sprung up to audit legal bills, and auditors claim they are finding such irregularities as law firms that have billed for more than 24 hours in a day.[9]

With lawyers so unpopular, even advertisers have joined in on the lawyer bashing: A Reebok ad declared that on a perfect planet there would be no lawyers; a Miller Lite commercial showed cowboys lassoing briefcase-carrying lawyers. Contemporary movies also tend to portray lawyers as greedy, cynical, powerful mercenaries who twist the truth to suit their cases: In *Regarding Henry*, a domineering and manipulative lawyer becomes gentle and sensitive, but only after being shot in the head; in *The Firm*, lawyers work for the Mafia and kill suspicious partners; and in *Philadelphia*, the city's top law firm forces out a good, young lawyer because he had AIDS. Movie theaters reported audience cheering when a dinosaur in *Jurassic Park* devoured a lawyer. Even in *Reversal of Fortune*—a movie in which the lawyer triumphs—the Alan Dershowitz character comes across as arrogant, self-righteous, angry, and perpetually overcaffeinated. As a reluctant witness tells Paul Newman in *The Verdict*: "You lawyers are all the same. You don't care who you hurt as long as you make a buck—you're a bunch of whores."

The current cinematic portrayal of lawyers greatly differs from what it once was. Years ago, lawyers were depicted as the Spencer Tracy–type character in *Inherit the Wind*. Gregory Peck's Atticus Finch in *To Kill a Mockingbird* and Jimmy Stewart's Paul Biegler in *Anatomy of a Murder* both loved the law so much they didn't care if they were paid in collard greens or hickory nuts, or not at all. Both emitted integrity, and both were highly effective. But nothing better illustrates the change in Hollywood's portrayal of lawyers than the two versions of *Cape Fear*, made 30 years apart. In the original film, Sam Bowden, the lawyer played by Gregory Peck, embodies all the usual virtues. But in Martin Scorsese's 1991 remake, Bowden, now played by Nick Nolte, is unfaithful, unethical, and unsympathetic. As if to underline the point, the now-aged Peck again portrayed a lawyer in the movie, but this time it was as a slick, sanctimonious windbag.

A LITIGATION BACKLASH AGAINST LAWYERS

In the contemporary climate of lawyer bashing, even clients are striking out at their lawyers. Increasingly, lawyers are being hit with malpractice lawsuits from their former clients. The causes of this malpractice explosion are varied. Some observers believe it is a justifiable reaction to bad lawyering. Hilton Stein, a legal malpractice expert, traces the surge in lawsuits to an increase in the number of incompetents practicing law. "I frankly think there's an epidemic of legal malpractice in this courty," he claims.[10] Others argue that the rise in malpractice litigation is a result of lawyers looking for more areas of litigation. It's a matter of "simple cannibalization," says Joseph Acton, publisher of *Lawyers' Liability Review*. "Lawyers are eating lawyers to maintain their own standard of living."[11] Still others claim that the malpractice boom is yet another symptom of a litigation culture. With the public increasingly eager to sue over any failure or disappointment, it is not surprising that if individuals lose their first lawsuit, they then turn against their lawyer. Consequently, more and more disgruntled clients see their lawyer as just another deep pocket.

The recent increase in malpractice cases both reveals and reinforces a change in the lawyer–client relationship. Although that relationship was once built on trust, it is ceasing to be so. In the past, lawsuits against lawyers were usually generated by obvious, irrefutable mistakes, such as missing a deadline for filing court papers. Today, however, malpractice lawsuits increasingly challenge lawyers' decisions. In the litigation culture that exists in America, legal malpractice claims have become just part of the cost of doing business as a lawyer. And because so many lawyers in a litigation culture tend to prosecute their cases with little involvement by their client, malpractice suits arise from alienated and disgruntled clients.

Clients can become nonentities in a litigation culture of lawyers immersed in an obsession with beating each other, and with little concern for the costs of doing so. Consider, for instance, a malpractice claim brought by an individual against one of the nation's top firms, Gibson, Dunn & Crutcher. In his lawsuit, the former client, disgusted with how the firm handled a real-estate litigation matter, alleged that Gibson Dunn spent 552 hours drafting the complaint and 323 hours of research, yet still missed the leading judicial decision regarding several issues in the case. Perhaps what incited the former client the most, however, was the huge bills, along with the seeming lack of progress. After a year and a half, despite more than 10,000 attorney and paralegal hours, and more than $2 million in billing, the case was still not ready for trial.[12]

The billing practices of lawyers have also exposed the profession to public outrage. For instance, the attorneys who represented Rodney King in his police brutality lawsuit against the city of Los Angeles presented the city with a bill of $4.4 million for legal fees. The bill included time spent on talk shows, taking Mr.

King to movie and theater premieres, and attending his birthday party. It was also $600,000 more than the $3.8 million that Mr. King received in his judgment against the city. "No wonder lawyers have such a bad name," said Federal Judge John Davies, who was in charge of settling the bill. Another case that resulted in a public outcry against legal fees was the wrongful death lawsuit by the families of 21 Texas children who were killed when their school bus was hit by a soft-drink delivery truck in 1989. According to calculations, the lawyers for the families recovered fees amounting to at least $25,000 an hour for each plaintiff's lawyer involved in the case.[13] Not only are lawyers' hourly returns on contingent fee cases continually rising, according to Professor Lestor Birckman of Benjamin Cordozo Law School, but research has shown that in automobile injury lawsuits, claimants without lawyers actually take home more money than those with lawyers who charge a contingent fee.[14]

As yet another sign of public hostility to lawyers, people are increasingly suing lawyers who threaten them with lawsuits. Growing numbers of delinquent debtors, for instance, are suing the lawyers who are trying to collect the debt. The debtors are accusing lawyers of violating the Fair Debt Collection Practices Act, which was intended to protect consumers from late-night telephone calls and other types of harassment by collection agencies. For their part, collection lawyers have invoked the kind of defense for which lawyers have become famous—they say that these accusations often involve technical violations, such as failing to use correct wording in their letters.

In an even more egregious reaction against lawyers, threats of violence have become "surprisingly common," according to legal experts.[15] "Most attorneys have had some sort of situation where they have been threatened," said one Chicago lawyer.[16] Yet the attorneys most likely to be threatened are not those handling criminal cases, but the ones representing clients in civil matters, in which the attorney's work is often accomplished apart from the client, in a maze of confusing paperwork and adversarial strategies that may drag on and ultimately result in a settlement that the client does not see as a benefit.

THE EVOLUTION OF LAW AS BIG BUSINESS

The rising levels of public mistrust of and hostility toward lawyers result partly from the evolution of law into a big business. Since the 1980s, law firms have undergone profound changes. Partnerships are no longer lifetime appointments, and clients regularly switch allegiances. The most valuable skill or quality lawyers can possess is not their legal knowledge but their ability to bring a wealthy client to the firm. Those who control the clients control the practice of law. Consequently, these lawyers become the superstars of the firm. Like the sports world, the legal profession has adopted free agency, bringing with it the megasalaries that have come to dominate professional sports. The average billing rate for a partner in a law firm is $173 per hour, with the rates of well-known attorneys such as Robert Shapiro in the $500 per hour range, and the average income for a partner is about $183,000.[17]

To pay these free-agent lawyers the high salaries they demanded, firms had to start making a lot more money—and they had to start acting more like big businesses. In the years between 1978 and 1988, for instance, the number of firms in the United States with 200 or more attorneys grew eightfold, and the number of lawyers practicing in such firms increased tenfold.[18] Besides the trend toward conglomeration, the legal profession also witnessed the emergence within law firms of a more commercially aggressive style of practice: charging huge premiums; filing frivolous lawsuits; loosening conflict-of-interest codes; and unofficially encouraging lawyers to press the limits of legal ethics.[19]

The new climate of competition for big-money clients means that the lawyers who reel in the clients, rather than those who set standards of public service and legal scholarship, are the ones richly rewarded by their firms. Whereas in the past, according to Sol Linowitz in *The Betrayed Profession*, respected lawyers were leaders in their communities, known for the kind of analytical thinking that helped resolve individual and social problems, in the present the lawyers most admired within the profession are those who can simply claim the power to channel a client's legal dollars.[20] In the contemporary legal profession, according to Anthony

Kronman in *The Lost Lawyer*, traits such as prudence and good judgment are no longer valued or compensated.[21] As a result of the legal profession moving away from its traditional identity as a helping profession, the public now tends to see it as a collection of greedy lawyers, uninterested in such things as justice and public service.

Most of the ways in which the general public now views and encounters lawyers involve their constant pursuit of more business. Filling daytime and late-night television are the parade of lawyer ads: "If you've been injured, there's serious money at stake.... Call now, we can help" or "Have you been put out to pasture because you're over 40?... Age discrimination is illegal. Call us to find out your rights"; and then a narrator's voice urges the viewers to dial for help by calling numbers such as 1–800–LAWYERS. The amount of money lawyers have spent on television ads has gone up every year—from $5.5 million in 1980 to more than $130 million in 1995.[22]

Increasingly, the law is becoming more a commercial calling than a stately profession. Cases and clients are sold like commodities. After disasters such as plane crashes or fires, a first round of lawyers scours the field of victims in the hope of signing up one or more as clients. Then, the lawyer sells the case, for a referral fee, to a litigation specialist, who might then refer it to another specialist for yet another referral fee. It is no surprise that in the litigation age, the image of lawyers has fallen as far as it has.

LITIGATION AS A LEGAL BUSINESS STRATEGY

Rather than just responding to clients' concerns and problems, trial lawyers on their own initiative are identifying potential areas for litigation and then drumming up whatever clients are needed to instigate a lawsuit. For instance, within days of Copley Pharmaceutical, Inc.'s recalling an asthma drug in 1994, a law firm ran a series of television advertisements inviting users of the drug to file a lawsuit against Copley. These advertisements occurred before there were any confirmed injuries relating to the recalled drug, yet in less than 10 days after starting the televised advertisements, the firm filed its first lawsuit against Copley.[23]

At meetings of the Association of Trial Lawyers of America, attorneys target the products or corporations that they see as likely subjects of future litigation. Then, they share information concerning how best to initiate and prosecute such litigation. In 1994, for instance, computer software was seen as a potential litigation gold mine for lawyers. Although software malfunctioning may be a nightmare to users, it spells opportunity to litigators. As one computer-litigation specialist put it: "There's actually more *opportunity* for technology to malfunction now than there was 10 or 15 years ago [emphasis added]."[24]

Perhaps class-action lawsuits illustrate the most blatant example both of how lawyers can single-handedly fuel the litigation explosion and how, in doing so, they can act in a manner contradictory to their clients' interests. As the class action lawsuit has evolved, it has become much more of a lawyer-lawsuit than a client-lawsuit. Frequently, the primary beneficiaries are the lawyers. In fact, clients have virtually no say in a class-action lawsuit, nor do they tend to recover any more than a pittance of their damages.

A class-action lawsuit is one in which a small number of defendants—frequently manufacturers of a particular product—are sued by many claimants, typically the purchasers or users of that product, all asserting that they have in some way been injured or damaged by a defect in that product. As originally intended, the class-action lawsuit is a means to efficiently gather in one action all the similar claims that hundreds or thousands of people might have against a defendant. Over the years, however, class-action lawsuits have greatly increased in both frequency and scope. According to the American Electronics Association, 63 percent of all Silicon Valley high-tech companies have been hit with such suits, with the average settlement being $8 million.[25] It is even common to have lawsuits purporting to represent so many claimants that the number and identity of those claimants are never known until the final settlement or judgment proceeds are actually paid out. For instance, in a price-fixing class-action lawsuit against the airline industry, the lawyers simply named a handful of defendants and then prosecuted the suit on behalf of all the unknown persons who bought airline tickets during a particular period of time.

Because of the magnitude of class actions, no claimant has any control over the lawsuit. The lawyers engineer the lawsuit as they see fit and negotiate whatever settlement they want. The only advocate on behalf of the claimants is the judge, who must give final approval to any settlement. Another feature of the class-action lawsuit is that all possible claimants are bound by the final settlement of the suit, unless they specifically notify the court in writing that they do not intend to be included in that settlement. Taken altogether, the nature of the class action is such that it becomes the lawyers' lawsuit, with the individual claimants playing a very passive and tangential role. This can be seen in the type of settlements that often occur in class-action litigation. For instance, in a class-action suit based on billing errors in their telephone bills, Chicago residents in 1995 received a 3-cent rebate while the lawyers representing the class received nearly $750,000 in fees. In a Texas class-action lawsuit against automobile insurance providers charged with rounding up premiums (i.e., if a policyholders premiums were calculated to be $700.50, then the bill would read as $701), lawyers asked for fees in the range of $30–40 million. Yet by their own admission, the lawyers calculated that in a typical scenario, a driver may have been overcharged only $35 over a 10-year period. In the 1990 price-fixing lawsuit against the airlines, the settlement yielded no cash for the members of the class—they received discount coupons for future air travel, laden with restrictions—but produced over $16 million for the attorneys.

CLASS-ACTION LAWSUITS AS LITIGATION-FOR-LAWYERS

Because of the immense profitability of class-action lawsuits, lawyers pursue them with a ravenous intensity. Once it is learned that something has happened that might give rise to a class-action lawsuit (i.e., a defective product made, misleading investment advice given, an error in billing committed) the lawyers rush to recruit a plaintiff and then to commence a lawsuit. In class-action suits commenced by shareholders against a corporation whose drop in stock price has left them suddenly poorer, lawyers race to the courthouse, often before they even consulted the shareholders. By using "professional plaintiffs"—people who hold a few shares in a large number of companies, and who make themselves available for such suits—lawyers are able to move swiftly. The first attorney to file a lawsuit is usually made the lead attorney when the class is later formed, and is well positioned to claim the lion's share of any legal fees awarded.

In class-action litigation, the lawyers, virtually on their own, can set up the case. By finding a plaintiff in the right part of the country, a lawyer can make sure that the case is tried in a locale well known for its large verdicts. For instance, the Texas class-action lawsuit against the automobile insurers was not filed in any of Texas's major cities, where most of the drivers would be. It was filed in a poor, sparsely populated county near the Mexican border, known for its proplaintiff attitudes and generous verdicts.

Not only do lawyers choose the location for their lawsuits, but they also actively recruit class members. In a class-action lawsuit by investors against Prudential Securities, for instance, the lawyers identified potential litigants through investor mailing lists and then invited thousands of these investors to seminars in dozens of cities across the country. At these seminars, the lawyers recruited litigants by boasting of the potential rewards of joining the class. In another case, which involved a class-action suit against Occidental Petroleum Corporation by people who claimed various injuries when a chemical leak had occurred at a nearby plant, a common link between most of the claimants was that "not one of them went to see their family doctor first or even last—all of them went to see their lawyer first and the lawyer arranged for [them] to be examined."[26]

Class-action lawsuits allow lawyers to create a litigation behemoth from a very small injury or damage. The Milli Vanilli class action is one example. When it was revealed that this music group was lip-synching with prerecorded music at concerts, a horde of class-action lawyers immediately filed suits. They were eventually consolidated in Chicago, where the judge approved a legal fee of $675,000 for the attorneys. Sometimes the final benefits to the class are so meager that they hardly justify a class-action lawsuit that produces millions for the lawyers. The airline price-fixing suit, commenced in 1990 and settled in 1995, illustrates this strange lopsidedness of class-action benefits. It was the disparity between the legal fees and the limited returns to the flying consumers that led many travel and legal experts to label this case a "lawyers' case."[27] As it turned out, none of the class members received any cash—they just got a limited number of highly restrictive coupons toward future flights. No matter how many coupons a single individual received, they could only be redeemed for a few dollars at a time—never for more than 10 percent of the amount of the ticket. As for the lawyers' take, however, five firms shared most of the more than $16 million in fees.

The airline case also reveals how class-action lawyers often end up benefiting their opponents, the defendants, more than their clients, the plaintiffs. The coupon settlement was very much to the airlines' advantage. Not only did the coupons not cost the defendants anything, but they actually served to boost ticket sales. The settlement actually ended up being an extremely successful marketing tool for the airlines, prompting consumers to use the coupons by purchasing more airline tickets. In fact, Alaska Airlines, one of the few large carriers not named in the original lawsuit, actually *asked* to be a defendant when it learned of the coupon program. "The airlines using those coupons are going to see substantial additional ticket sales because of them," predicted Louis Cancelmi, a spokesman for Alaska Air. "We asked to be named in the case because, once we saw the settlement, we realized it was to our competitive disadvantage not to do so."[28] In defense of the settlement, one of the four lawyers who served as cochair of the plaintiffs' committee said that the plaintiffs "should be satisfied" with what they received—"Coupons are better than nothing."[29]

Coupons have also been used in class-action lawsuits against

Ford Motor Company (alleging leaky Mustang convertibles) and General Mills (charging that some cereals were tainted with pesticides). Although the lawyers in the Ford case received more than $1 million, each plaintiff was given a coupon good for 1 year toward the purchase of a new Ford. In the General Mills case, the lawyers got close to $2 million, while their clients received a coupon good for a free second box of cereal when they bought a first one. Again, the coupons were called "a sophisticated marketing program."[30]

Such settlements are obviously a windfall to lawyers, who get the only cash that is paid out, and to the defendants, who use them to increase sales revenues. Courts, however, "are starting to realize what a scam and hypocrisy these types of settlements can be," according to Beverly Moore, editor of *Class Action Report*, a Washington publication.[31] Such settlements tend to be used by lawyers "who are not zealous on behalf of the class," according to John Coffee, professor at Columbia University School of Law.[32]

Coupon settlements illustrate how plaintiffs' lawyers and defendants conspire. The defendants give the lawyers a generous amount of fees in return for a settlement that is beneficial to the defendants, for once a class action is settled, even if the class members never knew that the case was going on, none of the members can ever sue any of the defendants for the same injury again. Thus, while the lawyers get a bundle, the defendants save money by not risking a more costly suit later on and by eliminating all future claims against them. Since lawyers representing the class members don't need their approval of any settlement, the lawyers are often willing to settle at any price, as long as their fees are sufficient.

CONFLICTS BETWEEN LAWYERS AND THEIR CLIENTS

Class-action lawyers can not only sell out their clients' interests, but they can also affirmatively harm the class members. In a class-action lawsuit against the Bank of Boston for its handling of mortgage escrow accounts, many of the class members actually ended up paying out money. One class member was charged $91.33 in legal fees for his recovery of $2.19 in back interest.[33] After receiving a host of complaints from similarly disgruntled class members, Senator William S. Cohen, Republican of Maine, sponsored corrective legislation. "There is evidence from around the country that in many instances class actions are benefiting lawyers to a much greater extent than their clients," he said.[34]

A typical plaintiff in the Prudential Securities class action, settled in 1994, received about 4 cents back for every dollar she had invested in a real estate fund sponsored by Prudential. Meanwhile, her attorneys pocketed nearly $6.5 million. Adding to the disappointment was the fact that some investors in the same fund who sued separately came away with far more money—sometimes more than 100 percent of their investment.[35] "The only people who make money in these [types of lawsuits] are the claimants' lawyers," said Samantha Rabin, senior editor of *Securities Arbitration Commentator*.[36]

Altogether, the attorneys in the Prudential case received almost $23 million, while each investor, on average, was awarded $679. The settlement would have been much worse for the investors if not for various regulators who stepped in to object. As it was being finalized, a number of federal and state regulators argued that the plaintiffs' lawyers did not deserve that much in fees, because the lawyers had actually endorsed a much smaller deal. Due to these objections, the lawyers had to go back to work to try to achieve a larger one. Thus, in the Prudential case, the class members were better represented by the regulators than by their own lawyers.

Because of the abuses of class actions, judges have begun taking harsh action. In one lawsuit in which a corporation was charged with conspiring to fix the price of Passover matzo, the judge not only refused to approve the settlement but even rebuked the lawyers for pursuing the case. According to the judge, the lawyers' clients "appeared to want nothing to do with the litigation."[37] The only cash to have been paid out in the proposed settlement was $500,000, all to be used for legal fees. "In short, class counsel are litigating this case without any clients.... It appears that the proposed settlement is simply a thinly disguised ploy for the recovery of ... attorneys' fees," said the judge.[38]

Many of the problems with class-action lawsuits occur because lawyers are in such a rush to file a lawsuit that they cannot possibly investigate or verify their clients' claims. In one case, the judge outrightly dismissed a shareholder class-action suit against Philip Morris, finding it to be a fabrication of the lawyers. The original suits on which the class was based, and which were supposed to be filed by different plaintiffs around the country, all contained identical allegations, apparently lodged in one attorney's computer memory of form complaints, and even contained identical errors (i.e., stating that Philip Morris was in the toy industry). Furthermore, the suits were filed on the very day that the plaintiffs' cause of action was said to arise, and the judge, in dismissing the case, expressed disbelief that shareholders across the country would have appeared at their lawyers' offices so quickly.

Because of a divergence of lawyers' interests with those of their clients, a judge in the breast-implant suit against Dow Corning Corporation ordered on March 21, 1996, that the lawyers negotiating on behalf of the class of women with implants be replaced with a new negotiating committee made up of the women themselves. The judge found that the lawyers' negotiations were inherently rife with conflicts of interests. "The attorneys' interests in these cases are not always exactly congruent with the claimants themselves," said Mark Roe, a professor at Columbia University Law School.[39]

The lawyer-driven aspect of class actions revealed itself once again when the same lawyers that prosecuted the breast-implant litigation turned their sights on Norplant—the silicone birth-control patches inserted into the arms of women. Both prior to and following commencement of the lawsuits, there was no medical evidence of any significant health risks associated with the device. Furthermore, the FDA had approved Norplant, and numerous studies had found the device safe. Surveys showed that virtually 100 percent of the women using Norplant were satisfied with it. According to the group that developed the device, there were no lawsuits in any of the 44 countries outside the United States where Norplant was marketed. Nonetheless, the U.S. lawsuits against the manufacturer of Norplant alleged a host of dangerous side effects. "The claims were virtually the same as with the breast implant [litigation]," said Dr. Elizabeth Connell, professor of gynecology and obstetrics at the Emory University School of Medicine.[40] A spokesperson for the manufacturer of Norplant noted that many of the suits contained identical typographical errors, even though they were filed in different states. This was no surprise, since the same lawyers involved in the breast-implant cases were now initiating the Norplant cases.

In the summer of 1995, class-action lawyers held a National Norplant Litigation Conference in Houston. The conference was essentially a series of seminars instructing lawyers and doctors on how to get in on the Norplant litigation boom. Lawyers were using everything they had done in the breast-implant cases as a model for their litigation against Norplant. Having scored big in their breast-implant litigation, the lawyers were now looking around for other products to go after. What attracted them to Norplant was the fact that the device was a silicone one, thereby allowing the lawyers to replicate all the procedures and experts they had developed in the silicone breast-implant litigation. As critics warned, the Norplant litigation revealed that roving bands of class-action litigators could seriously jeopardize the development and availability of new medical products in the United States.

THE OPPOSITION TO LEGAL REFORM

Lawyers have been extremely successful in warding off any significant reform of the litigation system. Their opposition to reform attempts shows once again that lawyers have moved far away from their clients' interests and the public interest. They are instead determined to preserve the system they have built for themselves. In 1993, for instance, lawyers succeeded in killing a proposal that would streamline the litigation process in federal courts—a proposal sponsored by the federal judges and supported by the Supreme Court. Lawyers justified their opposition on the grounds that the proposal (which called for lawyers from each side to voluntarily turn over certain information to each other) was "totally inconsistent with the adversary process."[41] However, according to a spokesperson from the Federal Judicial Center, the real reason why lawyers opposed the proposal was that "it threatened to reduce their income."[42] Since lawyers have a financial interest in opposing a plan that might shorten court cases and reduce billable hours, the lobbying against the reform measure was very intense. "Very few issues generate that kind of debate," said one observer.[43] Even the defense attorneys, whose corporate clients strongly supported the proposal, opposed it.

One reason lawyers have been so successful in derailing many reform attempts over the years (i.e., to place caps on fees, eliminate lawsuits over auto accidents, require the loser to pay attorneys fees, and limit punitive damages awards) is that their lobbying organization has been so strong. The Association of Trial Lawyers in America (ATLA) spends more per member on political donations than any other major lobbying group, including the American Medical Association.[44] According to a former ATLA president, the leaders of the ATLA "don't like to compromise and seldom do."[45] In the Congressional campaigns between 1989 and 1994, plaintiffs' lawyers individually contributed more than $18 million, while the major oil producers gave $7 million and the Big Three auto makers contributed $2.2 million.[46] Moreover, the $18 million was in addition to some $6 million in contributions made by the ATLA over the same period. In the 1996 battle over legal reform in California, lawyers were expected to spend about $10 million to defeat measures that would cap attorneys' fees and eliminates certain kinds of lawsuits.[47]

In addition to acting as a lobbying group, the ATLA also sponsors and supports various litigation groups, such as the Vending Machine Tipover Litigation Group, the Penile Implant Litigation Group, and the Automatic Door Litigation Group. These groups are among some 80 trial-lawyer networks searching out new sources of lawsuits and new defendants.

In the litigation age, lawyers have become, in many ways, quite separate and independent from their clients, and from the general public. They have been successful in designing and maintaining a litigation culture that feeds on itself and breeds yet more litigation. But if America has indeed become a litigation culture, lawyers are a suspect group of leaders.

CONCLUSION

The Empty Promise of Litigation

AN ENDLESS MAZE OF CONFLICT

The lofty promise of litigation was that it would establish an accepted set of principles to guide social behavior. With the precedence of its case law, the courts would create a framework through which disputes would be avoided or resolved without the need to file a lawsuit. Litigation would be the means by which the values of justice and fairness would shape American life.

Unfortunately, the legal system has not fulfilled that idealistic promise. In an age of the litigation explosion, the law seems to be doing nothing to diminish the occurrence of conflict nor to encourage the private resolution of disputes. In a therapeutic culture in which courts examine the emotional and psychological makeup of each party, the rule of precedence is of little value. With the abundance of lawyers in America, clients have no trouble finding lawyers who claim to be able to somehow avoid or escape whatever unfavorable precedent might exist.

Not only has the legal system not upheld the hopeful promises once set for it, but it has actually had a damaging social effect. The adversarial culture bred by the litigation explosion has contributed to the creation of a more conflict-oriented society. Like the proliferation of guns, the rapid expansion of rights has given everyone the weaponry to wage social warfare. Just as Ellis Island may have ingrained assimilation into America's mind-set a century ago, the litigation explosion is cementing conflict and adversity into contemporary cultural attitudes.

As the reverberations of the litigation explosion shake every corner of society, the conflict of the courtroom is transforming America into its own image—an adversarial image. Instead of providing a structure of values and principles that would make society a more harmonious place, the litigation explosion is preaching the message that conflict pays, and that filing a lawsuit is an accepted step toward pursuing the American dream. Instead of being a process seen as dispensing justice, litigation is perceived as an arena of orchestrated combat among gladiator attorneys. Trial lawyers even talk of their trade in terms of combat: Trial teams set up "war rooms" out of which to wage their litigation battles. Litigators draft complaints that will hurl an artillery barrage at the enemy, and researching associates search for the means by which to wage a flank attack.

In the modern age, litigation in America is not about dramatic verdicts and eloquent courtroom oratory. It is not about weighty contests of opposing ideas and values that engage the social imagination. Litigation is about discovery—that time-consuming process by which the opposing lawyers in a lawsuit meticulously investigate, and argue over, every conceivable and even inconceivable aspect of each other's case. It is because of this procedural maze of discovery that civil lawsuits drag on for years and then become too cumbersome to ever go to trial. The irony of the discovery process in civil litigation is that lawyers spend years and hundreds of thousands of dollars getting every aspect of the case ready for a trial, and then finally realize that the case is much too big and too complex ever to be tried. Yet, with each complaint that is filed, the lawyers begin once again their prodding game of discovery. Every document ever possessed or generated by the defendant is demanded by the plaintiff and vice versa. Then a series of motions are brought to the judge to fight over which documents may or may not have to be produced. Hundreds of written questions are served on either side, and it is the job of the lawyers to pretend to answer these, while yielding no useful information whatsoever. More motions are made to require more complete answers. Depositions are taken in which lawyers interrogate all witnesses having any possible information, no matter how trivial, concerning the case. The opposing lawyers fill the room with objections, hoping to derail the interrogating attorney and render the deposition a useless exercise. More motions are made to override the objections.

This discovery process, which may take years, does not focus on the substantive issues of the case. It simply involves what information one side can get from another. The battles are often irrelevant to, or not indicative of, the ultimate resolution of the lawsuit. Yet volumes and volumes of case law are devoted to the questions of how many documents one side can get from the other, or how long one side has to answer the questions posed by the other. It is this discovery process that is the most adversarial. It is here that lawyers, fighting over the answer to a question or the categorization of a document, accuse each other of being dishonest, manipulative, unethical, and sinister. Intimidation and accusations are generally considered by litigators to be useful discovery strategies. Though less than 5 percent of all civil cases actually go to a jury, 100 percent go through discovery, and discovery is strictly the lawyers' arena. But discovery produces no verdicts, no lessons for society, no principles of justice, no guidelines on how to avoid conflict in the future.

A CULTURE OF FEAR

Although discovery yields few, if any, valuable lessons for society, neither does the settlement of lawsuits. Increasingly, any case involving anything controversial—just the kind of case that might inspire public debate and lead to a deeper public understanding— is settled with a confidentiality agreement. Such an agreement, usually required by the party paying the money, buys the other party's silence. No mention is ever made of how the controversial dispute was resolved. When the next similar dispute occurs, the parties will start all over again, and they'll most probably settle it with a confidentiality agreement. For the rest of society, lawsuits serve simply as social teasers, piquing curiosity and then shutting it off.

The only social guide provided by litigation is the fear of litigation. The fear of being sued is becoming a universally held behavioral standard. People may disagree on everything else, but they'll join ranks if someone raises the threat of litigation. They may not know why they would be sued, or on what grounds, or even if the suit would have merit—they only know that they want to avoid a lawsuit. Avoiding litigation is becoming the all-American trait, the great social unifier. Physicians structure their practice and treatments according to the mandates of their malpractice insurers. Supervisors consider the propensity of particular employees to sue when managing them. Charitable organizations choose which tasks to undertake based on which ones may expose them to the risk of litigation. Personnel officers read from a list of lawyer-approved questions when interviewing applicants. Investment advisors try to convey as little information as possible, for fear of getting sued. Public swimming pools and playgrounds shut down because someone might get hurt and then sue. Fearing a lawsuit, city officials in Fresno, California, told volunteers to stop cleaning streets. An Arizona restaurant stopped serving free dinners to the homeless after being warned about the possibility of a lawsuit. Companies lay off productive employees, but retain the most disruptive—because it's the latter who are most likely to sue. The most hostile customer is coddled, while the reasonable one is dismissed. Factory forepersons focus their safety concerns on whether rules are being followed, not necessarily on whether a condition actually is or is not safe.

A fear of litigation may be commonly held, but it is not one that strengthens social unity. Litigation fears do not bring people together. They cause people to retreat from society and seek shelter within protected and insulated enclaves. The more that the threat of litigation is used as the currency of social discourse, the more mistrust and hostility will prevail. The more that the threat of litigation is used as a means of blackmail and extortion (i.e., "You give me this and I won't sue you") the more individuals will back away from each other. Strangely enough, at a time when speech codes at universities are forbidding anything to be said that might be offensive or insulting, angry threats of litigation are regarded not only as commonplace but also even admirable.

THE SPREADING LITIGATION CULTURE

Litigation has become so entrenched in the social psyche, so accepted in the course of social behavior, that it is spreading out beyond the lawyers' offices. No longer are potential litigants willing to be confined to the constraints of having to hire a lawyer. Increasingly, not wanting to be excluded by expensive lawyers, Americans are entering into the litigation arena on their own. In family court especially, the numbers are exploding. Fifty-three percent of all cases in Des Moines, Iowa, involve litigants representing themselves, and in Washington, D.C., the figure is 88 percent.[1] These lawyerless litigants, stumbling through the litigation maze for the first time, are clogging courts that are not accustomed to accommodating amateurs. According to California Superior Court Judge Roderic Duncan, "Lawyers have priced themselves out of the middle-class market."[2] Consequently, the nonlawyer population, after years of watching trials on "Court TV," "People's Court," and "L.A. Law," now feels ready to do it on their own.

All across the nation, the numbers of do-it-yourself lawyers have risen dramatically in recent years. An American Bar Association study in the Phoenix area found that in 1980, at least one of the parties was acting *pro se* in 24 percent of all divorce cases. Ten years later, the figure had soared to 88 percent.[3] Naturally, lawyers are not pleased with these figures; and they have been generally successful in restricting the availability of nonlawyer services that offer to the public various types of assistance in handling their own lawsuits. Arizona is among the most liberal in allowing the provision of legal services by nonlawyers, and not surprisingly, it is among the states witnessing the highest numbers of lawyerless litigants.

CRISIS WITHIN THE LEGAL ACADEMY

As America's litigation culture grows, the need for leadership and guidance of that culture intensifies. In the past, the nation's law schools served as a source of intellectual guidance and reasoned inspiration. Today, however, law schools have moved toward a more extremist fringe, and have lost some of the social and professional esteem they once enjoyed.

Although law schools traditionally espoused a careful analysis into the merits of initiating litigation, a law professor at George Washington University advocates a "Sue the bastards" approach.[4] Those words adorn the stationery posted by John Banzhaf outside his law school office, and he lists "suing the bastards" as his hobby. He teaches a course called "Legal Activism," which teaches students how to effect social change by instigating litigation. According to the course catalogue, students in his course learn "principles of maximizing legal leverage, legal judo, guerrilla law ... and unusual legal tactics." The students try out these tactics by filing complaints and acting as plaintiffs. One case brought by Professor Banzhaf's students was a sex-discrimination complaint against six hair salons for setting prices of haircuts based on gender. Another case, which Banzhaf won, was against dry cleaners who discriminated by charging more for women's shirts than for men's. According to one critic, Banzhaf "teaches [his students] how to make trouble in the courtroom.... He demeans some of the value of clinical education by focusing on cases that trivialize the litigation process and encourage students to be litigious."[5]

Advocacy and political activism have increasingly come to characterize legal education. But in focusing so much on advocacy, scholarly standards and objectivity can easily fall by the wayside. Due to a pervasive mistrust of majoritarian institutions among law school faculty, who during the Warren Court years were taught that law should be used to reform a corrupt society, the nation's law schools now often find themselves on the radical fringe of society. This was demonstrated during the Clinton Administration's failed attempt to appoint Lani Guinier to a high-ranking position in the Justice Department. What was most surprising, however, was Ms. Guinier's astonishment that her radical views on voting reform were regarded as extremist, even by the most liberal senators. Having taken root in an academic environment drastically out of touch with American political opinion, her views had apparently never been subjected to the kind of criticism that would have made her realize the degree to which those ideas differed from the climate of opinion in outside society. According to Harvard law professor Mary Ann Glendon, within the legal academy there is "a growing disdain for the practical aspects of law, a zany passion for novelty, a confusion of advocacy with scholarship, and a mistrust of majoritarian institutions."[6] So obsessed with "cutting edge" legal theories are the nation's law schools that they often encourage views that have little or no logical bases.

The evolution of Critical Legal Studies (CLS) in the 1980s further demonstrates the marginalization and extremism of some of the nation's most elite law schools. The movement, with adherents among the tenured faculty at many of the top law schools, is an attack on "the notion that the law is a body of neutral principles that, when applied to real-life disputes, produce results that are more or less consistent and more or less derived from considerations of justice rather than power."[7] According to CLS, the law is biased in favor of the wealthy and powerful, and is used to maintain an unjust and oppressive social and economic structure. The purpose of Critical Legal scholarship, its adherents argue, is to expose the entire legal system as a sham and a fraud.

Though it presents a radical view of the law, CLS is not the province of legal scholars on the fringe. The "typical Critical Legal scholar attended an Ivy League college in the 1960s or early 1970s, went on to study at an elite law school, perhaps spent a year clerking for a prestigious judge, and then proceeded directly to a position on the faculty of a top-tier law school."[8] If someone with that much education and training sees the law as a complete sham, then there may be good reason to believe that America's growing litigation culture is equally baseless.

Following in the footsteps of CLS has been the emergence in the 1990s of critical race theory and feminist jurisprudence. Like CLS, both critical race theory and feminist jurisprudence are antithetical to the traditional idea of law. They argue that the purported objectivity and neutrality of legal reasoning are a sham, and that law is merely a mask for white-male power relations. Consequently, critical race theory and feminist jurisprudence aim to overthrow all settled norms. One University of Pennsylvania law professor, for instance, urged her class to promote black deviance. She argued "that the black community should embrace the criminals within its midst as a form of resistance to white oppression."[9] She also urged blacks to discard the distinction between lawful and criminal activity, since law, after all, was simply the tool of a cruel, white race.

Like CLS, critical race theory dispenses with any traditional methods of legal scholarship, such as case analysis or logical reasoning. In their place is substituted a personal narration of experiences with oppression. Race and gender identities, as well as feelings about discrimination, are given top priority in analyzing legal problems. Reason and logic are replaced with emotion and group solidarity.

If developments in the nation's top law schools are any indication, the litigation explosion will not be producing any insightful or guiding principles for social behavior. Not even some of the nation's best law professors believe in law's ability to do so. According to them, litigation will simply continue unabated, the result of the clash of individuals in a multiracial society.

By itself, the litigation explosion does not require any indictment of the American legal system. To the contrary, the popular embrace of the courthouse is a testament to the public support of the judicial process. Furthermore, America has always been a fairly litigious, individualistic culture. What has plagued the nation recently, however, has been an excess of legalism and litigation. The law, and an adversarial law at that, has pushed aside many other social concerns and customs. Judicial decisions have smothered moral sentiments and civic values. To remedy the social and cultural consequences of the litigation explosion, as outlined in this book, is not to require outright prohibitions on lawsuits. It is instead to confine litigation to a necessary but well-defined area of American life, and then to let the remaining strands of the nation's social and cultural life breathe on their own.

Notes

INTRODUCTION

1. Jay Finegan, "Law and Disorder," *Inc.* (April 1994): 67.
2. Aaron Epstein, "Whistle-Blowers Win Millions," *Des Moines Register* (February 20, 1994), p. 1A.
3. Margaret Zack, "Law Sends Frivolous Cases to a Speedy End," *Star Tribune* (Minneapolis) (August 21, 1995), p. 1B.

CHAPTER ONE

1. Judicial Conference Committee on Long-Range Planning, "Conserving Core Values," *Report on the Judiciary* (Washington, D.C.: Government Printing Office, 1995), p. 11.
2. "Harper's Index," *Harper's Magazine* (February 1995), p. 13.
3. Margaret Jacobs, "Reliable Data about Lawsuits Are Very Scarce," *Wall Street Journal* (June 9, 1995), p. 1B.
4. Laura Mansnerus, "More and More Clients, More and More Lawyers," *New York Times* (August 14, 1993), p. 28B.
5. Center for Governmental Studies, *An Overworked Judicial System* (Chicago: Northern Illinois University Press, 1995), p. 14.
6. Theodore Boutrous, "Sue and Make a Million," *Wall Street Journal* (July 28, 1993), p. A15.
7. Patrick Garry, *Liberalism and American Identity* (Kent, Ohio: Kent State University Press, 1992), p. 185.
8. Lincoln Caplan, *Skadden: Power, Money and the Rise of a Legal Empire* (New York: Farrar, Straus and Giroux, 1993), p. 19.

9. "Harper's Index," *Harper's Magazine* (July 1994), p. 11.
10. Doreen Carvajal, "Civil Verdicts Delayed for Years," *New York Times* (April 17, 1995), p. 1A.
11. Wade Lambert, "Ever Hear the One About the Lawyers and Window Bars?" *Wall Street Journal* (March 23, 1994), p. 1A.
12. Elizabeth Kolbert, "A Fall Docket, but No Profits, for Court TV," *New York Times* (January 31, 1994), p. 4D.
13. William Finnegan, "Doubt," *The New Yorker* (January 31, 1994), pp. 48–67.
14. Seth Mydans, "New Dissonances Arise from End of Denny Trial," *New York Times* (October 25, 1993), p. A12.
15. Margaret Zack, "Judge Dismisses Whole Jury," *Star Tribune* (Minneapolis) (May 17, 1995), p. 1A.
16. Wade Lambert, "After the Verdict," *Wall Street Journal* (December 30, 1993), p. B1.
17. Jan Hoffman, "Courts Moving to Silence Lawyers Using Publicity as a Defense Tactic," *New York Times* (April 22, 1994), p. B7.
18. Janet Elder, "Does This Jury Count?" *New York Times* (February 13, 1994), p. 3E.
19. Carole Gorney, "Litigation Journalism on Trial, "*Media Critic* (March 1994), pp. 48–57.
20. Michael Janofsky, "Simpson Trial Eclipses California Politics," *New York Times* (August 14, 1994), p. 10A.
21. Ibid.
22. David Foster, "Sexual-Abuse Hysteria Cited for Climate of Fear," *Los Angeles Times* (March 20, 1994), p. A22.
23. Christi Harlan, "SEC Seeks to Beef up Safe Harbor Provision," *Wall Street Journal* (May 17, 1994), p. 1B.
24. Philip K. Howard, *The Death of Common Sense* (New York: Random House, 1994), p. 81.

CHAPTER TWO

1. Mark Habler, "The Persistence of the Frontier," *Harper's Magazine* (October 1994): 21.
2. Nina Easton, "The Law of the Schoolyard," *Los Angeles Times Magazine* (October 2, 1994), p. 19.
3. Peter Kerr, "Ghost Riders Are Target of Insurance Sting," *New York Times* (August 18, 1993), p. 13A.
4. Ronald Smothers, "Jury's $150 Million Award against GM Touches off Furor," *New York Times* (June 5, 1996), p. A9.
5. Paul Barrett, "Author Who Sued over Scornful Review is Now Scorned by the Publishing World," *Wall Street Journal* (April 7, 1994), p. 1B.
6. Edward Felsenthal, "Weekend Warriors Find a New Arena," *Wall Street Journal* (June 23, 1995), p. 1B.

7. Tonia Dorall, "A Campaign to Put Biblical Values in the Public Schools," *New York Times* (April 13, 1994), p. B1.
8. Andrea Gerlin, "With Free Help, the Religious Turn Litigious," *Wall Street Journal* (February 17, 1994), p. B1.
9. Elizabeth Gleick, "Onward Christian Lawyers," *Time* (March 13, 1995), p. 58.
10. Ibid.
11. Ibid., p. 65.
12. Patricia Edmonds, "In Court, Troubled Tales," *USA Today* (April 8, 1994), p. 8A.
13. Milo Geyelin, "Divorcing Couples Wage War with Domestic Torts," *Wall Street Journal* (February 2, 1994), p. 1B.
14. Ibid.
15. Ibid.
16. Shelby Blegen, "Putting Working Moms in Custody," *Newsweek* (March 13, 1995): 54.
17. Sam Verhovek, "Mother Scolded by Judge," *New York Times* (August 30, 1995), p. 7A.
18. David Dunlap, "Support for Gay Adoptions Seems to Wane," *New York Times* (May 1, 1995), p. 11A.
19. Edmonds, "In Court, Troubled Tales," p. 8A.
20. Felicia Waterston, "The Morning After," *Washington Post* (October 22, 1993), p. C1.
21. Peter Lewis, "Persistent E-Mail: Stalking or Courtship?" *New York Times* (September 16, 1994), p. B11.
22. Wayne Washington, "No Eyeful, So City Gets an Earful," *Star Tribune* (Minneapolis) (August 5, 1995), p. 1A.
23. Ellen Joan Pollock, "As Remedy for Certain Broken Promises, Professor Proposes Sexual Fraud Suits," *Wall Street Journal* (June 11, 1993), p. B1.
24. Jeffrey Rosen, "Sodom and DeMurrer," *The New Republic* (November 29, 1993): 16.
25. George de Lame, "Hawaii May Lead Way on Same-Sex Marriage," *Chicago Tribune* (May 15, 1994), p. 8A.
26. Mike Kaszuba, "Lesbians Sue Clinic," *Star Tribune* (Minneapolis) (April 10, 1995), p. 1A.
27. Enid Gulla, "Family Wins Right to End Their Son's Ordeal," *Star Tribune* (Minneapolis) (October 18, 1994), p. 1A.
28. Tamar Lewin, "Ignoring Right to Die Directives, Medical Community Is Being Sued," *New York Times* (June 2, 1996), p. 1A.
29. Tamar Lewin, "Students Seeking Damages for Sex Bias," *New York Times* (July 15, 1994), p. 11B.
30. Ibid.
31. Kurt Chandler, "Gay Teen's Suit against School Seen as Pioneering," *Star Tribune* (Minneapolis) (February 17, 1995), p. 1A.
32. Easton, "The Law of the Schoolyard," p. 21.
33. Ibid., p. 23.

34. Thomas Farnsworth, "Student Who Was Paid to Leave Will Not Return to Swarthmore," *New York Times* (September 3, 1994), p. A11.

35. Carol Simley, "Professor Strikes a Blow for Academic Freedom," *New York Times* (October 12, 1994), p. B8.

36. Asra Nomani, "Was Professor's Lecture Academic Freedom or Sex Harassment?" *Wall Street Journal* (March 7, 1995), p. 1B.

CHAPTER THREE

1. Michael Corin, "Quantifying America's Decline," *Wall Street Journal* (March 15, 1993), p. 15A.

2. The speech was printed in the *New York Times* (September 10, 1994), p. 9A.

3. Christine Gorman, "Dollars for Deeds," *Time* (May 16, 1993): 51.

4. Felicia Cowlings, "What is the Main Problem Facing the Country Today?" *Time* (February 7, 1994): 52.

5. William Bennett, *The Book of Virtues* (New York: Simon and Schuster, 1993).

6. Christopher Lasch, *The Revolt of the Elites: And the Betrayal of Democracy* (New York: W. W. Norton, 1994).

7. James Lincoln Collier, *The Rise of Selfishness in America* (New York: Oxford University Press, 1994).

8. James Q. Wilson, *The Moral Sense* (New York: Simon and Schuster, 1993), p. 61.

9. Gertrude Himmelfarb, *The De-Moralization of Society: From Victorian Virtues to Modern Virtues* (New York: Alfred A. Knopf, 1995).

10. Ichiro Ozawa, *Blueprint for a New Japan* (New York: Kodansha International, 1993), p. 31.

11. Andrew Pollack, "How Japan Hews to Tradition of Lifetime Jobs," *New York Times* (April 26, 1993), p. 1A.

12. Andrew Pollack, "Japan's Schools: Orderly and Crime-Free," *New York Times* (July 18, 1995), p. 1A.

13. Andrew Pollack, "Japan Says No to Crime," *New York Times* (May 14, 1995), p. A4.

14. Noda Yoshiyuki, *Introduction to Japanese Law* (Tokyo: University of Tokyo Press, 1976), p. 21.

15. Ibid., p. 23.

16. Ibid., p. 24.

17. Edward Felsenthal, "Are Civil Rights Laws Being Interpreted Too Broadly?" *Wall Street Journal* (June 10, 1996), p. B1.

18. Ibid.

19. Robert D. Putnam, "Bowling Alone: America's Declining Social Capitol," *Journal of Democracy* 6 (1), 1995: 73.

20. These statistics are taken from Putnam, "Bowling Alone," pp. 67–69.

21. Ibid.

22. This mind-set is also discussed in Philip K. Howard, *The Death of Common Sense: How Law Is Suffocating America* (New York: Random House, 1994).

23. Carlin Romano, "Down By Laws," *The New Yorker* (March 13, 1995), p. 104.

24. Robert Nagel, "Let's Kill All the Lawyers," *Washington Monthly* (January 1995): 46.
25. Michael Wines, "First Lady Makes a Pitch for Health Bill," *New York Times* (July 22, 1994), p. 1A.

CHAPTER FOUR

1. Robert Hughes, *Culture of Complaint: The Fraying of America* (New York: Oxford University Press, 1993).
2. David Guterson, "Moneyball," *Harper's Magazine* (September 1994): 45.
3. William Bukeley, "Sponsoring Sports Gains in Popularity," *Wall Street Journal* (June 24, 1994), p. B1.
4. Tim Jones, "The Boom in Sports on TV," *Chicago Tribune* (May 12, 1996), p. N1.
5. Ibid.
6. John Stravinsky, "He Shoots, He Scores, He Insults," *New York Times* (May 22, 1994), p. 13A.
7. Seth Mydans, "Nice Guys Finish Last," *New York Times* (April 9, 1994), p. A7.
8. Ibid.
9. Eleena DeLisser, "Abusive Fans Lead Amateur Umpires to Ask Courts for Protection," *Wall Street Journal* (August 1, 1994), p. B1.
10. Ellen Warren, "Is Learning Finishing Second to Winning?" *Chicago Tribune* (April 16, 1995), p. 1A.
11. Hiller Zobel, "In Love with Lawsuits," *American Heritage* (November 1994): 60.
12. John Marks, "The American Uncivil Wars," *U.S. News & World Report* (April 22, 1996): 68.
13. Elijah Anderson, "The Code of the Streets," *The Atlantic Monthly* (May 1994): 83.
14. Ibid, p. 94.
15. Pete Hamill, "End Game," *Esquire* (December 1994): 86.
16. See Martha Bayles, *Hole in Our Soul: The Loss of Beauty and Meaning in American Popular Music* (New York: Free Press, 1994).
17. B. Drummond Ayres, "Art or Trash?" *New York Times* (June 8, 1996), p. 6A.
18. William Grimes, "Burgeoning Civility Deficit Could Be Next National Woe," *New York Times* (November 16, 1993), p. 12A.
19. Ibid.
20. Angela Stofley, "Rude Doctors Sued More," *New York Times* (November 25, 1994), p. 9A.
21. Patrick Garry, *An American Paradox: Censorship in a Nation of Speech* (Westport, CT: Praeger, 1993), p. 56.
22. Gerald Graff, *Beyond the Culture Wars: How Teaching Can Revitalize American Education* (New York: W.W. Norton, 1992), p. 81.
23. Harold Bloom, *The Western Canon: The Books and Schools of the Ages* (New York: Harcourt Brace and Company, 1993), p. 212.
24. Richard Bernstein, *Dictatorship of Virtue: Multiculturalism and the Battle for America's Future* (New York: Alfred A. Knopf, 1994).

25. Richard Rorty, "The Unpatriotic Academy," *New York Times* (February 13, 1994), p. 13E.
26. Dirk Johnson, "Word Cops Monitor a Classroom," *Star Tribune* (Minneapolis) (May 13, 1994), p. 4A.
27. Daphne Patai and Noretta Koertge, *Professing Feminism: Cautionary Tales from the Strange New World of Women's Studies* (New York: Basic Books, 1995), p. 117.
28. Ibid., p. 151.
29. Robert and Jon Solomon, *Up the University* (Massachusetts: Addison-Wesley, 1993), p. 37.
30. Mickiko Kakutani, "Biography as Blood Sport," *New York Times* (September 20, 1994), p. B1.
31. Ibid.
32. Sam Dillon, "AIDS Curriculum: Fighting Words," *New York Times* (October 24, 1994), p. B1.
33. Ibid.
34. John Marks, "The American Uncivil Wars," *U.S. News & World Report* (April 22, 1996): 69.
35. Wendy Bounds, "More Students and Parents Take Their Schools to Court," *Wall Street Journal* (July 26, 1994), p. B1.
36. Sue Shellenbarger, "Work-Force Study Finds Loyalty Is Weak," *Wall Street Journal* (September 3, 1993), p. B1.
37. Margaret Jacobs, "Courts Conflicted over Religion in Workplace," *Wall Street Journal* (October 10, 1995), p. B1.
38. Frances McMorris, "Can Post-Traumatic Stress Arise from Office Battles? *Wall Street Journal* (February 19, 1996), p. 1B.
39. Ginia Bellafante, "Are Women Too Nice at the Office?" *Time* (October 3, 1994): 60.
40. Lisa Genasci, "The Perils of Plaintiffs," *Star Tribune* (Minneapolis) (October 11, 1994), p. 1D.
41. Thomas Lueck, "Job-Loss Anger," *Wall Street Journal* (December 12, 1993), p. 1A.
42. Anastasia Toufexis, "Workers Who Fight Firing with Fire," *Time* (April 25, 1994): 36.
43. Joan Rigdon, "Companies See More Workplace Violence," *Wall Street Journal* (April 12, 1994), p. B1.
44. Mathew Purdy, "Workplace Homicides Provoking Negligence Lawsuits," *New York Times* (February 14, 1994), p. 1A.
45. Dennis Farney, "Gay Rights Confront Determined Resistance," *Wall Street Journal* (October 7, 1994), p. 1A.
46. Ibid.
47. Paul Starobin, "A Generation of Vipers," *Columbia Journalism Review* (March 1995): 27.
48. Kenneth Walsh, *Feeding the Beast* (New York: Random House, 1996), p. 56.
49. Larry Sabato, *Feeding Frenzy: How Attack Journalism Has Transformed American Politics* (New York: Free Press, 1991).
50. Thomas Patterson, *Out of Order* (New York: Alfred A. Knopf, 1993), p. 71.
51. Ibid.
52. Adam Gopnik, "Read All about It," *The New Yorker* (December 12, 1994): 86.

53. Ibid., p. 93.
54. William Glaberson, "Cynicism Erodes Press Credibility," *Star Tribune* (Minneapolis) (October 14, 1994), p. 4A.
55. Peter Brown, "Gotcha Journalism," *Media Critic* (Autumn 1994): 66–73.
56. Ibid., p. 72.
57. Louis Harris and Associates survey, *The Privacy Study*, No. 902030 (March 1990).
58. Adam Clymer, "Taking Power in the Age of Defiance," *New York Times* (January 8, 1995), p. 17E.
59. Ibid.
60. "Partisan Hostility Strong in Wake of Carns Battle," *Star Tribune* (Minneapolis) (March 12, 1995), p. 15A.
61. Jan Ferris, "Village Boards Veer toward Uncivil Liberties," *Chicago Tribune* (September 25, 1994), p. 1A.
62. Katharine Seelye, "In Attack on Gingrich, Democrats Use His Tactics," *New York Times* (January 19, 1995), p. 1A.
63. Sharon Schmickle, "Federal Partisanship Is Culmination of Trend," *New York Times* (December 4, 1995), p. 1A.
64. Katharine Seelye, "Lawmakers Take Sour View as Session Totters to Close," *New York Times* (October 1, 1994), p. 1A.
65. Text of remarks appeared in *Chicago Tribune* (November 15, 1994), p. 7A.
66. Sam Howe Verhovek, "Retiring Senator Sees Turmoil Ahead," *New York Times* (November 16, 1994), p. 11A.
67. "Alabama Senator Is Fourth Democrat to Retire," *New York Times* (March 29, 1995), p. 10A.
68. Robert Whereatt, "Suspicion, Paranoia, Lies," *Star Tribune* (Minneapolis) (November 22, 1994), p. 1B.

CHAPTER FIVE

1. Source: Committee for the Study of the American Electorate.
2. "Promises, Promises," *New York Times Magazine* (January 29, 1995), p. 14.
3. Franklin Knoll, "Apathy on a Roll," *New York Times Magazine* (October 16, 1994), p. 37.
4. Poll results were published in "Congress Fails the Grade," *New York Times* (November 3, 1994), p. 10A.
5. Katharine Seelye, "Lawmakers Take Sour View as Session Totters to Close," *New York Times* (October 1, 1994), p. 1A.
6. From a *Time*/CNN poll taken from August 31 to September 1, 1994 by Yankelovich Partners, Inc., reported in Keven Phillips, "Fat City," *Time* (September 26, 1994): 55.
7. E. J. Dionne, Jr., *Why Americans Hate Politics* (New York: Simon and Schuster, 1991).
8. "The October Massacre," *The New Republic* (October 24, 1994), p. 7.
9. Adam Clymer, "Awash in Filibusters, Senate Limps toward Adjournment," *New York Times* (October 5, 1994), p. 1A.

10. Adam Clymer, "Rancor Leaves Its Mark on 103rd Congress," *New York Times* (October 9, 1994), p. 1A.
11. David Rosenbaum, "A Likely Long-Term Effect of Census Ruling: More Litigation," *New York Times* (August 10, 1994), p. 8A.
12. Rhonda Hillbery, "Warning: Signing That Petition Could Get You Sued," *Law and Politics* (July 1995): 19–22.
13. Joseph Berger, "Cottage Industry Fights City Hall, and It's Winning," *New York Times* (December 24, 1994), p. 11A.
14. Hiller Zobel, "In Love with Lawsuits," *American Heritage* (November 1994): 66.
15. Milo Geyelin, "Trial Lawyers Reach out to GOP with Revised Image and Strategy," *Wall Street Journal* (December 15, 1994), p. B7.
16. Tamar Lewin, "New Anti-Abortion Move: Malpractice Suits," *New York Times* (April 9, 1995), p. 1A.
17. Richard Schmitt, "Consumer Groups Get Windfall," *Wall Street Journal* (April 22, 1994), p. B4.
18. Kevin Diaz, "Closed Doors Prompt Open Quarreling," *Star Tribune* (Minneapolis) (September 21, 1994), p. A1.

CHAPTER SIX

1. Roseanne Arnold, *My Lives* (New York: Ballantine Books, 1994), p. 83.
2. Theodore J. Boutrous, "Lost Your Job? Sue and Make a Million," *Wall Street Journal* (July 28, 1993), p. A15.
3. Cullen Murphy, "Scapegroup," *The Atlantic Monthly* (April 1995): 22.
4. Margaret Carlson, "And Now, Obesity Rights," *Time* (December 6, 1993): 96.
5. Ibid.
6. Margaret Zack, "Man Says He Was Fired for Weight Problem," *Star Tribune* (Minneapolis) (June 19, 1994), p. 1B.
7. Carlson, "And Now, Obesity Rights," p. 96.
8. Amy Stevens, "Suit over Suicide Raises Issue: Do Associates Work Too Hard?" *Wall Street Journal* (April 15, 1994), p. B1.
9. Emily Bernstein, "Law School Women Question the Teaching," *New York Times* (June 5, 1996), p. B10.
10. Ibid.
11. Ibid.
12. Adam Nagourney, "So the Personal Does Turn out to Be Political," *New York Times* (September 1, 1996), p. E1.
13. Ronald Smothers, "Hate Fliers Inflame Mayoral Race in New Orleans," *New York Times* (February 27, 1994), p. 11A.
14. Charles Krauthammer, "Defining Deviancy Up," *The New Republic* (November 22, 1993): 23.
15. Ibid.
16. Christine Hoff Sommers, *Who Stole Feminism? How Women Have Betrayed Women* (New York: Simon & Schuster), p. 37.
17. Katie Roiphe, *The Morning After* (New York: Little, Brown, and Company, 1994), p. 38.

18. Christopher Byron, "The Joke That Killed," *Esquire* (January 1995): 84.
19. This project was funded in 1992 and carried out by the National Center for History in the Schools at UCLA, which released its report in November 1994. The report was endorsed by the American Federation of Teachers and the National Education Association.
20. See Tom Engelhardt, *The End of Victory Culture* (New York: Basic Books, 1994).
21. Walter Kronig, "History Hijacked," *Time* (February 13, 1995): 90.
22. Patrick Garry, *An American Paradox: Censorship in a Nation of Speech* (Westport, CT: Praeger, 1993), p. 57.
23. Ibid., p. 58.
24. Arlene Croce, "Discussing the Undiscussable," *The New Yorker* (December 26, 1994): 54–60.
25. Mark Schapiro, "The Fine Art of Sexual Harassment," *Harper's Magazine* (July 1994): 62.
26. Paul Robinson, "The Riot Defense," *Wall Street Journal* (October 27, 1993), p. 15A.
27. The study was conducted by Penn and Shoen Associates, Inc. in March of 1994 and was reported in the April 1994 issue of *National Law Journal*.
28. Milo Geyelin, "Late Tax Filers Offer New Plea," *Wall Street Journal* (April 18, 1994), p. 1B.
29. Ibid.

CHAPTER SEVEN

1. Barbara Ehrenreich, "Oh, Those Family Values," *Time* (July 18, 1994): 62.
2. Robert Wuthnow, *Starting the Journey: Support Groups and America's New Quest for Community* (New York: Free Press, 1992), p. 9.
3. Ellen Herman, *The Romance of American Psychology* (Berkeley: University of California Press, 1993), p. 5.
4. Robert Hughes, "Bitch, Bitch, Bitch ...," *Psychology Today* (September 1993): 29.
5. Mary Gaitskill, "On Not Being a Victim," *Harper's Magazine* (March 1994): 39.
6. Warren Berger, "Childhood Traumas Healed While U-Wait," *New York Times* (January 8, 1995), p. H33.
7. Hughes, "Bitch, Bitch, Bitch ...," p. 28.
8. Conrad deFiebre, "Linehan: I Just Want to Live a Normal Life," *Star Tribune* (Minneapolis) (August 29, 1994), p. 1A.
9. "Reading, Writing and Recovery," *U.S. News & World Report* (May 23, 1994): 22.
10. Ibid.
11. John Taylor, "Irresistible Impulses," *Esquire* (April 1994): 98.
12. Rolanda Jackson, "U.S. to Pay Weaver's Family $3.1 Million," *Star Tribune* (Minneapolis) (August 16, 1995), p. 1A.
13. Junda Woo, "Urban Trauma Mitigates Guilt," *Wall Street Journal* (April 27, 1993), p. 1B.
14. See Elizabeth Loftus and Katherine Ketcham, *The Myth of Repressed Memory* (New York: St. Martin's Press, 1994); Richard Ofshe and Ethan Watters, *Making Monsters: False Memories, Psychotherapy and Sexual Hysteria* (New York: Scribner's Sons, 1993); Mark Pendergrast, *Victims of Memory: Incest Accusations*

and Shattered Lives (Lexington, KY: Upper Access Press, 1995); and Lawrence Wright, *Remembering Satan: A Case of Recovered Memory and the Shattering of an American Family* (New York: Alfred A. Knopf, 1994).

15. Dave Ferman, "Modern America: Where the Buck Stops Nowhere," *Star Tribune* (Minneapolis) (May 4, 1994), p. 1E.

16. Walter Olson, "The Long Arm of Harassment Law," *New York Times* (July 7, 1996), p. E9.

CHAPTER EIGHT

1. Jan Crawford, "In Lawsuit Land, No Dispute Too Small for Courts," *Chicago Tribune* (February 20, 1994), p. 1A.

2. Philip K. Howard, *The Death of Common Sense* (New York: Random House, 1994), p. 49.

3. Joseph Pereira, "Employers Confront Domestic Abuse," *Wall Street Journal* (February 11, 1994), p. 1B.

4. Edward Felsenthal, "Potentially Violent Employees Present Bosses with a Catch-22," *Wall Street Journal* (April 21, 1994), p. 1B.

5. Ibid.

6. Mark Guyer, "Litigious Patients Are Able to Obtain Insurance Payments for Unproven Treatments," *New York Times* (March 28, 1994), p. A1.

7. Associated Press, "3-Year-Old Slapped with Court Order," *Star Tribune* (Minneapolis) (March 8, 1996), p. 1A.

8. Crawford, "In Lawsuit Land," p. 1A.

9. Bryan Miller, "Hey, Waiter! Now There's a Lawyer in My Soup," *New York Times* (March 12, 1995), p. E1.

10. Richard Schmitt, "One Thing to Say about Ms. McColin Is: She Sues People," *Wall Street Journal* (September 26, 1995), p. 1A.

11. Dean of Students, Antioch College, "Code of Sexual Conduct," (1992), p. 2.

12. Eric Fassin, "Playing by the Antioch Rules," *New York Times* (September 21, 1993), p. A13.

13. Michele Ingrassia, "Abused and Confused," *Newsweek* (October 25, 1993): 57.

14. Jane Gross, "Now Look Who's Suing," *New York Times* (February 26, 1995), p. E1.

15. Ibid.

16. Patrick Garry, "Dangerous Romance," *Law and Politics* (November 1994): 21.

17. Survey conducted by *National Law Journal* and reported in Margot Slade, "Law Firms Begin Reining in Sex-Harassing Partners," *New York Times* (February 25, 1994), p. B14.

18. Harvard Women's Law Association, *Presumed Equal: What America's Top Women Lawyers Really Think about Their Firms* (Cambridge, MA: Harvard University Press, 1995), p. 21.

19. Terry Pristin, "Firms Wake up to the Problem of Sex Harassment," *New York Times* (October 14, 1994), p. B14.

20. Frances McMorris, "Brawl Erupts in the Bar-Review Business," *Wall Street Journal* (February 23, 1995), p. B6.

21. Constance Johnson, "Attorneys Discipline More of Their Own," *Wall Street Journal* (August 14, 1995), p. 1B.
22. Christine Biederman, "Families of Crash Victims Say Lawyers Ignore Solicitation Ban," *New York Times* (June 4, 1996), p. A9.
23. George James, "47 Are Indicted in Scheme to Speed Insurance Claims," *New York Times* (September 22, 1995), p. 10A.
24. Sylvia Ranson, "Legal Woes," *Time* (March 21, 1994): 32.
25. Michael Duffy, "Culture of Deception," *Time* (August 15, 1994): 15–19; Michael Kramer, "Slippery Hillary," Ibid., p. 19.
26. Stephen Labaton, "Bentsen Denies Aides' Assertions of Briefings on Whitewater Talks," *New York Times* ((August 4, 1994), p. 1A.
27. David Johnston, "Agriculture Chief Quits as Scrutiny of Conduct Grows," *New York Times* (October 4, 1995), p. 1A.
28. Associated Press, "Campaign Paid to Settle Claim of Harassment," *Star Tribune* (Minneapolis) (December 16, 1994), p. 5A.
29. Robert Pear, "Judge Cites Misconduct by Officials," *New York Times* (December 2, 1994), p. 9A.
30. Jan Crawford, "Lawyers Group Chides U.S. Appeals Judges," *Chicago Tribune* (February 22, 1994), p. 7A.
31. Ken Armstrong, "More Bite Sought from Judicial Watchdogs," *Chicago Tribune* (June 23, 1996), p. 1A.

CHAPTER NINE

1. Lynn Elber, "End of 'L.A. Law' Era," *Star Tribune* (Minneapolis) (May 18, 1994), p. 3E.
2. Floyd Abrams, "Why Lawyers Lie," *New York Times Magazine* (August 16, 1995), p. 55.
3. Jeffrey Toobin, "Ito and the Truth School," *The New Yorker* (March 27, 1995): 43.
4. Ibid.
5. Philipp Gollner, "Consulting by Peering into Minds of Jurors," *New York Times* (January 7, 1994), p. A14.
6. Daniel Franklin, "The Menendez Quandry," *Washington Monthly* (July 1994): 50.
7. Victor Gold, "Beware the 'Hidden Persuaders,'" *Los Angeles Times* (November 29, 1994), p. 13A.
8. Henry Weinstein, "Legal Aftershocks Will Keep Lots of Lawyers Busy," *Los Angeles Times* (January 30, 1994), p. A1.
9. Junda Woo, "Like Recent Disasters, the Quake is Expected to Spawn Many Suits," *Wall Street Journal* (February 7, 1994), p. B5.

CHAPTER TEN

1. Judith Schroer, *USA Today* (October 7, 1993), p. 1B.

2. Mary Jordan, "More Attorneys Making a Motion for the Pursuit of Happiness," *The Washington Post* (September 4, 1993), p. A3.
3. Amy Stevens, "This Breed of Rodent Is Becoming a Pest at Major Law Firms," *Wall Street Journal* (August 20, 1993), p. 1A.
4. Amy Stevens, "Why Lawyers are Depressed," *Wall Street Journal* (June 12, 1995), p. B1.
5. Colin Covert, "Lawyers Losing Case with Public," *Star Tribune* (Minneapolis) (May 29, 1994), p. 1E.
6. Ibid.
7. "Lawyers Still Unpopular," *Wall Street Journal* (August 2, 1993), p. B2.
8. Roger Stageberg, "The Public's View of Lawyers," *Bench and Bar* (October 1993): 5.
9. Debra Sparks, "Law: The Worms Turn," *Financial World* (May 23, 1995): 53.
10. Richard Perez-Pena, "When Lawyers Go after Their Peers," *New York Times* (August 5, 1994), p. B12.
11. Milo Geyelin, "Many Lawyers Find Malpractice Lawsuits Aren't Fun after All," *Wall Street Journal* (July 11, 1995), p. A1.
12. Amy Stevens, "How a Lawyer–Client Relationship Went Awry," *Wall Street Journal* (July 31, 1995), p. B1.
13. Peter Passell, "Contingency Fees in Injury Cases under Attack," *New York Times* (February 11, 1994), p. A1.
14. Ibid.
15. Dionne Searcey, "Lawyers, Defend Thyselves," *Chicago Tribune* (May 5, 1996), p. B1.
16. Ibid.
17. "Six Facts," *New York Times Magazine* (April 16, 1995), p. 14.
18. Verlyn Klinkenborg, "Law's Labors Lost," *The New Republic* (March 14, 1994): 33.
19. Lincoln Caplan, *Skadden: Power, Money, and the Rise of a Legal Empire* (New York: Farrar, Straus and Giroux, 1993).
20. Sol M. Linowitz, *The Betrayed Profession: Lawyering at the End of the Twentieth Century* (New York: Scribner's Sons, 1994).
21. Anthony Kronman, *The Lost Lawyer: Failing Ideals of the Legal Profession* (Cambridge, MA: Harvard University Press, 1993).
22. Maria Shao, "Dial-a-Suit," *The Boston Globe* (October 10, 1995), p. 1.
23. Milo Geyelin, "Law Firm's Ads Pursue Users of Recalled Drug," *Wall Street Journal* (February 3, 1994), p. B1.
24. Milo Geyelin, "Faulty Software Means Business for Litigators," *Wall Street Journal* (January 21, 1994), p. B1.
25. Vincent Schodolski, "Law May Let Investors Sue If Stock Dips," *Chicago Tribune* (June 23, 1996), p. 1A.
26. John MacCormack, "Town Seeks a Fortune from a Chemical Leak," *New York Times* (May 5, 1995), p. A11.
27. Anthony Faiola, "In Settling with Airlines, There's No Free Ride," *The Washington Post* (March 20, 1995), p. A1.
28. Ibid., p. A10.
29. Ibid.
30. Barry Meier, "Fistfuls of Coupons," *New York Times* (May 26, 1995), p. C1.

31. Ibid., p. C5.
32. Ibid.
33. Barry Meier, "Math of a Class-Action Suit: 'Winning' $2.19 Costs $91.33," *New York Times* (November 21, 1995), p. A1.
34. Ibid.
35. Kurt Eichenwald, "Millions for Us, Pennies for You," *New York Times* (December 19, 1993), p. 12F.
36. Ibid.
37. Edward Felsenthal, "Lawyers Rebuked for Their Pursuit of Class Lawsuit," *Wall Street Journal* (August 12, 1994), p. B3.
38. Ibid.
39. Tamar Lewin, "Implant Judge Ousts Lawyers on Panel," *New York Times* (March 23, 1996), p. A9.
40. Gina Lolata, "Will the Lawyers Kill Off Norplant?" *New York Times* (May 28, 1995), p. F1.
41. Richard Schmitt, "Lawyers Unite against Plan to Speed Suits," *Wall Street Journal* (June 8, 1993), p. B1.
42. Ibid.
43. Richard Schmitt, "Effort by Judges to Streamline Civil Litigation Meets Roadblock," *Wall Street Journal* (September 15, 1993), p. B2.
44. Richard Schmitt, "Trial Lawyers Glide Past Critics with Aid of Potent Trade Group," *Wall Street Journal* (February 17, 1994), p. A1, col. 5.
45. Ibid.
46. Richard Schmitt, "Trial Bar's Political Heft Gauged in Campaign Contributions Study," *Wall Street Journal* (April 10, 1995), p. B3.
47. Margaret Jacobs, "Business Groups, Lawyers Face Off over California Litigation Reform," *Wall Street Journal* (January 15, 1996), p. B3.

CONCLUSION

1. Junda Woo, "More People Represent Themselves in Court," *Wall Street Journal* (August 17, 1993), p. 1A.
2. Ibid.
3. Jeff Donn, "Do-It-Yourself Lawyers Cite Cost," *Los Angeles Times* (March 20, 1994), p. A16.
4. Courtney Leatherman, "You Want Their Attention? Sue!" *Chronicle of Higher Education* (February 10, 1995): 13.
5. Ibid.
6. Mary Ann Glendon, "What's Wrong with the Elite Law Schools," *Wall Street Journal* (June 8, 1993), p. A15.
7. Louis Menand, "Radicalism for Yuppies," *The New Republic* (March 17, 1986): 21.
8. Ibid., p. 23.
9. Heather MacDonald, "Law School Humbug," *Wall Street Journal* (November 8, 1995), p. A23.

Index

ABC, 62, 111
Abrams, Floyd, 162
Abortion, 30, 31, 60, 74, 91, 96
Abuse, domestic, 142
Adventures of Huckleberry Finn
    (Twain), 72
AIDS, 72, 81, 98, 172
Alaska Airlines, 181
Allen, Dick, 62
Altman, Roger, 156
American Association of University
    Professors (AAUP), 70
American Association of University
    Women (AAUW), 39
American Bar Association (ABA), 153,
    171
American Center for Law and Justice,
    30
American Civil Liberties Union
    (ACLU), 31, 108
American Electronics Association, 178
American Federation of Teachers, 115
American frontier
    overseas, 25
    technological, 25
    urban–industrial, 25
    Western, 25–26
"American Gladiators," 65
American Medical Association
    (AMA), 186

American Psychological Association,
    123, 134
American society
    as an adversarial culture, 4–6, 61,
        65, 81, 89
    as an aggression culture, 79
    as an assimilation model, 4, 60–61
    individualism in, 51
    as a litigation culture, 7
    as a melting pot, 59–60
    multiculturalism in, 6
    as an oppositional culture, 66
    as a political culture, 6, 83, 85
    as a sports culture, 4–5, 61–62, 65,
        140
    as a therapeutic culture, 10, 125–28,
        130–32, 135–36, 138
American Telephone and Telegraph
    (AT&T), 114
American Trial Lawyers Association
    (ATLA), 11, 186
Americans with Diabetes Act, 27, 109,
    137, 143
Anatomy of a Murder, 173
Anderson, Elijah, 66
An Innocent Man, 161
Anorexia, 112
Antioch code, 35, 147
Anti-smoking, 95, 145
Armey, Dick, 85

Arnold, Roseanne, 104
Ashe, Arthur, 81

Bailyn, Bernard, 117
Baker and McKenzie, 75, 152
Bank of Boston, 182
Banzhaf, John, 194
Barry, Marion, 111
Bayh, Evan, 111
Beattie, Melody, 126
"Beavis and Butt Head," 67
Bell, Alexander Graham, 115
Bennett, William, 44
Bentson, Llyod, 156
Bernardin, Joseph Cardinal, 107, 133
Betrayed Profession, The (Linowitz), 176
Bettiol, Zoravia, 119
Beyond the Culture Wars (Graff), 68
"Blood sport," 7
Bobbit, Lorena, 121, 132, 138
Bocchco, Steven, 162
Bocat, Steve, 29
Bonier, David, 85
Bonilla, Bobby, 62
Book of Virtues, The (Bennett), 44
Boren, David, 86
Bork, Robert, 83
Boxer, Barbara, 111
Boy Scouts of America, 22, 52
Bradley, Bill, 86
Bradshaw, John, 126
Brown, Hubie, 63
Brown, Kathleen, 111
Brown, Ron, 158–59
Buchanan, Pat, 115
"Burden of Proof," 154
Bush, George, 91, 157
Butcher, Jamie, 36–37
Byrd, Robert, 86

California Interscholastic Federation, 63
California Lawyer, 171
Cape Fear, 173
Capital punishment, 91
"Capitol Gang, The," 65
Carns, Michael, 83
Carol Publishing, 50
Cases, "Baby Richard," 33–34

CBS, 90
Chapman & Cutler, 155
Chavez, Linda, 69
Chavis, Rev. Benjamin, Jr., 108
Chicago Council of Lawyers, 159
Chicago Theological Seminary, 69
Chicago Transit Authority, 105
Chicago White Sox, 62
Child abuse, 34, 120
Child care, 56, 60
Child custody, 32–34
Christian Education Association, 30
Cisnero, Henry, 58
Citicorp Credit Services, 109
Civil rights
   expansion of, 101
   violation of, 15
Clark, Marcia, 33
Class action, 12, 178–81, 184
Class Action Report, 182
Clinton, Chelsea, 111
Clinton, Hillary Rodham, 55–56, 77, 155, 157
Clinton, William Jefferson, 26–27, 44, 67, 80, 83, 91–93, 104, 111, 155–57
Closing of the American Mind (Bloom), 68
CNN, 18, 154
Cohen, William, 183
Colleges
   Antioch, 35, 147
   Bates, 146
   Carlton, 114, 148
   Swarthmore, 35
Connell, Elizabeth, 185
Continental Airlines, 149
Copley Pharmaceutical, 177
"Court TV," 62, 193
Craig, Jenny, 77
Criminal justice, 119–20
Critical Legal Studies (CLS), 195–96
Croce, Arlene, 118
"Crossfire," 5, 18, 81

"Dateline," 81
Dayton Hudson, 143
Death of Common Sense (Howard), 142

Defense
  as black rage, 121
  in riots, 121
Defenseless, 161
Deford, Frank, 63
Demographics, 60
De-moralization of Society, The (Him-
    melfarb), 45
Denny, Reginald, 19, 121–22, 165
Department of Transportation (DOT),
    76
Dershowitz, Alan, 173
*Diagnostic and Statistical Manual of
    Mental Disorders*, 128
Dictatorship of Virtue (Bernstein), 68–69
Dingell, John, 85
Dirkson, Everett, 83
Disabilities
  addictions, 109
  obesity, 109
Disclosure, 34
Discovery process, 190–91
Discrimination
  in age, 76, 177
  in race, 152, 196
  as victim of, 110
Domestic torts, 3, 32
Donaldson, Sam, 79
Dow Corning, 184
Downey, Thomas, 82
Dress codes, 56
Due process, 8, 140
Duke, David, 81
Durenburger, David, 83
Durso, Ed, 62
Dworkin, Andrea, 112

Edison, Thomas, 115
Ehrenreich, Barbara, 125
Elitism, 118
Ellis Island, 60, 190
Entitlement, age of, 167
Epstein, Richard, 145
Equal Employment Opportunity
    Commission, 75, 148–49
ESPN, 62
Espy, Mike, 158
Esquire, 66
Explosion rage disorder, 122

Family court, 193
Farrakhan, Louis, 81
Federal Aviation Administration
    (FAA), 35
Federal Drug Administration (FDA),
    184
Feeding Frenzy (Sabato), 78
Fein, Bruce, 133
Feminism, 112–13
Ferguson, Colin, 122
Filibuster, 92
"Firm, The," 172
Fizel, Douglas, 123
Foley, Tom, 94
Ford, Motors, 182
Foster, Vince, 155
Frank, Barney, 85

Gay rights, 30
Gays, 33, 36, 38, 69, 71, 74, 77–78, 93,
    129–30
General Mills, 182
General Motors, 29
Gephardt, Richard, 83
"Geraldo," 81, 126
Gibbons, Sam, 85
Gibson, Dunn & Crutcher, 174
Gingrich, Newt, 83–85
Glass, Lillian, 126
Glendon, Mary Ann, 195
"Good Morning America," 18
"Gotcha" journalism, 8
Goya, 119
Grace, W. R. and Co., 76
Grandy, Fred, 85
Greenfield, Jeff, 111
Gridlock, 7, 91–92
Grisham, John, 18
Guiliani, Mayor, 93
Guilty as Sin, 161
Guinier, Lani, 83, 195
Gun control, 95–96

Harding, Tonya, 140
Harper Collins, 77
Harris pol, 80
Harward Women's Law Association,
    151
Hayes, Helen, 104

Heflin, Howard, 86
Helmsley, Leona, 20
Hill, Anita, 149
Hitler, Adolph, 86
HIV, 18, 169
Homosexuality, 36, 71, 77–78, 117
Hooters Restaurant, 150
Hubbell, Webster, 158
Huffington, Michael, 111
Hughes, Robert, 60
Humphrey, Hubert, 110
Hunio v. Tishman Construction, 105

IBM, 151
Ideology
    combative, 71
    of conflict, 73
    of division, 82
Illiberal Education (D'Souza), 68
Imposters in the Temple (Anderson),
    68
Incivility, 67–68, 72, 86
Inherit the Wind, 173
Inman, Bobby, 83
"Inside Edition," 19–20

Jack-in-the Box, 111
Jackson, Michael, 132
Jagged Edge, The, 161
Jamieson, Kathleen Hall, 79
Japanese
    attorneys, 48
    schools, 47
    society, 46–49
"Jenny Craig Eight," 149
"Jenny Jones," 81
"Jerry Springer," 81, 126
Johnson, Lyndon, 83
Jones, Paula, 27, 158
"Judge Wopner," 62
Jury consultants, 163–64
Jurassic Park, 172

Kennedy, John F., 71, 99, 104
Kerrigan, Nancy, 140
Khomeini, Ayatollah, 74
King, Martin Luther, Jr., 131
King, Rodney, 20, 121, 165, 174–75
Klein, Joe, 155

K-Mart, 144
Ku Klux Klan (KKK), 115

Lake, Ricki, 111
"L. A. Law," 18, 162, 193
"Larry King Live," 18, 22
Law schools
    Columbia University, 182, 184
    George Mason, 141
    Northwestern University, 35, 168
    Regent, 31
    University of Chicago, 145
Law suits
    libel, 50
    malpractice, 174
Lawyers
    ethics complaints against, 153
    as free agents, 176
    public hostility to, 175
    solicitation in, 154
Lawyers' Liability Review, 173
Lehrman, Karen, 129
Lesbians, 33, 36, 40, 56, 71
Lewis, John, 85
Liability, risk of, 54
Life Dynamics, 31, 96
Lincoln, Abraham, 86, 115
Lindsay, Bruce, 159
Litigation
    fear of, 192–93
    as new frontier, 2, 3
    in religion, 2
Lombardi, Vince, 86
Los Angeles Times, 166
Lost Lawyer, The (Kronman), 177
Lussier, Thomas, 143

MacArthur, Charles, 104
MacKinnon, Catharine, 112
Malpractice
    explosion of, 173
    lawsuits, 174
Manne, Henry, 141
Mantle, Mickey, 104
Mapplethorpe, Robert, 67
Marcos, Imelda, 20
Maternity leave, 73
"Maury Povich Show," 81
McCain, John, 90

McCarthy, Joseph, 115
McDonalds, 10, 97, 105
"McLaughlin Group, The," 5, 65, 67, 81
"Meet the Press," 5
Menendez brothers, 120–21
Meredith, James, 124
Metpath, Corning, 4
Meyerson, Harvey, 154
Milk, Harvey, 120
Miller beer, 172
Miller, Tony, 22
Milli Vanilli, 180
Millner, Guy, 111
"Monday Night Football," 62, 146
"Montel Williams Show," 81–82, 126
Montgomery Ward, 144
Moral Sense, The (Wilson), 45
Moran, James, 111
Morning After, The (Roiphe), 113
Moscone, George, 120
Mothers Against Drunk Driving (MADD), 50
Multiculturalism, 6, 60, 91
Multiple Chemical Sensitivity (MCS), 27

Nagel, Robert, 56
Naked Maja, 119
National Association for the Advancement of Colored People (NAACP), 31, 108
National Education Association, 115
National Endowment for the Arts, 118
National Federation of the Blind, 143
National Health Laboratories, 3
National Honor Society, 72
National Opinion Research Center, 21
National Organization for Women (NOW), 39
National Public Radio, 63
National School Boards Association, 72
National Standards, 115–16
Native Americans, 116, 129
Nazism, 86, 127
NBC, 62
Newman, Paul, 173
New Republic, 92

Newsweek, 44, 78, 155
New Yorker, The, 18, 118
New York Mets, 62
New York Pride, 67
New York Times, 84, 90
New York Times Book Review, 29
"Nightline," 19–20
Nike, 63
Nippon Steel, 46
Nixon, Richard, 157
Nolte, Nick, 173
Norplant, 184–85
Northwest Airlines, 107, 131
Northwestern National Life Insurance, 76
Nussbaum, Bernard, 157

Occidental Petroleum, 180
Occupational Safety and Health Administration (OSHA), 53, 142
"Oprah," 103, 126
Osby, Daimion, 122
Overbilling, 12

Patterson, Thomas E., 78
Peck, Gregory, 173
Pena, Frederico, 158
"Peoples' Court," 17, 193
"Perry Mason," 161–62
Personal injury, 28
Pharr, Suzanne, 78
Philadelphia, 18, 172
"Phil Donahue," 126
Philip Morris, 184
Picasso, Pablo, 71
Planned Parenthood, 44
Playboy, 20, 84
Polarization, ideological, 60
Politics
    cynicism in, 86
    decline of, 102
    hostility to, 90
    interest group, 99–101
    negativism in, 86
    victim of, 112
Pollack, Jackson, 71
Posttraumatic stress disorder, 75
Prayer, in schools, 56
Presidential Legal Expense Trust, 15

Presumed Innocent, 161
"Prime Time Justice," 17
Product liability, 17
Professing Feminism (Patai and Koertge), 70, 129
Professional Plaintiffs, 180
Prof Scam (Skye), 68
Proposition, 187, 93
Prudential Securities, 180, 183
Punitive damages, 3, 28–29, 96–98, 107
Putnam, Robert, 52

RAND Corporation, 97
Rayburn, Sam, 83
Reebok, 172
Reeves, Christopher, 111
Referee, 64
Referral fee, 177
Regarding Henry, 172
Reversal of Fortune, 172
Revolt of the Elites (Lasch), 45
"Ricki Lake Show," 81, 126
Rifkin, Joel, 123
Rights, legal, 57
Rise of Selfishness in America (Collier), 45
"Rivera Live," 19
Robertson, Pat, 30
Robert's Rules of Order, 84
Robie, Derrick, 122
Rockefeller, John D., 115
Rodman, Dennis, 63
"Rolanda," 81
Romance of American Psychology (Herman), 126
Roosevelt, Franklin, 110
Roosevelt, Theodore, 110
Rose Law Firm, 156, 158
Rosen, Lee, 32
Rosenkowski, Dan, 159
Rutherford Institute, 30

"Sally Jesse Raphael," 81, 103, 126–27
Sanders, Deion, 63
Sauerbrey, Ellen, 94
Scheck, Barry, 18
Schering–Plough, 142
Schindler's List, 113
Schlesinger, Arthur, 100
Schools, development in, 52

Scorsese, Martin, 173
Searle, G. D., 97
Securities Arbitration Commentator, 183
Self-esteem, 128–30, 138
Serrano, Andres, 67
Sexual abuse, 120, 134
Sexual Harassment on the Job (Petrocelli), 136
Shapiro, Robert, 176
Siegel, Fred, 67, 109
Simon, Paul, 85
Simpson, O. J., 18, 20, 33
"Simpsons, The, 67
"60 minutes," 81
Smith, Eric, 122
Smith, William Kennedy, 20
Smithsonian Institution, 117
Snyder, Graydon, 69
Sommers, Christina Hoff, 113, 129
Spence, Gerry, 18
Steel, Ronald, 71
Stein, Hilton, 173
Steiner, Joshua, 157
Steinhilber, August, 72
Stephanopoulos, George, 157
Stern, Howard, 5
Stewart, James, 173
Strategic Lawsuits Against Public Participation (SLAPP), 94
Stroh's Brewery, 13, 150
"Summer Olympic Games," 62
"Swedish Bikini Team," 13
Syndromes
    adopted child, 123
    battered wife, 121
    chronic lateness, 137
    failure to file, 123
    meek mate, 122
    premenstrual stress, 123
    Super Bowl Sunday, 123
    survival, 123
    Tourette's, 18

Talmud, The, 70
Target Discount Store, 143
TBS, 116
Telephone, cellular, 21
Tenured Radicals (Kimball), 68
Term limits, 93

Therapy, 124, 133
  recovered memory theory, 134
  repressed memory theory, 133, 135
Thomas, Clarence, 83, 149
Thomas, Patrick, 142
Thomases, Susan, 157
Time, 44, 61, 79, 155
To Kill a Mockingbird, 173
Topol, Lisa, 146
Tourette's syndrome, 18
Tracy, Spencer, 173
Trials, non-jury, 16
Triumph of the American Nation (Todd
  and Curti), 116
Trust, decline of, 51
Tubman, Harriet, 115
Turow, Scott, 18
Twelve Angry Men, 19, 165
"20/20," 22
2000: A Space Odyssey, 13
Tyson, Mike, 20

Universities
  Colorado, 56, 144
  Campbell, 171
  Duke, 69
  Emory, 185
  George Washington, 194
  Georgia 69
  Illinois 69
  Johns Hopkins, 171
  Maryland, 70
  Michigan 90, 117
  Minnesota, 141
  Nebraska, 60, 160
  New Hampshire, 114, 148
  New York, 123
  North Carolina, 69
  Old Dominion, 114, 148
  Pennsylvania, 69, 79, 118, 146, 150, 196
  Syracuse, 78
  Tennessee State, 145
  UCLA, 90
  Valparaiso, 114, 148
  Vanderbilt, 68
  Virginia, 69
  Yale, 114, 148.

Up from Nigger (Gregory), 131
Up the University (Solomons), 71
U.S. Air, 167
USA Today, 81
U.S. Postal Service, 143

ValuJet, 154
Van Sustern, Greta, 154
Verdict, The, 173
Victimization, 9–10, 103–08, 110–12,
  119–20, 124, 127
  in speech, 115
  politically correct, 115
  obsession with, 116
Vietnam War, 116
Volunteerism, decline of, 52
Voting Rights Act, 94

Waldman, Steven, 78
Wall Street Journal, 158
Walsh, Kenneth, 78
Warfare, ideological, 69
Washington, George, 86
Watergate, 157
Waters, Maxine, 85
Watkins, David, 159
Weaver, Randy, 132
Webster, Daniel, 115
Western Canon, The (Bloom), 68
West Publishing, 152
White and Case, 152
Whitewater, 156–58
Whitman, Christine Todd, 113
Who Stole Feminism? (Sommers),
  112
Why Americans Hate Politics (Dionne),
  91
Williams, Maggie, 157
Wilson, Pete, 22
Winston and Strawn, 154
Wolf, Naomi, 112
Works Progress Administration
  (WPA), 119
Wright, Jim, 83
Wrobel, David, 26

Zobel, Hiller, 65